Adventures of a Currency Trader

Founded in 1807, John Wiley & Sons is the oldest independent publishing company in the United States. With offices in North America, Europe, Australia, and Asia, Wiley is globally committed to developing and marketing print and electronic products and services for our customers' professional and personal knowledge and understanding.

The Wiley Trading series features books by traders who have survived the market's ever changing temperament and have prospered—some by reinventing systems, others by getting back to basics. Whether you are a novice trader, professional, or somewhere in-between, these books will provide the advice and strategies needed to prosper today and well into the future.

For a list of available titles, visit our web site at www.WileyFinance.com.

Adventures of a Currency Trader

A Fable about Trading,
Courage, and
Doing the Right Thing

ROB BOOKER

John Wiley & Sons, Inc.

Published by John Wiley & Sons, Inc., Hoboken, New Jersey.
Published simultaneously in Canada.

Wiley Bicentennial logo: Richard J. Pacifico.

Financial charts throughout this book created using TradeStation software. Copyright ©
TradeStation Technologies, Inc., 1992–2006.

For general information on our other products and services or for technical support, please
contact our Customer Care Department within the United States at (800) 762-2974, outside
the United States at (317) 572-3993 or fax (317) 572-4002.

Wiley also publishes its books in a variety of electronic formats. Some content that appears
in print may not be available in electronic books. For more information about Wiley
products, visit our web site at www.wiley.com.

Library of Congress Cataloging-in-Publication Data:

Booker, Rob, 1971–
    Adventures of a currency trader : a fable about trading, courage,
and doing the right thing / Rob Booker.
        p.   cm.— (Wiley trading series)
    Includes index.
    ISBN-13 978-0-470-04948-8 (cloth)
    1. Foreign exchange market.   2. Foreign exchange futures.
3. Speculation.   I. Title.
    HG3851.B62   2007
    332.4'5–dc22

                                                        2006029332

Printed in the United States of America.

10   9   8   7   6   5   4   3   2   1

For Kris
Thank you for telling me to go upstairs and write my book.

Contents

Foreword

Trading technology has made exponential advances over the past decade. It is no longer necessary to work at a bank to trade currency, nor is it necessary to have a broker talk your ear off about why Pfizer should be taking off, when all you wanted to do was buy some Intel. These days you can do it all from home on your computer. It is this idea of independence and freedom that is attracting so many of us to the trading marketplace.

That old statistic about 90 percent of traders going belly-up within the first year . . . yeah that still applies, give or take a few percent. But Rob Booker has made it a personal mission to prove that it needn't always be the case. He has built a network of trading students all over the world and helped them to realize that focus and discipline are all that make a successful trader. Systems are a dime a dozen (or sometimes $3,000 each), but only the disciplined trader who denies distraction will make any money from them.

The market is overrun with books, courses, lectures, seminars, and webinars designed to teach us all how to trade for a living and perhaps acquire a sense of freedom by doing so. The problem is that each expert who presents such an offering is out to prove that it is the best and maybe the only good trading system out there. Rob will tell you that the system is not the most important piece of the trading puzzle. It is the ability to know exactly what you are looking for, wait patiently (or frantically, as long as you really wait) for it to happen, and then jump on it. And repeat. And repeat.

Trading can become boring and redundant. But it is about making money, not about excitement. It is about making money, not about being right or smart. And well . . . trading isn't even about the act of trading; it is just about making money, to afford the freedom that we all desire. This freedom is where the excitement really comes in. Freedom is the end. Hard work, discipline, and focus are the means. It sounds lame, played out, and cliché, but it is still true. When we lose sight of that truth and start feeling like genius traders, we start screwing up. Many people give up along the way, perhaps like the fabled gold miner who gives up digging just one inch away from the vein of gold.

One of the top five most important things Rob ever helped me with, was to not give up when I was losing and my financial situation was nearly demanding that I focus elsewhere. He helped me dust myself off, reassess my commitment to becoming a successful trader, and start over with a proper foundation for success over the long haul. (Thanks Dude.)

In *Adventures of a Currency Trader*, Rob explores—through the story of Harry Banes—the ups and downs of being a trader, the struggles many of us must face to obtain the freedom that we are reaching for, and the liberating sense of finally making it.

This book, which is unique in its format, gives traders deep ideas to think about: It presents a foundation to trade by and an example we can relate to.

MAXWELL FOX, currency trader

South Pacific
August 2006

Preface

Trading can bring you independence. Trading currency has brought that to me, and I hope that it can do the same for you.

It's not easy. It takes time and discipline.

It's an adventure. But you can do it.

I will show you how, with the help of my friend Harry Banes.

The story you are holding in your hands is told through his eyes—he is Every Trader. There's a little bit of each one of us in Harry. And as you read, you'll follow Harry as he learns from some of the best traders in the world, alongside his friend and mentor.

As you get to know Harry, I think you will like him. He doesn't start trading with a huge sum of money, and his ambition is larger than his ability. Knowing where Harry came from can help us appreciate how we all begin our trading careers: nervous, excited, unskilled, and unproven. His financial situation, his day job, his life as a new trader, and his relationships with those around him, are much like mine were, or maybe yours are right now. His challenges and obstacles might remind you of the struggles you are facing right now. But he is determined to become a trader no matter what gets in the way.

Even the humblest among us can go on to become great traders. Even the chump traders can become champions. Even the indebted can become financially independent.

Harry admits early on that he's a rookie trader, which doesn't adequately prepare you for how bad he is. He's the worst trader I've ever known. But we'll stand next to Harry as he picks himself up from the sidewalk on Wall Street and begins to implement the wise counsel of an experienced trader who agrees to mentor him. From Harry's experiences, you'll learn how to recover from disastrous losses, how to set yourself up as a full-time trader, how to talk to your loved ones about what you're doing. But that's not all.

You'll learn with Harry how some of his mentor's best and worst former students set up their charts, do their analysis, and take their trades.

What is more important, you'll learn how Harry eventually uses similar techniques to become a profitable trader and reach financial freedom. And most important of all, you'll learn not only how he made those profits, but how he was able to keep them.

I need to stress two more things: Every character in this book is fictional, although you might see a bit of yourself in some of them. For more details about Harry, his mentor, their friends, and everything else about the book, check out Harry's web site at www.HarryBanes.com.

I now invite you to go on an adventure with Harry.

Read on.

ROB BOOKER

Wheeling, West Virginia
December 2006

Acknowledgments

This book took me 20 years to write. Well, not this specific book. But just the act of finishing a book and getting it to a publisher. While I trade for a living, I have dreamed of being a writer since I was 10 years old and sat in the back of Mrs. Holmes's fifth-grade class in La Verne, California. But just because I had the dream didn't mean that I made it easy for myself. In the past two decades, I have allowed some people and experiences to get in the way of my dreams.

Other people have helped me clear away those obstacles. I want to thank them.

Mrs. Holmes was my first and greatest inspiration. I would never have put pencil to paper in my small yellow notebook if not for her. She encouraged me and started me on the path to writing; without her, I could never have believed in myself. Many times during the writing of this book, I thought of the faith that she had in me when I was still so young, and I was able to write another sentence or page. I owe more to her than I have ever repaid.

I met Maxwell Fox in Fort Lauderdale, Florida, at the first seminar I ever did. He is the best trading friend I have ever had; he has helped me overcome plot difficulties and name characters (including Harry); and he was the first person to read the entire manuscript. I am a better person for knowing Max. He leaves people better than he found them. He is also the single greatest trader I've ever taught, hands down. He is disciplined, he is dedicated to the science of backtesting, and he wrote the funniest ebook on chart patterns you've ever seen. You can get that ebook at http://www.HarryBanes.com.

Eric Beutler helped in a moment of need. At just the right moment, in fact. And then he helped again and again and again.

I could have dedicated this book to David Murphy. He has been by my side for more than 20 years, to help me at every major point in my life. He has endured my ego, my mistakes, my weaknesses, far more than I could ever repay.

Emilie Herman and Kevin Commins at Wiley were patient with me and helped me every step of the way. Kathy Lien and Boris Schlossberg introduced me to Kevin and generally cheered me on when they didn't even know that I needed it. Jesse Torres introduced me to Betsy from Deutsche Bank, who kindly showed me a trading floor.

I have been honored to work with some of the finest currency traders in the world. I would stand any of these people up to any other traders on the planet: I can't name all of them, but here are some from the past few years: Craig Taylor, David Elliott, Scott Kush, Derek McGuire, Roman Jakubas, Beth McNabb, Nina Hernandez, Louis Cooper, Angela Nitkin, Ben McDonald, Andy Eastabrook, Dan Ziembienski, John Law, Gary Young, Chris Ennico, Thomas Gibbs, Marie-Sophie Blanchet, Todd Bryant, Nona Bates, Nader, Alex Semaan, Elaine Sequeira, Jonathan Warr, Jeff Politis, Irene Beregszaszi, Stephen Nieri, Chuck Smalley, Joseph Burgos, Johnny Ream, Darin Carlyle, Matt Forsyth, George Roy, Damodar Patlolla, Greg Walker, Guita Al-Boudoor, Napaporn Nozawa, Darryl Martins, Chris Pyor, Carlos Angel, Steve and Dave Trehan, the Pip Brothers Szymon and Jerry, Gene Miller, Craig Brinton, Wasyl Szeremeta, Phranq, Paul Kurtz . . .

I could go on for a long time. But these are among the best people I know. I am lucky to know them. They all helped me to write this book.

Any success I have in life is possible because I married my best friend. Kris is the best example of courage in the face of opposition and trial that I know. And she has supported me more than I have ever been able to support her. Thank you for putting me through law school, and for helping me quit a legal career and follow my dreams.

And last of all, I want to thank my son Isaac. You found me at the brink of emotional disaster and you reached out and saved me. You came to us in the very moment when we needed you most. I wrote this book for you, too, even though you are too young to read.

R. B.

About the Author

Rob Booker is an active proprietary forex trader and forex educator. Mr. Booker has trained hundreds of forex traders around the world. He speaks about currency trading at conferences, expos, street corners, first class and coach seats, weddings, funerals, mornings, evenings, and pretty much whenever anyone will or will not listen to him. Rob focuses on helping traders deal with the mental, psychological, and discipline issues related to trading. Mr. Booker has authored a number of ebooks, including Strategy:10, which has been downloaded over 200,000 times.

Rob can be reached at rob@robbooker.com.

Adventures
of a
Currency
Trader

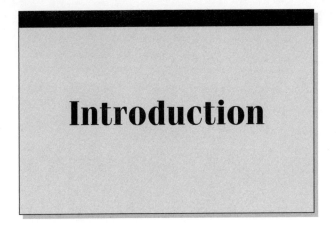

Introduction

My name is Harry Banes. I used to be the worst trader in the world. A real chump. I bought when I should have sold, and sold when I should have stayed out of the market completely. Ever do that? Of course not.

I was an expert at exiting my trades at just the exact moment when they would go from staggering loss to hugely profitable. Convinced that the trading gods wanted me to suffer, I nearly gave up on many occasions. When I say that I was a chump trader, I mean Super Chump. I lost thousands of dollars that my wife and I could not afford to lose.

It's a good thing that I never gave up. With the help of an amazing friend that you are going to meet in this book, I became a superprofitable trader. I traded my way out of the mess I was in.

If it were not for trading, I'd still be working in the filing room of the law firm Wakeman, Butterman, and Bailey, on 59th Street in Manhattan. That was the crummiest job I've ever had in my whole life. For 11 years, I worked there like a dog on a leash. Two years ago, I broke the leash and walked away, and I became human again.

You see, I reached my trading Independence Day. And I have never looked back.

I want you to do the same. That's why I am writing this book.

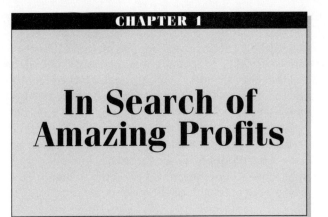

CHAPTER 1

In Search of Amazing Profits

I started trading because I saw a commercial on television about how simple it was to make money trading currency. A company called Amazing Forex Profits, supposedly based in New York City, the financial capital of the world, had agreed to unleash the powerful secrets of professional traders to the common man (me) for an unbelievable price. Making the decision to buy the software was easy: I needed money fast, and the advertisement seemed to promise that all I had to do was buy an easy system for making loads of cash every day. I called the toll-free number and right there, in the middle of the night, I spent $2,000 on that software. Now I only had to wait for the package to come in the mail. The road to riches was lined with profits from the forex (foreign exchange) market, and I was on it.

I didn't say a thing about this to my wife. I knew that the best way to handle this situation would be to get the software, have Scott, my assistant, install it on my computer at work, and start making a boatload of money; then I would buy something really nice for my wife and announce that I was going to be a full-time forex trader, a millionaire, and a hero to our family. The plan was foolproof!

Waiting for the software was agonizing. At the age of 35, I found myself racing home to see what had come in the mail that day. (Why had I not opted to spend an extra $49.95 for expedited shipping? The kind sales operator from India had insisted I would want to get started as soon as possible, so why didn't I listen?) It seemed as if an eternity passed before the package arrived, but arrive it did. So eager was I to start (and having learned from the infomercial that the forex market was open 24 hours a day), I called Scott and asked him to meet me downtown that very evening. I told my wife that I had some important matters to discuss at the office, kissed her and my kids goodbye, and hopped on the subway to 59th Street.

Everything seemed to be coming together. Although we had a lot of debt, I figured that with this new trading venture, I could make some serious profits. Some of the people on the commercial were making thousands of dollars a day—and this was not some fraudulent get-rich-quick scheme. I had met people who day-traded the stock market. They did their homework, they treated it like a job, and they were making real money. Some of them had made a lot of money in the late 1990s and although the market had fallen, they were still in the game. I liked the thought that I was going to join the ranks of people who could make money for a few moments of work per day.

When I arrived at the office, it was past 9:00 P.M. and everyone had long since gone home. Waiting at my cubicle was Scott Needleway, a junior filing clerk who had attended the same high school that I did (only he graduated seven years after me). He had long hair. He was brilliant with technology. He also won the "most likely to go to jail" award in his high school yearbook.

"So what're we doin' tonight?" he asked. I could tell that he had either been drinking or smoking something stronger than cigarettes. His days at the firm were numbered already, so I let it pass. Especially considering that I needed his help that night.

"I've got the software. I need you to show me how to get it running."

Scott had essentially run my computer for me for the past five years. Thank goodness, my job didn't require much work on the computer, and an attorney who needed to contact me would simply e-mail Scott. He, in turn, would tell me what was going on. Now I was excited to do some of my own computer work.

He took the CDs and quickly installed the software without a hitch. As promised on the commercial, the software was fairly straightforward. It was like a news feed—with headlines popping up on the screen, telling me to either buy or sell a particular currency pair. On another section of the screen, it showed all the current open positions. Most were colored green, showing me that they were making money.

All this had only taken 10 minutes, but I could tell that Scott wanted to go home, or go wherever he went when he wasn't at the office. I told him that I would see him tomorrow and he darted out of the office without another word. He hadn't even asked what the software did! Right there, he had walked away from an opportunity to improve his financial situation. Well, he could stay and work at Wakeman, Butterman, and Bailey for the rest of his life. Not me.

Instead of going home, I dove right into the software. I took my time getting used to clicking around the screens. I read the help manual twice,

I clicked through every screen in the software to learn about the different trades I could take, and I read an article about how currency pairs were quoted. I learned that currencies traded in pairs, meaning when you traded currency you were always buying one currency and selling another, or selling one currency and buying another. You could not trade currency just as a stand-alone financial instrument—and that made sense. Here is what I read:

> *If you think the U.S. Dollar is going up, you have to ask yourself: going up against what? Obviously, another currency. So you choose a currency that it is going up against, and you buy that other currency. And because you buy it with U.S. Dollars, you are selling Dollars and buying that other currency.*

It took a while to sink in, but within a couple of hours, I was a former filing clerk turned currency guru. I knew the major currencies were the Euro (EUR), the Great Britain Pound (GBP), the Japanese Yen (JPY), and of course, the U.S. Dollar (USD). I figured out how to read a currency quote. This is what one looks like:

GBP/USD 1.8000/1.8005

This meant that the Great Britain Pound against the U.S. Dollar could be sold for 1.8000, and could be bought for 1.8005. Simple enough. I also learned that if the Pound moved from 1.8000 to 1.8001, just one point, that would be called a one *pip* move—a pip, in other words, referred to a Percentage in Point in the world of foreign exchange. And the software was going to tell me how to do all this stuff.

The next morning I submitted all the necessary documents to open a trading account at a firm suggested by the Amazing Forex people. Within 24 hours, I was promised that I could fund my account with a credit card. More waiting, and this time it would be even more excruciating. Imagine the profits I was missing out on! All night, I had watched as the software called for buys and sells on currency pairs. Trade after trade was profitable. On a sheet of paper next to my computer, I calculated the point gains I could have made just by following along: over 110. It was going to be difficult to concentrate on my job that day knowing that I was letting more of the same profits go by. The challenge was not going to be making the money—it was going to be finding a way to trade as much as possible.

I hadn't slept that night, but it had been worth it. More motivated than ever to start trading, I felt invigorated and determined that during my lunch break that day I would schedule out all the times of day that I could trade. Although it would require me to get less sleep and steal some time from my employer, the payoff would be huge. Definitely worth any sacrifice!

THE ANSWER TO MY FINANCIAL PROBLEMS

Most people never do anything about their problems. When I was 10, I broke my "Tommy Baseball Home Run Challenge" electronic handheld game. After realizing that I could not fix it by shaking the game, or reinserting the batteries backwards, or praying to God, I hid the device away deep in my closet, behind the winter blankets and underneath my T-ball uniform. I put it there for two reasons. First, so my parents would not discover that I had broken an expensive toy when I celebrated a home run by spiking the game to the floor as if it were a football. The second reason? I knew that underneath the protective and magical cloth of my T-ball uniform, there was a chance that the baseball gods would heal the toy and bring it back to life.

I learned soon enough that this was not a useful method for fixing my problems. When my parents divorced later on that year, it became clear that simply hiding my father underneath my T-ball uniform was not going to keep my parents from yelling at each other (and in any case, the game was still using that space under the uniform). But hiding my problems, or storing my biggest challenges away in a closet, became one of my most frequently utilized methods for approaching difficulties in my life.

But when I purchased the Amazing Forex Profits software, I took control of my financial situation. I was doing something. This felt really good. I knew that my wife would be skeptical, so it was important to hide my decision from her at first. This small deception would turn out to be an inconsequential necessity on the road to riches. When she understood how much money I could make, it would seem less like a lie and more like a surprise.

Surprise is actually a good word to describe how we both felt about the results.

I BECOME CONVINCED OF MY GENIUS

A week passed; it was far more difficult to open the trading account than I had imagined, especially considering that I needed to fax the forex broker copies of my passport, utility bills, and everything except the results of a prostate exam. During this time, I watched as the Amazing Forex software lived up to its name. During the hours at work alone (as I stayed late every evening and kept an eye on it during the day), it was racking up hundreds of point gains every day. This was nearly too much for me to bear, as I realized how much in dollar terms this could mean.

Knowing that the forex broker (Universal Currency Brokers, based in Florida) would alert me by e-mail when the account was opened, I decided to dedicate this unintended downtime to becoming more capable with my e-mail so that I would know immediately when I could fund my account. Scott even took an entire day to teach me to use a BlackBerry, so that I could receive the e-mail no matter where I was. The more I used e-mail, the computer, the Amazing Forex software, and the BlackBerry, the more I realized how powerful all this technology was. Perhaps I could run the software on the BlackBerry and trade no matter where I was. The possibilities were endless. This claim of reaching financial freedom through trading did not seem unrealistic at all.

Tuesday, March 16, 2004, at precisely 12:06 P.M. Eastern Standard Time, I received the e-mail. I was in the conference room with the insurance litigation team, who were debating the merits of charging Wakeman clients in 6-minute increments versus 15 minutes. I was thrilled to be in the meeting, because it was easy to keep an eye on the BlackBerry, avoid doing any real work in the office, and then make a short presentation about how it was possible for our attorneys to bill a bit extra for administrative time by classifying "filing" as "research." I was near the end of my presentation when my BlackBerry buzzed and I knew that the moment had arrived.

"I'm sorry, I've got to take this," I said, excusing myself, "our daughter is in the emergency room and I've got to check on her."

Every attorney, especially the ones with small children at home, was quick to excuse me for this important break. Of course I had told a whopping lie, but once again, this was a minor indiscretion on the way to a more important goal: my own enrichment.

Outside the conference room, I read the blissful news: The trading account was open and I could fund it with my credit card at any time. I dropped into my cubicle, took out my credit card, and called the forex dealer.

It only took a few moments, but I was so wrapped up in funding the account with $1,000, that I didn't realize that I was being watched. John Murphy, a young attorney who did lots of work with contracts, stood near the entrance to my cubicle.

"I heard you reading out your credit card numbers," he said. "I didn't mean to pry, but is everything all right?"

I nodded. "Yeah, thanks." Dang! He knew that I was lying about my daughter going to the hospital. I probably owed him an apology.

"Well if you need anything, let me know. Did you have to pay out-of-pocket expenses for the ER?"

Hooray! He had no idea I had lied! "Yes," I told him, adding another small lie to my growing list of Minor Indiscretions on the Path to Riches.

"If you need anything, let me know. Your insurance ought to cover it. I know we've got problems with the benefits here, so I will see what I can do to help."

I thanked him, then I thanked God that I hadn't been caught, and then I totally forgot about John Murphy and the ER and the lie. It was time to trade. I booted up the Amazing Forex software and my trading account, pinned the "Out to Lunch" sign outside my cubicle, and made sure my computer monitor was still positioned so that only I could see it.

Barely had I signed into Amazing Forex (Login: SUPERTRADER_2000, Password: G$TRICH) that I noticed Scott standing behind me.

"You got your account set up?"

Just hearing his voice was disturbing. Right now I needed privacy! The clock was ticking down, and I only had 37 more minutes of lunchtime to make as many trades as I could.

"Yeah, Scott. Got it set up. I am going to check it out now, see what's going on, you know, during my lunch."

He nodded. "Gonna make some coin at the office! Nice."

"No," I replied, showing some frustration in the tone of my voice, "I am going to just take it easy today and watch." I didn't mean this either. The lying was coming easier, and right now I was grateful that I could use a plausible distortion of the truth to distance myself from unwanted intrusive eyeballs.

"Well, then I might stay and watch."

I sighed and realized that arguing with Scott would steal precious trading time. "You can stay but just keep quiet. I am trying to learn this and it's not easy for me."

"Looks like you have a buy alert on the Gee-Bee-Pee," he replied.

He was right. There it was, my first order alert! I quickly toggled to my trading platform, hit the GBP/USD quote, and up popped an order window. Without a moment's hesitation—for there could be other trades just waiting to be taken—I clicked the okay button and boom! My trade was opened with a slick whooshing sound. There, in the open trades window, I saw it, but I was already down $50! How could that be?

"How could that be?" I found myself saying out loud.

"You already suck at trading," Scott said. I considered poking out his eyes with a pen, but that would also rob me of precious time that could not be wasted.

I toggled back to the Amazing Forex software screen. It told me that the GBP/USD trade, the one that I had just taken, should be negative 5 points (or $50, since I had traded for $10 per market point) right then. Phew! Knowing that the Amazing folks were experiencing the same quick loss helped ease my mind. I faintly remembered that nearly all trades in the system started off unprofitable. Good. I planted my feet firmly on the floor under my desk and waited for the next order to appear.

Then my cell phone rang. The ring tone told me it was my wife, Gini. Scott had set that up for me so I would not miss her calls.

"You gonna get that?" Scott asked, knowing it was my wife. This time I considered taping his mouth shut, but all I had was clear office tape and that would not do the trick.

I took the call, if only to appear that I was cool and calm, even though my palms were sweaty as I opened the phone. My nerves were rattling as I spoke.

"What's up?"

"Hi sweetie," she happily chirped. "How's your day?"

I answered that it was going fine in the tone of voice that a husband uses when he wants to tell his wife that she has called at a bad time, but does not want to actually say that she called at a bad time.

"Is this a bad time," she asked. "I wanted to know what you wanted for dinner."

"Anything is great."

"Any-thing," she replied, speaking slowly as if she were writing it down. "Got it. I will check at the market for Anything. Want to say hi to your son?"

"Not now," I quickly answered. It was impossible to hold my cell phone up to my ear and toggle back to the trading account. I tried, but all I managed to do was switch to a screen that showed my e-mail. Now I couldn't see anything!

"Okay, I just wanted to say hello and that I love you," she told me, and I could tell that she wanted to talk more even though she was kindly willing to end the call if I insisted. Which is what I did.

"Not now," I barked. "I gotta go."

I immediately felt terrible, but I hung up the phone anyway. I didn't even give her a chance to respond; I was now sweating badly and having trouble keeping my right leg from bouncing on the floor, which is what I always do when I am nervous.

Scott didn't say anything about the way I hung up with my wife. I clicked on the trading software and up popped my account. I looked at the current profit on the open trade: Three hundred dollars. Three hundred dollars!

Scott's jaw dropped down. My sweat turned cold. I heard my heart beating, and my foot stopped drumming on the floor. I think 10 seconds passed, but to Scott and me time had ceased to have meaning, and I cascaded into a deep trance.

I imagined quitting my job that day. I could see my wife driving a new sporty sedan, the kids happily cheering her on as she sped through the EZ-pass gate on the way to our summer home in the Hamptons; then I could see myself diving into an oval of midnight blue water, with reggae music playing in the background and leggy blondes sunning themselves around the edges of the pool. This was the life! Trading had brought it to me!

Scott knocked me from the daydream by gripping my shoulder and shaking. "Dude, dude, you gotta take that money!" he told me, and he was right. I had no idea what Amazing Forex said, but there was no way I was going to miss out on three hundred bucks. I clicked once on the open trade window, and up popped a box that asked me if I wanted to close the trade.

"Darn right!" I said, speaking much louder than I should.

"Woo hoo!" yelled Scott, happy for me and now much more interested in the Amazing Forex software than he had been the week before.

I clicked a button and all of a sudden, my account value had gone from $1,000 to $1,300. Holy moley, I thought. This really is simple. This really is the answer to my financial problems. In less than a minute, I had made enough to buy a new iPod for my wife. I determined that this was exactly the present I would give to her to tell her all about the trading.

Scott wanted me to see what the software was telling us, so I switched back to look at it. But something was wrong. The trade was still there, but it was showing a 34 pip loss, not a gain.

"What's up with that," Scott asked. "Did it go the other way?"

I spent a moment looking over the screen for clues. It wasn't hard to find.

"Sheez, Scott. We bought when we were supposed to sell."

Scott was speechless.

I had taken the wrong trade! Immediately, I checked the trading account again. Yes, the sweet profits were still safely secure in my "account equity" window. This meant that Amazing Forex Profits' suggestion to sell the GBP/USD had been a horrible idea—but that we had mistakenly taken the opposite trade and profited. As I watched the sell trade go deeper into a loss, I actually felt happy.

I smiled. We had cheated the Amazing Forex software! We were victorious. It stood to reason, in my moment of complete insanity, that I could beat the software. I was that good.

Scott agreed, and appropriately took credit for first misreading the software's recommendation to sell. I patted him on the back and promised to share some of the profits with him over time. Maybe he could be my technology right-hand man. Surely there were other programs out there like the Amazing Forex Profits software, and we could install a few of them.

I determined that I owed my wife a phone call, instead of doing any more trades. It was the right thing to do and she happily accepted my apology. I told her I had a surprise for her when I got home. She giggled on the phone, and I realized that my superpowers as a trader were only exceeded by my Amazing Relationship skills.

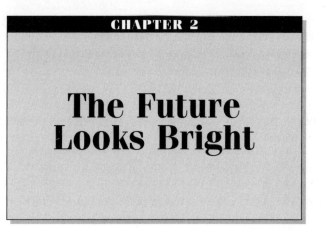

CHAPTER 2

The Future Looks Bright

After work that day, I bought my wife an iPod and hopped on the subway, smiling the entire way home. Of course, I needed to make a lot more money before I quit my job, but that day I felt as if I had already given notice.

When I arrived home, I was so consumed by thoughts of trading that I forgot to give my wife her surprise present. But that doesn't mean I wasn't happy to see her. I found her in the kitchen, and I wrapped my arms around her waist and hugged her tightly.

"Not so tight," she said, laughing. "Caroline's in there!" Caroline was our five-month-old fetus, growing strong and healthy and on schedule. My wife was starting to grow bigger now, and was as beautiful as ever. I kissed her neck and she turned around to face me.

"I am happy to see you, too. We're late for our rent payment again. I don't mean to ruin the happy moment."

I knew she loved me, and I knew she had to remind me that the rent was late. Otherwise, I was going to pretend that it wasn't happening. We were knee-deep, or deeper, in debt. I hated to face it. My usual response, as I said before, was to ignore financial problems and hope they would disappear. Once I got around to admitting there was a problem, I would dwell on the depressing state of affairs until I had a knot in my stomach and a headache. That evening, admitting that the rent was late was, for once in my life, not so terrible: I could face it, knowing that during 60 seconds of my lunch break I had made enough money to pay a nice chunk of the rent.

After dinner, and when the kids were in bed, I retreated to our small family room and I opened my wallet. Here is what I found:

- Regular identification
- Six credit cards

I took out the cards one by one. I shifted them between my fingers. These would soon be history! My wife walked in and noticed what I was doing.

"I didn't mean to worry you about the rent," she said.

"I'm not worried at all," I replied happily and put the cards away.

As I got ready for bed, I started to calculate in my mind everything that we owed. The total came to $24,000, give or take a few hundred. Our monthly payments on the cards were low—interest rates were falling—so that wasn't so bad. Sometimes I paid our rent from one of the cards. But what was going to happen when the introductory low rates ended? What was going to happen when we ran out of credit? Without trading, we were going to be screwed. I couldn't believe how lucky I was to have found trading—it had come along at just the right moment. My wife was trying to be as supportive as possible. But I knew that a big talk was coming between the two of us, and it was not going to be an easy one. I wanted to be optimistic. Ignoring the problems wasn't optimism, though. I had been lying to myself, living in a daze, expecting to ignore my problems.

But now I didn't have to ignore them anymore. I could face them, three hundred dollars at a time!

THE FIRST NIGHTMARE

At 2:00 in the morning, I woke up with my wife tossing violently at my side, and my golden retriever, Franklin (who slept in the bed with us), nudging me to do something because he was worried but did not know how to help. I rubbed my eyes and looked at my wife, who was whispering something while she thrashed back and forth. It was obvious that she was having a nightmare.

"We will pay you," she said. It was eerie to see her speaking and tossing around, with her eyes closed the entire time.

"We will pay you. We will pay you."

She said it twice more, and then I put my hand on her shoulder to keep her from rolling over onto the floor, and spoke her name loud enough to wake her up, but not so loud that it would scare her.

She bolted upright in bed and gripped my hand that had been on her shoulder, and then let out a huge gasp for air. She was covered in sweat and trembling.

I hugged her. "You were having a bad dream."

A few moments passed before she could speak. "I did. I did have a nightmare."

I got her a drink of water and sat on the bed next to her. She laid her head on my lap. "I heard you talking in your sleep," I told her. "I heard you talking about paying someone."

"I'm worried about money, Harry."

"I know."

Franklin was now awake as well and was up on all fours, panting and ready to go to battle for my wife.

"It's okay Frank," I told him. "I'm all right. Sorry we woke you up."

"We can't pay our rent," Gini reminded me. She had only been awake from the nightmare for a few moments, but she was speaking clearly as if she had never been asleep. I heard the traffic outside our open window that was definitely not providing enough cool air. I kicked the sheets off the bed.

I could feel my heart pounding. This was not something that I could ordinarily feel. Gini continued.

"And Judy needs a uniform for Girl Scouts."

"Can we use a credit card?" I hated to even say the words.

She shook her head and I heard a sniffle. A street lamp sent light into our room, and onto her face, where it reflected off a teardrop. She wiped her nose and sniffled.

"I don't think we have any more credit." She was probably right, especially since I had charged $250 to a credit card to buy her the iPod.

Out of credit. Not good. Franklin stirred a bit, as if we had just destroyed his plans to order some dog biscuits online. I spoke up. I needed to take control of the situation and stop playing like I didn't care.

"I think I know a way we can get out of this."

She perked up a bit. It was obvious that she was so upset that any solution seemed like a good idea, even if she had not heard it yet. I could have told her that I was going to start a meth lab in our walk-in closet, and she probably would have gone along with it for a few moments. She felt as bad about not buying that Girl Scout uniform as if she had been unable to feed the family. It was coming down to this: We were so far down the well that we could no longer see the light at the top.

"How?" she asked.

"I might be able to do some trading."

Her head shot up. She wiped her nose and smiled. "Really?"

Her eyes were brighter.

"What does that mean? Is it expensive?"

"No," I said as I chuckled. "In fact, so far it has been paying for itself." I explained the late night commercial, the clandestine purchase, the all-nighter at the office when I learned to use the software, and how I had already started making money.

"How much?" she asked.

"Three hundred dollars."

She lifted her head from my lap. "Three hundred dollars?" I could tell she was amazed. Well, that's what the software promised! This was good! This was not a crazy scheme to ask for another raise, especially now that I was probably the highest paid (overpaid) file manager in any U.S. law firm. This was a way to make money on the side! This was being sensible! This was what the provider does! He thinks of real solutions that make sense to wives.

In that moment, I remembered the iPod and felt even more proud of myself.

The obvious question came next: "What kind of trading is it?"

I hesitated. My wife was excited and I didn't want to have an endless discussion of the risks associated with trading. Honestly, I had hardly listened to the risk disclaimers on the commercial, and thank goodness I hadn't paid more attention. I might never have bought it.

But I owed her the truth.

"It's forex trading."

"Flo-recks?" She was perplexed.

"No, forex, like 'foreign exchange,' or currencies. It's like trading stocks, only you trade currencies."

"Wow. I didn't know they did that." I was really happy that she did not blow up the idea immediately. This emboldened me.

"Honestly, neither did I," I admitted. "But it only took me about a minute to trade today."

"So you can do it at work?"

"Well, at lunch. And after I get home."

"At night?"

I nodded. "Yes, it's a 24-hour market, so I can trade it anytime. It's perfect for keeping my job now and doing this on the side."

"Can you make that much every day?" she asked, perhaps now more hopeful than I was. I decided a bit of restraint was in order.

"Well, not every day. Maybe that much. Maybe a bit less."

She was doing numbers in her head. "That's like nine thousand dollars in a month." I could tell she was having trouble comprehending that I could make that much money.

"Well, there isn't any trading on Saturday. So it's less than that."

"Still," she spoke, putting her head back down on my lap. "That is so much money. We could be out of debt in a few months." She then said nothing for a few minutes, and I knew what was coming next. Her head popped back up: "Is this risky?"

I shrugged, trying to act cool. "For a beginner. For someone who doesn't know what he is doing. Sure. But I've got the software, and I am going to play it safe."

"Can we lose the thousand dollars you put in?"

"I don't think so. I'm only going to trade when the software tells me to. There are people making a lot of money from this. I watched it for a week and it was just as amazing as they say—it was really making some incredible trades."

Skeptical but satisfied, she told me she just wanted to go back to bed now. I told her that before she did I wanted to give her a gift. I went into the hallway, opened my briefcase, and brought her the present.

When she unwrapped the iPod, she threw her arms around me and kissed me. "Can we afford this?" she asked.

"We can now," I laughed. And with that, we went back to sleep, peacefully and with hope of the brighter future that was now within our reach.

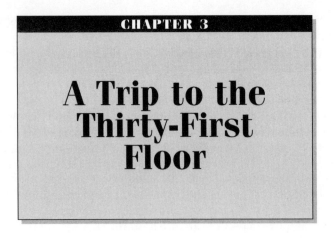

CHAPTER 3

A Trip to the Thirty-First Floor

I worked in midtown Manhattan for 11 years. I worked at the law firm of Wakeman, Butterman, and Bailey, and all I did—and I am not making this up—is file stuff away. Motions, briefs, interrogatories, settlements . . . you name it, I found a way to file it. This may sound like a boring job, and that's exactly what it was. It was like watching *Brady Bunch* reruns while poking my eyeballs out with a fork. This is the type of job that a man will do anything to get fired from. And believe me, I tried. There were times when I wanted to eat my leg just to inject an interesting event into my day.

While I never ate my leg, I did all sorts of other things to pass the time. I spent as much time as possible walking in between lawyers' offices and the filing area: We had 145 attorneys at the time, and I could waste a good 25 minutes on the way to a lawyer's office. I still finished all the work that I was supposed to do.

What got me the job in the first place was a pretty well connected father. Mine, to be exact. Harold Banes Sr. worked in the New York Metropolitan Transit Authority. He wasn't an engineer. He didn't dig tunnels or do anything cool like that either. He was a janitor. To put this into perspective, you need to pretend that you are in charge of cleaning up an area the size of a football field, only it's made of secret passageways, it's always either below zero or above 90 degrees, you enjoy the company of rats, and you consider it a pleasure to call the police about once a week because someone is living (or dying) in your work space. He's retired now, but I imagine he has nightmares in the same way as do Vietnam vets or abused pets.

He happened to work the same station that just about every single lawyer from Wakeman, Butterman, and Bailey walked through every day. And over the years, he spoke to every one of those lawyers. He became good friends with many of them, and when I graduated from high school, I had already worked three summers in the filing office of the firm, thanks to his relationships.

I wasn't making a lot of money at the time, but I didn't know it. I think they were paying me $15 an hour, back in 1992. That seemed like a ton of money to me then. But I certainly didn't protect the money as if I thought it was a lot. I spent it like money was coming out of the fire hydrants, and I lived like there would be a raise every year. And that was fine for a long time because it was just me, and I was living at home.

Soon enough though, my high school girlfriend and I were deciding to get married, and soon enough after that, we were having kids. Three, to be exact, in the first seven years of marriage. And now we had one more on the way.

Every day for the past 11 years, I had taken an elevator up to the 44th floor of a shining Manhattan skyscraper, to go to work at a job I didn't much care for, for people I didn't really think about unless they were standing in front of me, to earn about $300 less per month than I needed to survive (until now, ha!). And on the way up in that elevator, I passed floor after floor of other offices. I never really stopped to wonder who worked on those floors.

Anyway, when I got up to my cubicle, Scott was waiting for me just as he had done every day, for the past five years.

Today, he looked worried. This wasn't normal. He was about the most laid-back guy in the world, but right now he looked as if someone had caught him smoking behind the front desk. For a moment, I worried that this had something to do with trading.

"You didn't make any trades on my account, did you?"

He shook his head. I felt relief wash over me. I did not want him touching the account or the software. I didn't mind that he was now interested in trading, but I didn't fully trust him.

"Dude, Herbie wants to see you," he said, trying to seem as matter-of-fact as possible but really coming off as worried.

"Mr. Johnson?" Scott called him Herbie, always out of earshot, but all the same I hated when he did that. When I heard the name "Herbie," the name played over and over in my mind, and I worried that I might blurt it out sometime in front of Mr. Johnson.

Scott nodded quickly, like a child would do.

"Did he say what he wanted?" I asked, already dreading the encounter I was about to have. I had a lot of filing in front of me for the day, plus I wanted to trade again. I wanted to show my wife another good day of profits. Maybe I could go one more point past 30 today, and get $310. That would be awesome.

"No, he didn't say what he wanted," Scott replied, interrupting my daydream. "In fact, he just left a voice mail for you, which as usual I checked because you never do."

I smiled weakly. "I wanted to check the market before I got started with work today. It's why I got here early."

Scott nodded. "I'm sure you have a few moments. Let's fire it up."

We did. And things were hopping! There were already seven Amazing Forex orders open—all but two were profitable. I looked at the most recent order: It was an order to buy the British Pound against the U.S. Dollar—the GBP/USD—and the trade alert had just come through 5 minutes ago. It was only 10 points in the negative right now.

Scott brightened up: "You can trade that right now and get a better price than they suggested." I thought about it, and he was right: They had suggested buying the GBP/USD at 1.8100, and it was now at 1.8090. That meant that we could get in on a profitable buy trade and at a better price than had originally been suggested. I opened my trading platform and entered the order.

Whoosh! I liked that sound. Now we only had to wait for the profit to appear. We also had to keep an eye on the Amazing software, so that we would know when to exit. Yesterday we had exited in a gleeful pandemonium resulting from my first profit. But now I was committed to exiting the trades when the software told me to. I rubbed my hands together. I forgot about the filing that I needed to do. I expected the profit to come quickly again, but after a few moments had passed, the trade still did not budge. I was down $50.

"Why is it negative from the start?" I wondered aloud.

Scott answered quickly. "You've got to pay the spread. You can buy at a price higher than what you can sell for. That's how the broker makes his money."

"Ahh," I answered. The spread. Okay. That made sense. So I would be negative from the start of every trade. But Amazing Forex had been giving such good trades that usually I didn't notice this. Minutes passed.

It was 8:29 A.M.

I heard a booming voice down the hall. It was Mr. Johnson. I heard my name being called and remembered that the big man wanted to see me. Oops. I had an open trade! I expected it to be closed by now. I was becoming uncomfortable with this trade out there in cyberspace. I should have some profit by now!

"Harry, he wanted to see you first thing when you got in."

"I know."

"And he knows you get here every day at eight-fifteen A.M."

"I know."

What could I do?

Scott smiled at me and said: "I will get out of the trade right when the software says to. You go talk to Herbie. Here's a pen and a pad so you can take notes while he is yelling, and here is a tissue in case he spits on you." He handed me these things as if he were preparing me for battle.

I did not want to leave Scott in charge of my trade, but I had no choice. "Don't do anything else. Just close it when the software says to close it." "I will. I won't move."

I started on my way to Herb's office, glancing over the top of my cubicle on the way out. I couldn't see the screen because I had moved my monitor. This meeting with Mr. Johnson could last for a half minute. Or it could take an hour.

Herb Johnson was the managing partner of the firm. Newly elected, he was in the position he was because he could get things done. He was a first-class operator. This Napoleon-shaped man could return two phone calls, scribble down a defense strategy, and scream at an associate lawyer all at the same time. He had earned more money for the firm in fees than any other attorney in the firm's history, he had brought in more clients, had a reputation for speaking his mind clearly and loudly, and scared the crap out of anyone who worked for him. When I arrived at his office, he was already screaming. Not at me yet, but at someone on the phone.

Instead of ending the phone call like most humans do, he simply put down the phone—didn't hang up, just put it down on the desk—and stared me down for a good 30 seconds.

Was he going to fire me? Maybe.

Promote me? No way.

Yell at me about missing documents? Oh, yes. That was going to be it for sure.

"Banes, you've done it again," he growled. I heard what he was saying, but I was really thinking about my trade. Could it be possible that I was already making some money? Ohhh, money. How I loved it. How I longed to see the trade! It must be very profitable by now. I wondered how long it generally took an Amazing Forex Profit System trade to reach its profit target. Maybe I would call the company later that day and ask. But for now, I could nearly smell the profit wafting over the cubicles to me; it was a sweet scent that I hoped to smell again many times that same day.

I imagined myself sitting by the midnight blue water, reclining on a lounge chair. An attentive server was approaching me:

ATTENTIVE SERVER: Mr. Banes, would you like another drink?
ME: Why yes. I'll have another virgin strawberry daiquiri.
ATTENTIVE SERVER: Of course.

Mr. Johnson was still yelling when I snapped back into the present tense. He was blabbering about some lost file, some letter that surely demanded legal redress for the wrongs done to our firm's client blah blah blah.

When Herbie was really upset, he growled, and his growling increased as he talked. "It's the most important file in this whole damn office, Banes. It's the Anderson case, the trader. The bonus discrimination case."

He said this as if I actually cared about Anderson, or his case, or whether the file had been shredded with the receipts of Herbie's gifts to his mistress. I did care about trading, though, and when Mr. Johnson said, "trader," it made me even more excited to go check with Scott to see what had happened.

I wrote some notes down on the pad of paper that Scott had given me while Mr. Johnson continued his tirade. I didn't have to take any notes about the case, which Mr. Johnson was now describing in the most specific detail. I knew this case because it was on the front pages of every New York business section. We were representing a Wall Street firm—one of the biggest securities firms in the world. The firm was accused of paying a smaller bonus to a physically handicapped trader, or something like that, to force the trader out of the firm. I didn't know all the details, but I knew that the case was Herb's, that it was producing huge amounts of filing work, and that meant that it was producing huge fees. I stopped drawing my portrait of the managing partner, and asked: "Which document specifically do you want me to find?"

He stopped talking and stared me down again for what seemed like forever. I thought at any moment he would pounce on me, his little Danny DeVito frame scrambling across the desk to rip out my throat or something. I took a step back.

The phone was still sitting on his desk, and I could barely hear a voice calling out to him, wondering where Herb went. I think Herb was partly glad I had interrupted him so that he could get back to billing three people at once.

"It's a letter," he answered, as he started walking around his desk to pick up his briefcase. As he described the letter, he was already in the process of doing something else entirely. When he finished letting me know what I was supposed to go look for, he looked up at me and said, "Take it down to the 31st floor, personally, and tell Mr. Anderson that I want him to call me and let me know that you delivered it."

So this was the punishment: I was messenger boy for a morning. That was perfectly fine. I could stand that, especially since there were mountains of Anderson files that my team and I were going to have to work on for the rest of the day. And now I could check on the trade!

As I ran back to the file room to grab the letter, which I immediately recognized and which I had personally placed in the correct location only 24 hours before, I noticed Scott walking down the far hall of the office. He was more than 50 feet away and it was impossible to yell loud enough to get his attention. That meant that he wasn't watching the trade!

I bolted back to my desk to get the update. But the screen was blank—just a screen saver. The Amazing software was closed; the trading account program was no longer open. And I had no idea where to find Scott. And I needed to deliver the letter pronto.

Then I heard Mr. Johnson's voice booming from down the hall. Reluctantly I left my desk, determined to never again leave it while I had an open trade. Having to delay my knowledge of the outcome was going to kill me.

MY EYES ARE OPENED

I needed a special code to even get the elevator to stop at the 31st floor. On exiting the elevator, all I saw in front of me was a small lobby, with furniture that appeared to have never been used. Brass letters spelled out ERNEST WELLINGTON AND COMPANY above the secretary who guarded the desk, and behind her was a steel door that fit in very nicely with the wood trim in the rest of the small room. I stated my purpose, she made a phone call to check my identity, and then she turned around, swiped a card through a slot, and the steel door unlocked. She pushed it open, and while turning around and leaving me, said something which I never heard. In fact, I almost had to cover my ears to protect them from the noise I now encountered.

I could feel the door close behind me—it hit me in the butt—but I hardly moved. I was staring at the trading floor of a major Wall Street firm, and I thought I had been teleported to another planet.

There were at least 20 rows of desks, formed in a giant half-circle, starting directly in front of me, and extending out all the way across the floor to the other end of the building. At least 200 men and a few women were yelling, pounding on their computers, and watching their screens. There was so much happening right here, just a few floors below where I had been working for 11 years.

I forgot entirely about Anderson, and just wandered onto the floor. Glass windows looked out on midtown from the west side, and every other wall had glass conference rooms, one after the other, mostly empty. Above the conference rooms were screens: Some screens showed what were obviously quotes on stocks or bonds or whatever, and some showed what appeared to be news conferences from around the world, with closed captioning but no sound. I felt as if time stood still for me and was moving at 1,000 miles per hour for everyone around me.

It was chaos.

Walking a few feet forward, I stood next to a guy who was probably 21 years old, and he was screaming into his phone something about selling stock in November for some price that I cannot remember. The man next to him was at least twice his age and had his head in his hands, and didn't look very happy. The woman down one more seat was poking her finger into her trading screen, and saying something to the guy next to her about Commitments of Traders, and how she was owed a case of beer.

And this scene was repeated, row after row, until I was dizzy. I heard people talking about millions and millions of dollars. As I walked further toward the center of the floor, I heard a trader say to the guy next to him that he had just dumped a million shares of GE. A million shares of General Electric? That must have been worth tens of millions of dollars. How did he get those shares? Upon whom had he dumped them? Why did they buy them? How did the dumpee feel about all of this?

There is a time in one's life that is a wake-up call. This was mine.

Maybe it doesn't happen to everyone. It might have happened to you when you learned about trading or peered over a friend's shoulder to see him making trades. It's a moment when you feel as if you are just waking up out of hibernation and realize that you have been missing life for at least a few years, if not your entire prior existence. I forgot completely about my open trade on the GBP/USD and thought: These men and women are making enormous amounts of money by trading. I had thought that $300 was big time.

No, this scene in front of me was big time. It was the biggest time of all.

I had never seen so many people this animated, this excited, this depressed, this wild—all working in the same room, talking about dumping tens of millions of dollars of shares on someone else. Something clicked inside me. Or it was more like something snapped.

I knew this is what I needed to be doing. Already I knew that I wanted to trade. Already I knew that I had the talent to do it—but this trading floor, this mass of chaotic buying and selling: This is what I wanted to do for the rest of my life.

There could not have been a more ridiculous thought at the time. I had taken just one trade of my own. I was a file manager in a New York law firm, with ninth-grade math skills and a diploma from Ben Cardozo High School. Surrounding me at that moment were men and women educated at some of the finest universities in the United States—I probably was standing among more than a hundred Harvard Business School graduates. It was just as likely that I'd be made partner that same day in my own law firm without a law degree, not to mention a college degree.

But I knew what I wanted. I wanted to do what these people did.

Now, I remembered my trade. Seeing all these people in a state of violent anxiety over their trades made me feel part of the group. A member of a brotherhood of traders who worried about whether their trade was profitable. Just like me.

"Hey, Mack, you lookin' for somebody?" a voice called out to me.

I could not tell where it had come from, so I just answered while I was looking around the room, "Anderson. Looking for Anderson."

"Over in front of you, keep walking, to the conference room. You look like you stepped in something."

If I had been able to identify who was talking to me, I would have asked about the current price on the British Pound.

Copies of the *Wall Street Journal* were everywhere, but most of them were unopened. The sports sections of the *New York Daily News* and *New York Post* were opened across one out of three desks, at the least. Most traders wore casual clothes. If a guy had a sport coat of any kind, it was strewn over the back of his chair or on the floor.

Everywhere I looked around the trading floor, there were computer screens and on those screens, charts. Not so different from the charts I would see if I watched business news on television, which was mostly never. Every trader I could see—in fact, all of them—had at least three flat panel computer monitors, and some had four. At least one of those screens on each desk was showing some form of financial charts. The charts still made no sense to me. But obviously they were indispensable. It was one more thing I was going to have to learn.

Instead of spending more time gawking at the trading operation, I decided I'd be better off just getting over to see Anderson, and then getting back upstairs to check on my trade.

I hurried to the conference room where I saw a thin, blond man, with wire glasses and a bow tie, standing by a sea of papers on a glass conference table. Although he had boyish looks, it was obvious he was an important person around here, just from the way he stood at the table in deep thought, with his hand rubbing his chin. Maybe it was his ability to look so calm while there was so much madness happening right on the other side of the glass conference room.

He grinned at me when I opened the door.

"You must be Harry Banes," he said in a quiet voice. I would not have heard him if the glass conference room walls had not been surprisingly soundproof.

"Yes, that's right. I brought this letter from Herb."

He put out his hand to take the letter and smiled warmly. "How long have you been with the firm?"

"About 10 years."

"How is it, working with Herb?"

I was not about to lose my job from a stupid comment, so I answered as honestly as possible. "We'll be working more closely now that he's the senior partner."

"True. Where did you go to school?"

I didn't really understand what he was asking, so I said, "Cardozo."

"Oh, that's a fine law school," he said.

For a moment I thought about correcting him—I hadn't gone to Benjamin Cardozo law school. I'd gone to Benjamin Cardozo High School. What he didn't know wouldn't hurt him.

"You from the city?" He asked.

"Yep, born and raised."

"Who did you have for Corporations?" He asked, never letting his eyes off mine.

I must have let my eyes fall out of my head at that moment, because it was easily apparent that I had no idea what he was talking about. So I acted like I hadn't heard him and stared out the window.

"Busy day today on the trading floor," I told him. I said this with a matter-of-fact tone, as if I visited trading floors all the time and was pleased to see everyone busy at work.

"Sure is. CPI rocked the markets this morning. Sent stocks way up in a hurry."

Stocks were irrelevant. My buy trade on the GBP/USD was far more important.

"And the dollar?" I asked.

He grinned. "So you're a student of the markets, I see."

I nodded. "I do a bit of trading myself."

"Well, then," he said, "You'll be happy if you're short dollars today."

Short dollars? That meant selling dollars. I had bought British Pounds. This should not have been so confusing, but it was. I had bought the GBP today, which meant that I had sold USD, which meant that I was short dollars. And he was telling me that the dollar had gone down! That meant that more sweet profit was waiting for me upstairs.

"Actually," I told him, "I should be short dollars as we speak."

This pleased him immensely. "Fine, very fine. We need to make sure that we keep in touch. Anyway, about Corporations, who'd you have?"

Now I was screwed. "I'm embarrassed to say that I don't even remember."

With a quiet chuckle, he let me off the hook. "Too much trading, I presume! Understood. Skipped corporations myself. By third year, I was skipping class and calling my broker to place trades. I paid more in commissions in my third year than I made in profits on every trade." And then he patted me on the shoulder. Thankfully, our discussion about my law school experience, which I never had, was nearly over. He continued.

"Well, catch up on some of your corporations material—because we're going to form an in-house forex fund, and we're going to need a lot of help on that. We've got investors from all over the place—some in mainland China, some in the Middle East. Will probably raise some eyebrows and need some background checks. This is not just the ordinary setup. We're putting five billion behind this to start."

Five billion dollars? Whoa! I am happy he hadn't asked how much money I was making on my trades.

"Tell that to Herb when you get back. Tell him we might need some help with the fund and he should call me."

All I could say was, "Will do," and then I got out of the conference room as quickly as I could stumble over myself.

I walked across the entire trading floor to make my way back. Once again, it seemed as if time stood still for me while it moved for everyone else. I felt like I was on a people mover, or a ride at Disneyland; I couldn't quite wrap my head around what I was watching and hearing. It didn't matter that I took my time, anyway, because I knew my trade was okay, and I knew that I wanted to soak up as much of this experience as possible.

This was a wild ride that I was going to have to repeat.

On the way back to the office, I hoped that Anderson and I could talk again. Imagine how much he could teach me about currency trading!

Since I knew that my trade had done well, I stopped by Herb's office first. Poking my head in his office, I gave him a thumbs-up sign, to let him know I had delivered the letter. He was talking on the phone, had two other attorneys in the office with him, but still took the time out to say, "Don't ever misplace a file again, or you're fired."

I don't know what came over me at that point, maybe all the yelling and testosterone from the 31st floor had rubbed off on me. I looked him in the eye and said: "Well, don't look in the wrong place next time, or you'll have to call me again."

Then I walked away, positive that I was going to get fired and feeling really good that I had stood up for myself. Wow! Just a few minutes in the midst of all those traders, and I had recaptured my optimism. It hit me so hard when it came back that I got chills up my spine.

I could be working down on the 31st floor, I told myself. If I wanted to, I could work there. And if Herb fired me, I could just start trading on my own. I should be trading for a living already. That was where I belonged.

The job didn't really matter. The overdue rent didn't matter. The credit card debt seemed so much smaller. No matter how suddenly I had found this new path, it was pointing in the right direction. And I was going to take it.

As I walked down the hall, I heard Herb loudly call to the other attorneys, "Well, let's hope to God he didn't talk to Anderson that way. Head of

---

trading for the entire operation, and he probably walked in there and told him to find his own letters from now on."

I stopped cold. The head of all trading? Anderson? The thin, pale guy with the Nerd Club for Men glasses? That's the person I had talked to? Most excellent! My new friend on the 31st floor was a master trader!

The wheels started turning in my head. Could I go back down there? Could I ask him a bunch of questions about currencies? Would he offer me a job? What would I say? In this moment of supreme confidence, it seemed like a great idea.

Even if Anderson didn't want to sit and talk about currencies with me—he was certainly a very busy man—maybe he would let me just watch the traders for a while and learn while sitting there. Yes! That was a good idea. I literally propped myself up against my cubicle to keep from falling. How much time had just passed? Twenty minutes from the time I went downstairs until now? An hour at the most? Maybe I should go back down there immediately and ask if I could watch the traders for the rest of the day.

But I had a trade to check on. How much profit had I made? Another $300? More? When I get a flash of euphoric optimism, I believe that I am king of the world and all humanity should bow down before me and do my bidding.

I found Scott in the break room pouring himself a gigantic cup of coffee. He smiled when he saw me. "You're gonna be happy."

"I knew it! I knew it! Tell me the good news."

"You got 20 pips, bro!"

"Pips?"

"Points. They call them pips in the forex market."

"Just 20? Not more?"

He lowered his voice, like he was about to tell me a secret. "Well, it was something like four hundred dollars in profit."

I knew he was lying. Making $400 was impossible on the trade if he just got 20 points, or pips. I had traded again for $10 per point, and he had made 20 pips. That was $200, not $400. I told him this.

"Well, that's true. But I exited your trade at 10 pips when the software told me to get out. And it kept moving up, so fast, so I got in again."

I was nervous, happy, and upset all at the same time. "You got in again? Did the software tell you to?"

"No, but it was moving up fast! I had to get a piece of that for you."

"And you got 10 more pips?"

"Yep. I traded three times your usual trade size so I could make more money for each point."

Oh, gosh, I thought. I had never thought of that. I could trade for more value per point, or pip, when I really thought the market was moving fast.

Scott was right in doing that for sure. But I was still not happy that he had taken a trade without permission from the software.

He was drinking his coffee in big gulps, obviously excited about his performance that morning. And I could not be too angry with him. Why, I had started with $1,000 a day ago, and now I had $1,700. If I could nearly double my account value every couple of days, this was going to be the easiest money I had ever made.

CHAPTER 4

Two Promising Conversations

Because I knew that I could trust John Murphy, I stopped by his office later that day.

He was happy to make time for me. "How is your daughter?" he asked.

I gave him a blank stare and said, "She's fine," in a way that clearly told him it was a strange question. I had forgotten the lie that I had told the day before about the emergency room.

"You've got a great new office." The view was amazing from where we sat—we were looking out over midtown Manhattan.

"Thanks. This actually used to be a partner's office. Charlie Flank. He left to start his own practice on the East Side, writing wills for rich people who want to leave everything to their poodles. Anyway, when Charlie left the firm last week, Herb let me move in." It was obvious that John hadn't had much time to move in. Some of Charlie's stuff was lying on the floor near the door: a photo of Charlie with Mayor Bloomberg, a coffee mug with "MS Walk 2002" on the side, and a box of business cards. John continued: "Of course, I begged Herb to let me have it, so I could finally have a view. So what's on your mind? Is this about the firm's benefits?"

I then remembered my lie. "Oh no, not that. My daughter's doing much better now and everything worked out. I appreciate that." He nodded, happy to know that he had cared deeply about a problem that I had never even had. "Actually, I wanted to ask you about trading. Have you ever been down to the 31st floor?"

"Sure. I've got a friend who works down there. It's pretty amazing."

I then told John about my errand down to the 31st floor and that I had met with Anderson that day.

"Anderson told me that they are going to be starting a new forex fund."

"Did you tell that to Herb?"

I shook my head.

"Why are you telling this to me?"

"Herb scares me," I admitted, "So he doesn't deserve the news just yet."

John smiled widely. He seemed to like that.

"And," I continued, "I heard Anderson say some stuff that I want to figure out."

"Shoot. I'll help where I can."

I took a deep breath. "Could they really be raising five billion?"

He looked at me sideways. "Oh, yes. Definitely. They could probably raise twice that if they wanted to. Forex—currencies—it's hot right now, white-hot. They are probably raising capital to do their own fund, rather than sell people shares in other forex funds. Other firms are doing it now, and it's big business. These companies take high-net worth clients, even corporations, and put their money in a fund that only trades international currency."

"What do all those guys do for a living down there? What are they doing?"

"They're trading. Some of those guys are actually my classmates from law school."

"Trading? From law school?" Just like Anderson.

"Yes. Some of the guys in school just didn't want to practice in a firm. So they interviewed on Wall Street instead. These firms are looking for a pedigree, and Harvard Business or Harvard Law do equally well. It might be a bit tougher for the law guys, but there are fewer of them in the first place that want to go down there and scream and yell for a living. To tell you the truth, it's the guys down in the bottom of the law school class that went to work on Wall Street."

"Why is that?" I speculated that the smart guys were getting the good job offers, and that at the bottom of the class you had to settle for a job on Wall Street. It almost sounded like they were taking a step down when they went to work as traders. John confirmed that and then rejected it.

"They are taking a step down, right, in a certain sense. Those guys didn't do well in law school because they were always going to Red Sox games instead of Constitutional Law. Or they were sleeping in. Or they were reading the business section or the stocks tables, or watching CNBC. Some of those guys just had it in their blood. One of my friends dated the girl at the front desk on 31—and then spent every day for two weeks at a trading desk down there, acting like he was busy. He had a computer setup and everything. He didn't attract attention, didn't go to lunch with anyone, but he sat there for two weeks like he owned the place. He called me a few times a day and started shouting into the phone to act like he was doing something."

"What happened to him?"

"Anderson caught up with him."

"Did he get thrown out?"

John laughed. "No. He got hired on the spot. Anderson knew about it from day one. You can't get anything past that guy."

Except, I thought, that I was not an attorney. John continued: "Anderson watched Craig sit there and act like a trader for two weeks, dressing the part, banging on the keyboard, yelling into the phone. And Craig knew his stuff. He was smart, he knew currencies—and Anderson picked up on that. He interviewed Craig right there, right in the middle of the trading floor."

I was stunned. Maybe I could do the same thing. This guy Anderson seemed like the kind of person who would understand. If he threw me out, I really didn't need the job anyway. At $400 per day, my own trading was plenty enough. Then John continued: "In fact, Craig begged him at first not to throw him out. Craig thought he was going to be arrested. But Anderson wanted to talk shop. He started asking Craig what he thought about the value of the Euro to the Japanese Yen. He made some passionate speech about interest rates or trade balances, and the current outlook for each economy, and that now was the absolute perfect time for a buy based on his technical analysis. Anderson logged into Craig's computer and right there, bought five million Euros against the Japanese Yen."

"Whoa."

"Right. And the trade worked out, and Craig got the job. Good story. So," he continued, clearly satisfied with his telling of the story, but now pressed for time, "What can I do for you?"

"I want to talk to Craig. Or Anderson. Or anyone who knows about trading."

"Why? You want to be a trader?" He wasn't making fun of me. Rather he appeared to be sincere.

"Right. I want to be a trader. Maybe not down there. But maybe on my own."

"Caught the bug, have you? That's awesome."

"So do you think I could meet Craig?"

Even though he wanted to help me, I could see that I was stretching the bounds of our relationship. He probably didn't know if Craig would really want to answer all my questions.

"Listen," I said. "I have never been passionate about this job. I do good work for the firm. I've been doing good work for 11 years, before you even got here. But something happened when I went down there. It must be what you felt like when you first walked into a big law firm for an interview."

"Probably not, but go ahead," he said.

"I just want to talk to him. Find out what is going on down there on the trading floor. I swear, I would sneak in there and do what Craig did if I had the guts. But I don't. I would barf all over the desk on the first day."

This was the best job of begging that I could do, but John wasn't going for it. I could see that something was bothering him. Most likely, it was the fact that he was going out of his way to help me when I had nothing in return to offer him. Or did I?

"How much is this forex fund deal worth to the firm?" I asked.

He shrugged. "It's a lot of money. It's not just the offering documents, but registrations, compliance issues, ongoing legal support—maybe even some introductions to some of our clients, and of course the background checks that Anderson mentioned to you. Probably over two million dollars in fees."

"Herb doesn't know about this yet."

John stopped shrugging and looked me straight in the eye. "What are you saying?"

"You get me lunch with Craig."

"And?"

"I'll get you a meeting with Anderson about the forex fund."

"You really think you can set up a meeting with Anderson and me?"

I nodded. "I'm positive. He nearly hired me on the spot to start work on it." That wasn't exactly true, but it wasn't all wrong, either.

"And Herb?"

Now it was my turn to shrug. "What about Herb?"

"What if he finds out?"

I grinned. "I won't be working here any longer anyway. And you'll have to go to Herb, anyway, and tell him about the deal. The most you'll get out of this is credit, but it will be big credit."

With that, we shook hands and the deal was done. John called Craig, right there, and while they were talking—even from a few feet away—I could hear the roar of the voices on the trading floor. It sounded like sweet music to me.

WHY TAKE PROFITS WHEN I CAN RISK MORE?

To say the least, my wife was impressed with the profits. We had a conversation that I will never forget. Word for word, I can remember it perfectly six years later.

MY WIFE: Do you think we should take some of the money out?
ME: Definitely not.
MY WIFE: Why not?
ME: I can now increase the size of the trades.

From the look on her face, I could tell that my wife was not privy to the obvious wisdom of this strategy. It was frustrating to have to explain to her the intricate details of how I was on my way to becoming a currency trading tycoon, that I was on a hot streak, and that I was going to have a pool with midnight blue water and with attendants who served me drinks. I needed to be trading for more money per pip now, and I'd need all the money in the account.

I told her about my experience on the 31st floor as well.

"Do you think you could get a job there?"

"I don't think so," I told her. "Those guys all have Harvard degrees."

"You could do it. I am sure you could do a great job there," she told me, and this made me happy. It pleased me greatly to hear that my wife could tell that I knew what I was doing.

"I think I would like working there. I would never have expected it or thought about it. But when I walked through that steel door and saw that trading floor, something clicked inside me. I couldn't hear anything but yelling and screaming. But for the first time in months, maybe years, I felt peaceful about our financial problems. I started to see how we could pay our rent consistently. Something clicked. I was standing on . . . well, it sounds lame but I was standing where I should be. It was like I should have been there all along." She was smiling at me now. She realized that I had never felt this way about a job before. "All along, I should have been working as a trader. I don't have the degrees, I don't have the math, but I do have a secret weapon."

"What's that?" I could see that she was practically giggling. My wife! Happy! Pregnant, poor, wife of a lowly file manager, but happy!

"Connections. I am having lunch today with Craig Taylor, one of the traders at Ernest Wellington. He's going to help me do even better than I've done so far."

I wanted to trade again that night, but the kids and my wife got in the way and I didn't get the chance. I determined that tomorrow I'd make more trades. If I really wanted to turn up the heat and make some coin, I was going to have to make more trades every day. One or two trades was just not enough.

CHAPTER 5

Lessons Learned

The next day, Craig took me to lunch at an outdoor café. He was a bit over 6 feet tall, with an athletic frame and a cheerful, charismatic face. This was the type of guy who you knew had been elected class president and who set up the weekly poker tournaments in the dorms, stayed up all night taking money from his friends, and then ran in a track meet the next day. I immediately liked him.

Even better still, Craig was happy to help from the first moment that I met him. He didn't seem to mind that I was totally using him. I had a zillion questions, and he was ready for them. He didn't even care that I interrupted him during an answer, so that I could ask another question. This was a good omen. I had a friend on the inside. It was lunchtime, and I still had not traded yet for the day, and talking to Craig was making me more anxious than ever to get back to making money instead of just talking about it.

"How long have you been trading?" was my first question.

Craig took a bite of his sandwich and spoke with his mouth full. "Four years. About as long as John Murphy has been wasting his life at the law firm."

"Why did you want to trade instead of practice law?"

He grunted happily. "Besides the fact that I was at the bottom of my law school class and I was interviewing at public defenders' offices, while my classmates were already interviewing top law firms, and I had $100,000 in student loans?"

"So you did it as a last-ditch effort when you couldn't . . ."

"Oh, not at all. Sorry that I made it sound like this was a job that I didn't want. But really, this was the only job I wanted."

"And you knew that from the start?"

He smiled. "Well, I knew it when I walked onto the trading floor."

"And you didn't worry about your student loan debt?"

"Nope. I knew I was going to do everything necessary to make it work. Failure was not an option in my mind. I knew there would be bad days. But I was not going to give up."

"Were you a good trader from the start?"

"Oh, no. Very no. I was terrible. But," he added, "I knew I was going to be a trader. And that is all I needed to know."

"That is how I felt, too. I knew that I was supposed to be a trader."

He looked at me and furrowed his eyebrows. "You sure you want to trade?"

"That's why I'm here."

"Well, it's not easy."

I couldn't agree entirely with him, but I nodded. "I know."

"And," he continued, "trading on your own is way more difficult that trading in a firm. Are you trading stocks?"

"Forex."

His eyes widened like he didn't believe me. "Forex? On your own? Dude, you do need help. That's a Wild West market—you can get cleaned out fast. What kind of leverage are you using?"

"Leverage?"

He laughed. "You're really out there on a ledge, Harry. Leverage is credit. It's a way for your forex dealer to loan you money that you don't have."

"How's that?" I hadn't heard about this before.

"Let's say you have an account of $10,000 to trade with. These crazy forex brokers will let you trade $1 million in currency with that $10,000. That's 100 to 1 leverage. This means that for every $1 you put up for the trade, your dealer allows you to trade $100 worth of currency."

"Holy moley," I said. "How much is each point worth on a $1 million trade?"

"$100 per pip."

That means that when I was making $10 per pip, I was trading $100,000 in currency. That made sense. That meant that I was using leverage, too. I started to remember something about getting 400-to-1 leverage at my dealer. I decided that Craig didn't need to know this.

"At Ernest Wellington, we might use 2-to-1 leverage. That's it. We don't mess around with crazy leverage. We'd all wash up. We're not that good."

I didn't know how to reply to this, so I said nothing at all. Talking about trading, even the dangers of it, wasn't worrying me. It was making me want to get back to the office to make some trades.

"I am glad you are telling me all this," I told him. "In your opinion, is it better to trade stocks or something else instead?"

He shook his head. "No. You can trade forex. What you trade doesn't matter. Whether you trade it with discipline is what makes the difference." And he gave me some advice that I wish I had listened to much more carefully.

CRAIG'S TEN-MILLION-DOLLAR LESSON

ME: You said that at first you were not successful at trading. But John told me that you had a trade on the Euro against the Japanese Yen that Anderson took for you.

CRAIG: That's true. That one trade made ten million dollars for the firm.

ME: John told me it was five million.

CRAIG: No, that's not correct. Anderson at first bought five million Euros on the trade—but we made a little over ten million dollars on the trade when I finally got out. I knew that the Euro was falling back to a solid point of support on the charts, and I knew that the economic outlook for the Eurozone economy was much brighter than it was for Japan, which was still in a huge economic slump and had set interest rates at an unbelievably low point. After a brief move downward, the EUR/JPY was ready to pop upward. I had been doing my homework, calling around to other young traders that I knew, and we were all convinced that there was no way the currency pair could break and stay below 119.00. This was late September 2002. I didn't have any secret information, but I was convinced that I was right.

ME: How did you know you were right?

CRAIG: Mostly it was my own research. Besides what I've already told you, I called some analysts around Wall Street, asked them for their opinion on the British Pound against the Yen, the Swiss Franc against the Yen, and the Euro. Everyone was telling me that there was going to be a sharp sell-off that would end soon. They sent me some charts that confirmed what I already suspected—119.00 was a technically important barrier. Price had a hard time breaking above it in the first place. In fact, in the first week of 2002, nine months before, price had hit that same level and fallen back 300 points in just a few days. It took nine months and two weeks to finally break above it. By then it was the last week of September, and price had risen to 122.00, and on that day that Anderson sat down next to me, price was nearly exactly at 119.00.

ME: And that's how you knew that you should buy?

CRAIG: Oh, heck yes. For sure. I wanted to put my own money in this trade. I told Anderson all this. He didn't say a word for the entire time. Just listened to me make a speech. He didn't even ask any questions. I love that man. As soon as I finished, he took my keyboard and made the first trade (see Figure 5.1).

ME: So you bought it right at exactly 119.00?

CRAIG: Well, Anderson did, yes. And then I bought more after that at 119.50. Five million more Euros worth. And then ten million more at 120.00. And then again and again until I had put five hundred million in the trade. I was so sure of the trade that with any pullback, even slight ones, I added to the winning position.

ME: Then what happened? When did you exit the trade?

CRAIG: I closed it about two months later. It immediately moved about 300 pips in my direction, and I felt like the smarted guy in the world. Then it backed off a bit and bounced around in October and most of November. Then in the first few days in December, it skyrocketed. My positions were worth millions of dollars, and I nearly threw up on December 2, 2002. It moved 200 pips upward, breaking all resistance. I didn't sleep for four days for more than a couple of hours at a time. I

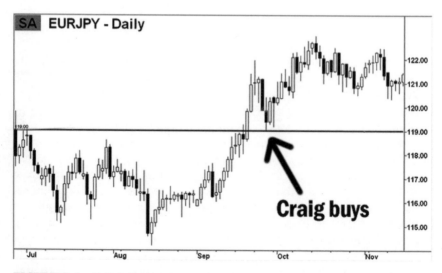

FIGURE 5.1 Craig's first trade.

glued my face to the charts at work and called in for quotes around the clock.

ME: Why were you so concerned?

CRAIG: I couldn't stand to see all that money in profits and not take it. I had sat on my hands with a trade that was up by a million dollars or so, and then all of a sudden, every trade moved into ridiculous superprofitability. Never before had I seen that much money in one place. I understood that if the currency pair fell down again, I would lose all that money. It was nearly the end of the year and I was thinking about what kind of bonus I could get for having done a ten-million-dollar trade. I had taken some other trades during this whole period—lots of short-term trades, and all of those netted out at breakeven. This was my huge winner.

ME: So you closed it?

CRAIG: Yes. Super yes. They stood up and gave me a round of applause on the floor that day. Everyone except for Anderson.

ME: This must have felt really good. My first trade was a winner, too. I remember that feeling. Why didn't Anderson applaud you? Didn't this trade make him a ton of money, too?

CRAIG: Oh, yes, I am sure he looked good for having hired me. But he understood that I had just cut off a huge position that was totally profitable, that had taken me months to build.

ME: Seems greedy to me.

CRAIG: Getting the most out of your best trades is not greed. It's being smart. You let your worst trades run to a loss. Why not let your best trades run into mad, psychotic profitability?

ME: You have a point. Did this one go up even further? Did you regret closing it?

CRAIG: You bet I regretted it. I had let my emotions ruin the trade. I had picked 131.00 as my profit target—with a round number, and a point of support or resistance that the pair had stopped at in 1997, 1998, and 1999. If it got that high, it would be the first time in three years that it reached that level. It would stop there for sure.

ME: Did it get there?

CRAIG: Damn right it did. If I had held on, I could have made a lot more on that trade. I would have had to hold it for four more months, but I would have made an additional thirty million dollars on this trade alone. Forget a round of applause. I would have been promoted to managing director or something wild like that. It would have been a monster trade. I really stepped on my own foot on that one. Ride your profits, Harry. That's the lesson here. Learn to ride your profits (see Figure 5.2).

FIGURE 5.2   Craig learns to ride his profits.

ME: I've got to ask this again—if you had a profit target picked already, then why did you not keep it?

CRAIG: I reacted before I thought about what I was doing. In a furious moment of insanity, I pushed buttons on my keyboard, letting my heart do all the trading.

ME: But in the end, when it was all settled, this was an awesome way to start your job. First few months on the job and you had made the firm ten million bucks.

CRAIG: That's the other thing. Making money on my first trade at the firm was probably the worst thing that I could have done.

ME: Huh? Why?

CRAIG: As I learned quickly, it turned me into a cocky son of a gun.

ME: What's so wrong with that? You made millions for Ernest Wellington, and you had barely been hired.

CRAIG: And I thought that I could keep making that much money every time I traded.

ME: You couldn't?

CRAIG: Oh, no. I could not. Not even close. I lost on my next 13 trades. All of them.

ME: Unlucky 13!

CRAIG: Luck had nothing to do with it. This was all purposeful implosion of my trading capital. In the next 13 trades, in January 2003, I lost the ten million. And then some. By February, I had dug myself a fourteen-million-dollar hole.

ME: What?

CRAIG: Yep. I got bold when I should have sat on my profits. Think about how I made the money in the first place: I planned a trade using all sorts of research. I planned the entry with knowledge of important support and resistance areas. I didn't put all my trading capital into the first position. Instead, I built it up over time. It took me over two months of research to put the trade together. I'd been piecing together my plan for weeks before I ever sat at the trading desk at Ernest Wellington. That's why I was so confident about it. The planning that I put into it.

ME: And the other trades?

CRAIG: I kept buying and selling the EUR/JPY. I thought it had some magical quality—that it had been built just for me and was my new best friend. So I took oversized positions, trying to buy it up to 131.00, but I couldn't stay in the positions for long because I was trading huge amounts of capital from the start, instead of building the position over time. I had no idea what I was doing.

ME: Sounds like you were trying to get back the position you had before you closed it.

CRAIG: Right. But I couldn't buy the pair at 119.00 anymore! When I closed the big trade, I lost the right to hold the EUR/JPY at a super-duper discounted price. So when I started trading again, I wanted to get all that lost profit, and took monster-size positions. What a mistake.

ME: Why didn't you just go back to planning big, long-term trades all over again?

CRAIG: Right. I should have done the same preparation all over again. But I was angry that I had not made as much money as I wanted! I was upset and greedy and wanted more. So I started trying to learn short-term trade, so that I didn't have to wait so long to get my lost profits back. And then I met my mentor. The greatest trader in the world taught me that the fear of missing out was the second greatest mistake that I could ever make.

ME: And the first?

CRAIG: Believing my own B.S. Believing that I actually knew how to trade. I didn't know anything then. I proved it when I lost more than I had gained in just a few weeks.

ME: Did you get it all back? Could you climb out of that hole?

CRAIG: Oh, yes. The year 2003 was great by the end. But it was my most difficult year.

ME: Can you tell me about that?

CRAIG: Some other time, yes. There were some awesome trades that year.

CRAIG GETS ANGRY

Craig stopped talking about his trading at that point. He was obviously still upset about his huge mistake in his first month. The regular charismatic Craig had turned a bit angry, even, and I could imagine how disappointed in himself he must have been. He expressed his determination that I should never make a similar mistake, and I assured him that I absolutely would not. I decided that before I traded again, I would request a withdrawal of $500 from my forex trading account, so that I could pay off the iPod purchase for my wife and make sure that I realized some of the profit. It felt like the right decision from the moment I made it. I told Craig that I planned to do this.

"You will be so happy you did. You are doing what it took me a long time to learn to do. You are taking your gains. Good for you." This got him smiling again. He then changed the subject: "John Murphy told me that you two are conspiring to get him an appointment with Anderson about some deal."

I nodded. "That's part of it. My end of the promise."

"Well, if you can work that out, it will be quite a coup."

By telling me that I was going to have to work it out, Craig let me know that if I wanted to conspire to get John and Anderson together, I was on my own. That didn't bother me.

"That would be a sizable legal deal," Craig said before he bit down on his sandwich. "Might even keep John at the firm."

I didn't know what to say—was John in danger of losing his job? That was news to me, certainly, and I wasn't going to spend any time delving into that problem. Maybe that's why John was so excited about getting a meeting with Anderson to do the work on the forex fund.

"Well, keeping him at the firm seems like a good idea to me," I said.

"Really? Is that what John told you?"

"No. I just thought it sounded like the right thing to say."

"So John didn't tell you," he said.

"Tell me what?" Now I was more interested.

"He wants to leave the firm and come down and work with me."

This made sense. If John got the deal to do the forex fund work, he could meet Anderson—and then he would be right in line for a job on the trading floor. I said this to Craig.

"Not really."

I was confused. "Why not? He would know Anderson; he could get to know him better."

"But then Anderson would lose an attorney he really likes, assuming he gets to know John. And who knows what kind of trader John would be.

He's my good friend, but honestly he's not passionate enough, too straight around the collar, a bit too organized for trading as a career."

"Too organized?"

"Too organized, too methodical. Not enough feeling. Anderson won't like that. John has to plan out every move that he makes. He used to make four-color calendars for our study groups in law school. He is a planning maniac. It could help him be a good trader in some ways, but Anderson won't go for it. In five minutes, Anderson knows if he wants to hire you or not. All the things that he won't like about John, Anderson will understand immediately. He reads people instantly. While you're still trying to think of something smart to say, you've already been hired or not. That's why I haven't introduced John to Anderson yet."

This was bringing up more and more questions. "But wouldn't John already know this about himself? Haven't you spoken to him about it?"

"Oh, yes," he replied, finishing off his sandwich, at which point he started looking around for something, as if this conversation had brought to mind a forgotten task. He pushed back from the table a little bit, and bent down to grab what looked like a drink coaster from his briefcase. He shoved it in his shirt pocket and forgot about it.

He continued: "I talked with John about it. I told him that he was going to have to let it go a bit, become a bit more of a risk taker. He promises he can do it, but I can tell he just wants to make the switch because of the money. Like I said before, Anderson will be able to figure that out before John barely opens his mouth."

I shook my head. How could a lawyer's salary not be enough? "He's got to be making plenty of money at the firm."

"How much do you think he makes?" Craig asked.

"I don't know. Over one hundred."

He nodded. "John made more than one hundred his first year with the firm. He's making at least two hundred right now, and he is doing well enough that he is clearly on the path to partner in a few more years—and then he'll make at least five hundred grand a year. That's good New York money."

I had never thought about it. I had spent a lot of time thinking about how much I made, but never very much about how much the attorneys in the firm were pulling down. Of course I knew they were wealthy. More than $100,000 per year meant wealthy to me. But I had no idea that the attorneys back at the office considered themselves so poor.

"That seems plenty to live on to me."

"What? One hundred? two hundred? five hundred?"

"Yeah. Easily enough."

Craig looked me squarely in the eye, and said, "A good trader could make that in a month on the trading floor."

A month! I nearly spit up the sandwich that I had only taken a bite from. A month of working on the trading floor for $100,000? Was that even possible? Was I dreaming? I reached under the table and held my right leg down, which was starting to bounce up and down from my nervousness. I thought that I might pee in my pants right there. I wanted to laugh out loud, scream, and throw up all at the same time. I had thought that $300 per day was good money. There was an entirely different league of traders out there.

"I never knew," I admitted.

Craig nodded. "From the moment I met you, I had the feeling you were going to say that. You had no idea at all how much traders make. This is not about the money for you, is it?"

I stopped at that moment. I could tell the truth, and he would think less of me, or I could lie and he would continue to talk with me, and perhaps even help me. Lying seemed like such a good idea at the moment. I said: "No, it is about the money. Honestly."

He laughed. "How could it be about the money if you never knew how much we were talking about?"

I shrugged and decided to clarify this slight misunderstanding. "It's about the money in the sense that I need to do better at supporting my family. I am hungry for more. I didn't know what 'more' was until I walked onto the trading floor. I suppose you could tell me that those guys were making the same salary I am, now that I think about it. Yeah, you could tell me that those guys are all making forty-five grand a year, and I would be like, okay, where do I sign up? Because for the first time in my career, when I walked onto that floor, it wasn't about exact dollar amounts. It was about potential. I could smell money there. It was being created by doing things that I don't understand, with people I don't know, with computers I haven't learned to use. But I could sense that there was a huge amount of potential for me to build something for myself as a trader. Not on the trading floor, necessarily. But trading for myself at the least."

Craig was just staring at me and listening. I could tell that he liked what he was hearing. So I continued, "And I think that I imagined that these men and women on the floor were way too unsophisticated to be making as much as lawyers. They were . . . wild . . . down there on the trading floor."

I laughed and so did Craig.

"But it didn't matter to me—I knew they were making more money than I was, or at least I was pretty sure about it. And I knew that they were on a roller coaster ride at their job. Some of them looked like they were on top of the world. Others looked like they needed barf bags. But they were feeling something. Anything! The last time I felt anything at work was when I handed a set of files to Herb Johnson's secretary and accidentally touched her where her bathing suit covers."

We laughed. By now I knew that I was overstaying my welcome. I had asked more questions than I can remember and write about here, and he had happily answered all of them. He spent his time so willingly with me that day that it seemed like he was paying me back for something that I had done for him, which obviously was impossible.

"I know you gotta go," I told him.

"Yes. I do. We've got some economic news coming out at two. Fomsee interest rate decision."

"Fomsee?"

He spelled it out: "F-O-M-C. Federal Open Market Committee. Alan Greenspan and Company of the Federal Reserve make a decision on whether to raise interest rates. This decision—even no decision—can move the dollar 100 points in sixty seconds."

That might not have sounded thrilling to any of the people sitting around me. But now I considered trading my future, and I was determined that as soon as I got back to the office I was going to log on at my desk, and spend as much of my employer's time as possible trying to find out what the FOMC said about interest rates and how it moved the U.S. Dollar.

I thanked him for meeting with me.

He nodded and said that a few years before, someone had done the same for him, and he owed it back. So that's why I had the feeling that he owed me something. Well, it wasn't me, but it was someone else. Maybe it had been Anderson?

We shook hands, and he started to leave. But before he left, he reached into his coat pocket and reached for the drink coaster, but then hesitated. He was thinking deeply.

"What's up?" I asked.

"I have a card for you." He was really thinking hard about this one. "But I don't know if I can give it to you."

Was it a business card from the human resources people at Ernest Wellington? Another contact? Craig's mentor or friend? He was hooking me up! Of course, I wanted to play it cool and not seem so anxious that I scared him off.

"It's okay if you can't for right now," I lied to him. I was probably willing to kill him right then and there for the card, but I knew that a homicide was going to look bad on my employment record, and probably affect my ability to get back to the office in time to trade again.

"Well," he replied, "Technically, I shouldn't give it to you right now. So I won't. Just know that when the time is right, I have a friend that I want you to meet. He can help you. He helped me. I still have my job today because of him."

"Anderson?" I guessed.

He nearly choked on a laugh. "Oh, gosh, no. Not Anderson. Not anyone at the firm. Someone else."

I felt stupid for suggesting that Anderson was his secret mentor but realized that it didn't matter. Now I had a plan and at least a view of the path ahead. I couldn't have the job interview today, or maybe tomorrow. But maybe in a week or two. And the name on the card? I would know it soon enough. Maybe I didn't need it anyway. I was doing all right with my trading already.

"I understand that now isn't the right time. Hopefully, we can talk again," I suggested.

He agreed that we could meet again soon. Then he scribbled words on a napkin, handed me the napkin, and it said:

Rule Number One: Don't Become Cocky

While I stood staring at the words, Craig raced off to trade. Before he left, he put cash on the table for the bill and said, "I'd stay longer, but I'm one of the only guys on the floor up there that knows how to read that report in sixty seconds. Last month I banked over 200 points on this report."

"200 points?"

"It's not about the money. But it meant over a million in profits in the first two hours after the minutes were released."

Craig then rushed away. And I also wanted to get back to the office. The FOMC interest rate decision was going to be out in 40 minutes, and I needed to be ready.

CHAPTER 6

A Turn for the Worse

I didn't know it at the time, but Craig wasn't just a good trader. John met me when I returned to the office and explained it all.

"Craig is a Supertrader, with a capital S. He might be the best trader under 40 years old down there. He personally makes more than $100,000 every month. For himself. That's his cut. He could probably make a million dollars for himself this week on this FOMC trading stuff. They love him down there."

"I'm surprised that he took the time to meet with me," I said.

John shook his head. "I'm not. That's the kind of guy he is. He helped people put resumes together in law school and left his for last. He probably walked away from some great trades today by talking to you. He eats lunch at his desk every day."

I looked at the napkin and showed it to John:

Rule Number One: Don't Become Cocky

John laughed. "I've got one of those, too. And he's right. I've made some bad mistakes in my trading by being too cocky."

Yeah, right, I thought. Whatever. If I was making $100,000 per month, I'd have my shoes shined at my desk and my wife would have a hundred iPods. I'd work for a month and take the rest of the year off.

I wondered if John had met Craig's secret mentor. From the way that John was looking at me, I got the feeling that he was wondering if Craig had mentioned this same friend. I wanted to talk about it with John, but we had the FOMC report in just a little while, and I decided that I needed to get my trading account up and ready.

"So are you trading still?" I asked, hoping to get a bit more information about John's plans.

"Yes. I'm having some trouble pulling the trigger on my trades. Some of the best ones in fact. But it will pass. I am down for the year still, but I am confident that will change. And you?"

"I only have a small account. But it's positive right now."

"How much?"

"I don't know," I answered. And then I calculated the percentage gain in my head. "Seventy percent so far."

He nearly choked. "Seventy percent? Your account is up 70 percent for the year?"

What was the big deal? At the rate I was going, it would be up 100 percent by today. I told him, yes, it was up that far but I really still had a lot to learn. I felt badly that I was doing so much better than he was doing. Now I felt my leg start to shake a bit. I wanted to start trading again as soon as possible. I had profits to make, and all this talk was driving me crazy.

I raced back toward my desk, thinking about how great the day had been. A great day in a great week in what was going to be the most Amazing great year of my life so far.

And now I was going to trade.

Or at least that is what I thought I was going to do. Scott Needleway was standing at my cubicle when I got back from lunch. He did not look happy.

"Herbie is pissed and wants to see you *now*."

I didn't care if Herbie was experiencing chest pains and shortness of breath. I was going to be trading for the next half hour and there was nothing that could be done to stop me. Scott did not share my enthusiasm.

"You should see him now. He's not happy."

I shrugged it off. "We both know it's just another missing document and that he's doing twenty-five things at the same time right now. He won't even care that I take my time getting over there."

Scott did not share my confidence in the matter. But it didn't occur to me that his usual laissez-faire attitude had been replaced by an expression of serious concern.

From all the running around that day and the day before, it seemed like an eternity since I had last traded. All that profit lost! I could have taken another two or three trades at least. It felt good that now I was going to have the chance to make up for all that by trading when the FOMC minutes were released. From what Craig said, this could really shake up the market, and I was going to be ready. I felt like I had a secret weapon: A real Wall Street trader, who was probably a millionaire, had given me a heads-up. My fingers twitched with anticipation for the trading they would do. My right leg started hopping on the floor. This was a good feeling. This was the rush of adrenaline that the traders on the 31st floor felt every day. Trading for a living was never going to be boring.

Scott was feeling it, too. The look of concern disappeared, replaced by what could only be described as bliss: He knew that we were going to witness something amazing.

"You going to turn on the Amazing Forex software?" he asked.

"Oh, yeah," I told him. "I almost forgot. I have a feeling that all we need to do is follow the direction of the market right after the minutes are released. From what Craig said, this economic report can move the market 100 pips in just seconds."

"Gotta have a quick trigger finger, then."

"You bet. I might make up for all the lost opportunities that I had this week."

It was 2:14 P.M. Eastern Time when the Amazing software triggered a sell order on the GBP/USD. The current price was 1.8135. I had my finger on the trigger to take the trade, and then boom! All of the sudden, the price on my trading platform started to skyrocket upward. Scott gasped, and I took my hands off the keyboard. Whoa! It was flying up 10, 20, 30 pips instantly! I wanted to be a part of that. Once before, the software had been wrong, and we had profited from inadvertently trading in the opposite direction of the signal. So that's what I did this time. With absolute confidence, I bought the GBP/USD at 1.8170.

I traded two standard lots, or $200,000 worth of currency, which equaled $20 for every pip the market moved (see Figure 6.1).

"Doubling up!" Scott exclaimed. "Sweetness!"

I was automatically in the red on the trade, because of the spread. So I was losing $100 right now, or 5 pips (the spread) times $20. I had seen this on the other trades we had taken, so I was mentally prepared. No freaking out just because I started off at a small loss.

We checked back with Amazing Forex Profits. It had a boatload of orders popping up on the screen. Here they were:

Buy USD/JPY,

Buy USD/CHF,

Sell EUR/USD,

Sell GBP/USD,

Buy USD/CAD,

Buy USD/SEK,

Sell NZD/USD,

Sell AUD/USD.

FIGURE 6.1   Harry trades two standard lots.

And many more. I had never seen that many orders popping up at the same time. And they were all going in one direction: buying U.S. Dollars and selling other currencies. Not one order went the other way.

Now I felt conflicted. Craig had told me the market could jump really fast, even 100 pips in 60 seconds. That meant I still had plenty of profit potential on the trade—it had only moved up 35 pips when I bought. So that left at least 65 more pips to come. At $20 per pip, I was looking at a profit of $1,300. That was easily enough to cover the extra money we needed to make our rent payment. With enough left over to give my wife a gift certificate for some online music. While I felt more nervous about this trade than the others, it was just because of the amount of money that I stood to gain. I had never made this much money this fast before.

Then I glanced at the Amazing software. What was I to do when it was telling me to go the other way? And with so many orders? I wondered if I could call Craig. I didn't have his number, but I am sure that John Murphy had it. I half sat up in my chair to leave. Scott backed away a bit. He suddenly remembered that Mr. Johnson wanted to see me. I saw the trade dip down to negative 10 pips—$200 in the red. That was more money than I had lost on a trade before. My right leg was bouncing, and I held onto it with my hand.

"You gotta go see Herbie," Scott told me.

He was right. Damn! This was happening again—a forced choice between watching the trade and doing my job. I couldn't wait for the day when I could walk away from the office and never come back. Just trade full time. Especially now that I had an open trade that had the potential to bank at least $1,300. It was unprofitable now. Maybe I could trade the other direction on another currency pair, and that would mean that no matter what, I would stand to profit from one trade immediately, while I waited for my first trade to make money.

"Harry, you really gotta go," he said.

"I will, I will," I replied testily. "I don't want to leave the trade. If he wants to see me so badly, he can walk over here."

Then I heard a terrible, familiar, angry growl from the entrance to my cubicle.

It was Mr. Johnson.

A GOOD DAY GOES BAD

Herb was not happy. Every vein in his forehead was visible and pulsating, supplying needed oxygen to the brain that would form the words that would come flying out of his mouth any second: "You got something you wanna talk with me about?"

Did he find out I was trading on company time? Had Scott said something? John? Or maybe this was another case of a missing letter. Lost files, misplaced papers, disappearing disks, it didn't matter, perhaps he was calling on me (with an angry booming voice) to find something he needed 10 minutes ago. This tirade would pass like all the others and in 15 minutes he would have his file, I'd have my peace and quiet, and we'd both be happy. I would be able to go back to my trade, which by the time I'd helped him would probably be profitable and closed.

Maybe the interruption was a good thing. Now I would focus on something else for few moments.

I could imagine Craig downstairs, pushing buttons, making trades, earning more money in a few minutes than I could all year long. Had he bought the GBP/USD? Had he sold? Did he have an Amazing Forex software tool, something the company had built for him? I wondered if his charts were showing big support or resistance levels or yearly highs or lows.

All these thoughts about Craig convinced me that the reward for passing through this predictable storm of tempers over lost files would be to find Craig's number and call him. Surely an hour from now he'd be out of his trades and we could talk about what he did, and what I did, and compare notes. Two traders just hamming it up after a day of hard-won profits in the currency trenches.

"Mr. Johnson," I started, "I did ask Scott to completely go over all the Anderson files to make sure that nothing was out of place. I'll make sure we get whatever you need right away."

Scott nodded quickly and heartily, eyes wide open. I thought he might suddenly jump out of my cubicle and go running down the hall screaming.

Mr. Johnson huffed. He did this in the way the boss does when you're talking about something so remote from whatever had caused him to be angry in the first place, that he cannot possibly believe how stupid you are. After a furious mental inventory of every file I had stored away in the last week, I began to realize that I might not be able to cut this conflict short. Not a good sign. Not with my trade doing who knew what (there was no way I was going to glance behind me at the computer screen at this moment).

With every pulse of the veins in Mr. Johnson's forehead, I thought I could hear his heart pounding. Or maybe it was mine.

My right leg was now shaking.

"Anything else about the Anderson case you wanna talk about?" The grunting, growling, and huffing had ended, replaced with words that just came out as a bark. I had never seen him this angry. Certainly not at me. Both his tiny hands formed fists at his side, and I guessed from the way he stood that his butt cheeks were clenched hard enough to crack a walnut. I don't know why I thought about that at the time, but I did. My emotions were all over the place. The pulsing in my chest increased. My leg would not stop shaking. I could have set it underneath a car and it would have not stopped.

At that moment I realized that Herb Johnson was going to kill me. He barked again: "I said, is there anything else you wanna tell me about the Anderson files?"

I looked at Scott. His face was white.

Turning back to Mr. Johnson, I shook my head like I had years before when my mother asked me if I had been peeing in the neighbor's backyard. I could remember standing on the black and white checked linoleum floor in the kitchen of our small home in Queens, right leg shaking, mind searching for exactly the right half-truth to get me out of this mess:

Mom: Were you back there in the Gonzales yard going pee?
Me: [silence]
Mom: Well, were you?
Me: [silence]

Now, in the office, I could pretty much replace "Mom" with "Herb." You can understand why I was preparing my behind for a spanking. I wanted to reply: Do I know anything about the files? Hell no. I'm just the filing manager! Talk to Scott! I make him do all my work!

Now I was flat-out petrified. I couldn't talk. His evil barking, his clenched butt cheeks, the near-bursting veins, his ability to summon my mother from the dark recess of my childhood—it was all too much for me to handle.

I couldn't believe this was about the Anderson files. I had made sure that the files were in order just that morning, and then I had gone to lunch, and now Herbie was barking at me. Maybe this was about my extended stay on the trading floor? About my lunch with Craig? Maybe he didn't like me fraternizing with members of Ernest Wellington while we were representing them?

Pretty much all day I had been scheming not only to enrich myself with a new job as a trader, and also to benefit the firm with a $2 million fee. And the thanks I got!

Then I realized why he was so angry.

He knew. He knew about the deal with John and Craig, about me trying to get a job at Ernest Wellington & Company, about me brokering a client-for-job-interview deal. He was like my mother! He could see what I did at all times, he was Momnipresent. No wonder this man had frightened me for 10 years.

A job-spanking for John Murphy, and possibly the loss of his cushy new corner-office location. For me? Maybe fired. Maybe worse. Gosh, I thought, I had even put Craig Taylor's job in jeopardy. Maybe he was down there on Floor 31 getting beat down, and totally missing out on tasty pips from the FOMC interest rate decision.

What had the FOMC decided?

Maybe I should have checked that before I traded.

Craig said it could move 100 pips in one minute. What about after that?

Would Anderson interview me for a job now?

How could I get myself out of this mess and back to looking at my trade?

My mind raced onward, toward nothing in particular. My brain had been melted by the white-hot rage coming from Herbie (Herbie? I was going to kill Scott) and my body had given absolute control of itself over to my heart, which seemed to have grown to the size of a watermelon and with every beat, was causing my body to shake.

Mom: I saw you, so don't you try to tell me you didn't do it.
Me: [silence]
Mom: Do you have anything to say for yourself?
Me: [silence]
Mom: Well, do you?

Only the truth could save me now!

Me: I had to go real bad!
Mom: Do you think that is an excuse?
Me: It really hurt!

Wait a minute. I couldn't tell him that it hurt when I peed.

HERBIE: Well, do you have anything to say for yourself? I want to know
    where you get off with behavior like this.
ME: [silence]
ME: I promise I delivered the letter like you asked me to do.

My only answer: the truth. Oh, I would have given up all the profit in
my trading account just for a good lie. The only thing that I could do was
talk. Talking could save me. Continued conversation would soothe the
beast.

"I did talk to Anderson about the forex fund, sir." I was not in the habit
of calling anyone sir, but I did it this time. Sir Herbie. "Sir, I talked with him
about the fund and he did tell me that I should mention it to you."

"What fund?" he asked. Now he was confused on top of angry. The idea
to use extended dialog to return Herbie to a happy state had failed.

He didn't know that I hadn't told him about the fund? Then what in the
world was this all about?

"Well, Banes," he grunted. "What the hell are you talking about?"

I stated in the most confident manner possible, with my right knee
jerking around like it was trying to send me flying to the floor: "The florex
fund. They're starting an in-house florex fund and they need the firm's
help."

I said it wrong because many, many synapses in my brain had snapped
and my communication skills were flushed down the toilet of neurological
implosion, along with physical control of my shaking body.

"Anderson told me that they're going to need legal help to get the fund
started. He doesn't know that I am telling you this, but it sounds like it
could be a two-dollar job for the firm. And he offered me a job."

Yes, I actually said two dollars, as in $2. And yes, I really did say that
Anderson offered me a job. I was living proof that your IQ can move up and
down depending on how afraid you were.

"Two dollars, Banes? What are you talking about?"

"Uh, I mean two million."

"How would you know something like that? And what's this about him
giving you a job?"

"Well, he did," I said, protesting even further that I was telling the truth
when in fact I was serving up whoppers one after the other.

This was like having to go down the entire road of deception just to
avoid one spanking. Why was I lying? When I did something like that, there
were disastrous and unintended consequences.

Mr. Johnson could tell I was lying. "We'll get him on the phone right
away about that, you can be sure of that, but first you and I have business to
settle. You've got me off track now and I'm putting us back on the subject."

Over the years I had seen at least 20 people fired from Wakeman, Butterman, and Bailey. Firings there fell into two categories, much like hurricanes: amicable firings, like when someone had been incompetent but was so good-looking or otherwise likable that human nature demanded it be done respectfully (the type of firing that Craig Taylor would presumably get); and angry firings, where someone always ended up with spittle on his face and his life destroyed because he had put himself in the path of such a disaster.

Herb was giving me category number two. Now he would yell at me until I walked away, then he was going to accuse me of walking away while he was "talking" to me, and then he was going to tell me to gather my things together and leave. He might even throw something.

Suddenly I had visions of credit card companies coming to take my furniture, my car, my wife, my kids—then kicking me in the crotch—and then it would, in fact, start hurting when I peed. And suddenly it was 20 years ago again:

Mom: It hurts when you pee? And you were bleeding?
Me: [nodding head sheepishly, unable to expand the lie with words]
Mom: We'll, let's take a look then.

Uh oh.

Certainly the forex fund was juicy news to Herbie, but he was so incensed that he wasn't giving me any points for scoring him inside information. Ten feet away from us, a fire hydrant hung from the wall. I thought that he glanced over at it. He was going to grab it, swing it at me, and take my head right off. He would murder me and then fire me! Twice as bad! So I tried one last strategy. I would beg him to back it up. To start over. This would unquestionably return us to calmer waters. So I said, "I have no idea what you're yelling at me about." I paused. Then my mouth opened to finish the thought and extinguish all hope of continued employment at Wakeman, Butterman, and Bailey. "Herbie, I'm telling you the truth."

Herbie. That was it. I had ended my life at the firm with that one word. Herbie. No one around there called him Herbert, let alone Herb. But Herbie. That was a blunder of classic proportions, to be logged forever in the annals of verbal mistakes. Herbert Walker Johnson III might have been shaped like a Volkswagen Love Bug, but he was outfitted with dirt-racing tires, a supercharged engine, and now was going to steamroll over me.

He bellowed: "Banes, gather up your things." No more words. No explanation. No "this is why I am firing you" speech. He stormed away and I couldn't blame anyone but myself, even though I still had no idea why he had been angry in the first place.

When he left, I looked at Scott. He was a ghost. Totally emptied of all thought, feeling, and life. I struggled to remember important details like my own name, where I was, and what I was doing. I looked around my cubicle. These were my things. The possessions that I would be taking back home with me today.

"Are you going to check your trade?" Scott asked.

I did. Maybe some happy news awaited me about the trade.

The GBP/USD was trading at 1.8155. I had lost only 15 pips. Negative $300. Not a big deal still. It should be moving a lot more than this, I thought, but I had to give it time. For sure, I wasn't going to eat a $300 loss just to see it go up and move far enough to have given me $1,300. I remembered well what Craig had said about letting my good trades run to profitability.

Now that I thought about this trade in light of Craig's advice, I realized I didn't need the stupid job anyway. I would hold on to this trade and make more money in a day than I'd ever made before. Three or four times as much. Soon I would be making serious money from trading. Soon I would be $1,300 richer; by the end of the hour for certain. I determined that the last thing I would do before I left Wakeman, Butterman, and Bailey forever would be to bank my hard-earned profits on the trade.

"I'm going to wash up," I told Scott. "Watch the trade if you don't mind, and then I'm coming back to gather up my stuff."

When I returned, Scott had vanished. On top of my desk was a box, just about the right size for all of my belongings, and inside the box, an envelope. The envelope contained a check made out to me for the sum of $3,386.75 (after taxes), and a release form for me to sign that gave me the money in exchange for a promise not to sue the firm. Sue them for what? Boss abuse?

I fell into my chair and put my head into my hands. The trade was going good, but what was I going to tell my wife? Why had I been fired?

For a moment I forgot all about the FOMC report, about Craig, about trading. I just thought of my wife and kids. How was I going to explain this? My financial life flashed before my eyes: We had $40 in a savings account, and negative who knew how much in our checking account. We had some savings in an IRA. We had some nice furniture that our parents had bought for us when we were married. We had a big screen television. We had kids. We had pictures on our walls of faraway places my wife dreamed of visiting.

What if the trading didn't work out? What if I couldn't repeat the success I had? What if Craig was right, that success at the beginning of a trading career was the worst thing that could happen to me?

I started to list everything I owned. At the moment, I was probably half-insane, and probably just wanted to remember the possessions I had, the stuff that I could still call mine. It helped put my feet back down on earth and my mind back into the present.

I then pulled from my pocket the napkin from lunch. It still read:

Rule Number One: Don't Become Cocky

Right then I was anything but arrogant. Upset. Confused. Angry, certainly. I took a moment and added up three month's rent in my mind.

And before I could think twice, I was walking back to Herbie's office, where I found him already doing three other things, not thinking at all about the fact that he was kicking me in the teeth professionally. When I looked inside his office, he stared right back at me.

HERBIE: What.

It wasn't a question. It was a demand.

ME: I'll sign the release for $6,400.
HERBIE: Done. Sign it, bring it back to me.

He went back to his work. Not one bit of emotion. I should have asked him for three times as much. Then I should have jumped on his desk and kicked him in the head.

Instead I returned to my cubicle and signed the form. By the time I was on my way back to his office, Bill from accounting met me in the hallway. He had an envelope in his hand, which he handed to me in exchange for the signed release. Now I had a check that would cover three month's rent. The firm had my promise not to sue for wrongful termination. I had also written in on the firm's copy of the form that they were to buy me a Porsche 911 and a private jet.

This is the part in a book where the protagonist usually tells you that he left the office, head hung low, fearful of his wife's reaction to the news, fated to never work again as a mail carrier or whatever. Not me! I had a good trade going and three month's rent. And now I was going into the file room and make a list of every Wall Street firm we had ever represented and the name of the head trader if I could find it.

I called Scott on his cell phone. He rushed over to my desk within seconds. He had been hiding out. He looked at the box on my desk.

"I'm sorry," he said. He didn't ask why I had been fired.

"I need you to cover for me for a few minutes."

He looked reluctant. "I don't know, man. I don't want Herbie to find out I'm helping you. I can't afford to lose my job."

"In twenty four hours you're going to have my job. There are only two of us here. They are not going to fire you. So congratulations. Now help me for five minutes."

"Five minutes. Okay."

I told him to call me on my cell phone if anyone approached the filing room.

In 20 minutes I had the names and numbers of nine Wall Street traders. I then left as fast as I could. When I got home, my wife was in such a good mood that I decided not to tell her that I had been fired. I took her and the kids to the park until the sun went down, then put the kids to bed, and then we both fell asleep early. I had forgotten entirely about my trade.

CHAPTER 7

Trying to Awake from the Nightmare

That night I had a dream. I was running on top of a cloud bank, toward the setting sun, up as high as you would be if you were in a 747. I was running really fast, and I was skipping across those clouds toward the setting sun.

The clouds were dark behind me—storm clouds. I kept my eyes focused on the setting sun—the pink clouds, the last light of the day. But every couple of seconds, I could see a flash of light from the corner of my eye, and the thunderclap was so loud that it shook my entire body. And after each clap, the booming sound stayed in the air, echoing out and then back, out and back, out and back. Each time it hit me, it punched me in the chest. I thought my chest would cave in with each pulse. But I kept running.

I couldn't make any forward progress, in the same way that earlier that week on the trading floor, I felt I was standing still while time and space passed me by. Only on the trading floor, I was filled with optimism and possibility.

This time it was only fear.

Far in the distance to my left, I saw my wife. I saw my children: Nathan, and Judy, and Jonathan. I passed them by so slowly that it seemed as if they were moving and I was not. And I saw Caroline—she hadn't been born yet, but I could see her, as if she had been born and had grown to at least five years old. She was standing in a white dress, and she was the only figure that I could not run past. She was smiling at me. She had my wife's pretty smile and curly hair. I could tell she was calling out to me to come to her—but I couldn't make any progress.

So I ran harder. It didn't help. I stretched out my hands, and that didn't help. I considered crawling on all fours and scraping for more traction. It didn't make a difference either. I was losing ground fast. The thunder was louder, the pulses more powerful, the pain in my chest greater, the lightning was brighter, and Caroline's voice was softer.

And softer.

Until I could no longer hear her.

Until I could barely see her waving to me.

Until she was no longer smiling.

And then the darkness wrapped around me, I lost sight of Caroline, and I woke up screaming.

YOU NEVER FORGET YOUR FIRST MARGIN CALL

When I woke up from the nightmare, my first thought was the open trade. Covered in sweat, with Franklin standing at attention by my side of the bed, and my wife sitting next to me, combing my hair back with her hand— I was thinking about my trade.

I knew it was bad. I hadn't seen it yet, but I knew it was really bad. Now I wanted to check on it. We had a computer in the next room. It didn't have any of the software on it, but I could load it on there and check on the trade. Just imagining the Amazing Forex software put a pit in my stomach.

"What can I get for you?" Gini asked.

"I need to take a walk."

"In the middle of the night?"

I nodded. "I need to cool off."

It was 2:00 A.M. I got up out of bed, put on a robe, and walked into the living room. I flipped on the television, looking for SportsCenter. On the way there, I passed by the Bloomberg Channel. I stopped. They were talking about the FOMC interest rate decision.

FANCY HOST: So the Federal Reserve kept interest rates low today.

FANCIER EXPERT: Yes, they did, and thank goodness. The easy money policy is really keeping the stock market on track for a good year. No need to ruin that.

FANCY HOST: Currencies didn't move much on the news yesterday. Why is that?

FANCIER EXPERT: They were looking for another 25 basis point rate cut, and didn't get it. Or at least a substantial change in the FOMC's statement.

FANCY HOST: What's next for the Fed?

I lost track of what they were saying and pulled a chair up to the computer desk. In the next 20 minutes, I tried to load the software, but I could not get it to download correctly and discovered that I needed a "pass key" to install the Amazing Forex Profits software on more than one computer. All the while, I missed any further discussion of foreign exchange rates on Bloomberg.

So I Googled "forex prices" and got a zillion results. One of the results was for "Professional Currency Charting Software," and I clicked on it. I downloaded a free trial of the program and started it up. The software was thankfully easy to use. I chose GBP/USD from the menu of available currencies, and here is what I saw. I have added some notes to the chart (see Figure 7.1).

The trade had completely blown up. For sure, I had lost everything.

It had fallen over 100 pips from where I had bought the GBP/USD. All that had happened as I was riding the subway home, just probably 20 minutes after I'd left the office. I had traded for $20 per pip. That was over $2,000 in losses. Did I owe money to my forex dealer now?

I scrambled over to my briefcase, knocking over a plant in the process. I didn't bother to pick it up. Soon I found the phone number for my forex broker. A pleasant-sounding customer service representative answered on the first ring.

"Thank you for calling Universal Currency Brokers! How may I help you?"

"I want to check on a trade."

FIGURE 7.1 Harry's trade dies.

I quickly read her my account number. Maybe she would give me a break? Perhaps they had a one-time policy of offering mercy to hopeless traders who had been fired earlier in the day? Surely they had the power to reverse the trade. I could claim that I hadn't made the trade, and argue that I should not stand to lose money on what I didn't mean to do in the first place. None of this made any sense, but it was two o'clock in the morning.

"Your account has no open trades at this time, sir."

Oh, no. "Do I owe you money?" I asked. "I had a terrible trade today, I think."

"You did have a losing trade," she answered quickly. "You bought the GBP/USD at 1.8170 this afternoon. The trade was closed just a little while later. You got a margin call."

"A margin call?"

"Well, you put up $500 in margin to trade two standard lots. This reduced your available margin to $1,200. When your losses reached $1,200, you had used up all the available margin. So we closed your trade automatically as a service to you. This leaves you with the $500 in margin in your account."

"As a service to me?" I noticed on my charts that the price had risen back up afterward. I told her so. "Why not keep it open for me?"

"We did that up until a few years ago. But traders were leaving losing trades open so long that they owed us money. That was worse."

I immediately agreed. That left me with this fact: I had lost $1,200. One thousand two hundred dollars. In one day. One trade.

I then hung up the phone.

When I looked up, my wife was standing beside me, looking at the computer screen over my shoulder.

"Did you make a trade?" she asked. "This late at night?"

What was I going to tell her?

MY WIFE'S ANGRY EYES

I told Gini everything, starting with the lunch with Craig all the way up to the time when I called the dealer and found out that my trading account had burst into flames.

She was angry. Not about the trade—which surprised me—but about my job.

MY WIFE: How could you let this happen?
ME: [silence]

There wasn't anything smart for me to say. My wife needed to hear the truth, but the problem was that the truth didn't make any sense, and she was only going to think it was a lie.

I told her: "I am not sure I had any choice in the matter at all. I mean, it was over before it began. I got back from lunch with Craig and wham! Herbie fired me."

"But how? On what grounds? You've been there 11 years!" Calling my boss Herbie didn't help; it only increased the notion that I wasn't serious or worried about any of this.

"I don't know." I'd been right. The truth came off worse than a lie would have. I could have just told her a lie and it would have been much better. Something like this:

MY WIFE: But why? Why did they fire you?

ME: I told you that I don't know. It might have something to do with the handicapped person.

MY WIFE: What handicapped person?

ME: The firm is suing a handicapped person—a quintiplegic Rwandan refugee—and I sneaked a peek at the files while I was scanning them into the system. We are suing this poor man for $20,000 because he hit Herbie Johnson right in the crotch with his wheelchair. The firm has seven attorneys working on it [I wipe a single tear from my eye].

MY WIFE: How terrible! How could you stand for that?

ME: Well, I didn't. I copied the entire case file, with some very damaging evidence that proves that Herbie was not in fact fitted with a prosthetic you-know-what. That medical report is the smoking gun document in the case. And I gave the entire file to the poor handicapped man's attorney today. And my forex dealer promised to donate my losses from this one trade to this poor man from Rwanda.

MY WIFE: You did the right thing! You are my hero!

"Hello? Hello, Harry! Are you listening to me?"

I fell back to earth and my wife's angry eyes were staring at me. I never got the chance to explain to Gini all about the Rwandan refugee. She just started crying.

"So you really have no clue as to why he fired you?" She was drying her eyes with her robe and sobbing quietly on purpose so that she did not wake the children.

All this was very distressing. Especially because we hadn't even started to talk about the bad trade, which was going to make matters even worse. And we couldn't even get to that horrible subject until I could tell her why I lost my job. Maybe I would get the chance to tell her about the quintiplegic and the wheelchair.

"And we're going to lose our benefits," she noted. "How are we going to pay for the pregnancy?"

I shook my head. Her worry was starting to transfer itself head on, right to me. My leg was going to start shaking any moment, because I realized that the delivery of a healthy baby would cost over $10,000. We were only a few months away. How was I going to raise that kind of money? I should have demanded an extra 10 grand from Herbie.

Instead, I said: "I don't know! Really! I don't know. This was my worst day in forever. It was terrible. Herbie came after me like he was hunting me down. Angrier than I have ever seen him. Something was very wrong, something that he thinks that I did. Something so bad that he wanted to blame someone for it. He needed a scapegoat, and I was going to be the one. I think that's why they offered me so much money to leave. They'd needed to place the blame on someone and I fit the description."

She sniffled. "That would explain why he didn't tell you why he was firing you. Because he knew you didn't do anything wrong, and he didn't want to give you a chance to defend yourself."

"And now they can place the blame on me and say they've taken care of the problem."

I wondered if it was Herbie who had done something wrong. "You know," I told her, "I could probably still talk to an attorney. There is no way I could have done something so wrong to deserve being fired."

"You were a good employee."

I shrugged. We were both calming down by talking about it. "I wasn't a good employee. I was a great filing manager, but I took advantage of them a lot. I had even started to do my trading on the job."

She didn't argue. She knew how much I disliked the job and wasn't going to blame me for not being thrilled about going to work every day.

"Do you think you can still trade?"

This was unexpected. I deserved a beating for the way I had acted with forex trading. In fact, I had half decided never to take another trade. Better to get out with a five-hundred-dollar overall loss, than trade the rest of the account into the toilet. On the other hand, what were my job prospects? Wakeman, Butterman, and Bailey would give a rotten reference for me if they agreed to offer one at all. And I had no other marketable skills. And I liked trading. And I had Craig, and perhaps Craig's mentor.

And as simply as that, I decided that from that time onward, I was going to be a full-time trader.

"I think I can still trade," I told Gini.

She smiled. My heart jumped. A smile popped onto my face. My skin tingled, and a shot of happy adrenaline shot up my spine.

I could do this!

CHAPTER 8

Charlie Flank Goes to U.S. National Bank

I called Craig the next day.

CRAIG: Don't think of this as a wrench in the gearbox. Think of this as a chance for you to pay some rent with the severance; sit down and make a trading plan; and think about how you want your family's future to look. I was forced to do this after my big trading loss—most trade traders put themselves in some kind of disaster scenario at the beginning. But you can choose what you want to do about it.

ME: Did you trade after the FOMC interest rate decision?

CRAIG: Yes, I sure did. I bought the British Pound for a quick profit. I might have been getting out just as you were getting in.

ME: How did you know to do that?

CRAIG: I followed the immediate movement. I was ready to buy Pounds right away, as soon as I saw price move up quickly. Price jumped up in the first minute and then fell back down, but as soon as it continued higher than the first move, I bought. I got in at 1.8130, and a few moments later, I was positive by 40 pips. I was tempted to take the money and get out. But I have a profit target at a previous level of support and resistance, where price stopped cold several times this year, and as recently as just a week ago. People were yelling and screaming around me to get out of the trade as it went into the red, but I am holding out for 1.8600. That's 470 pips away, but it can get there. I made up my mind before I took the trade today (see Figure 8.1).

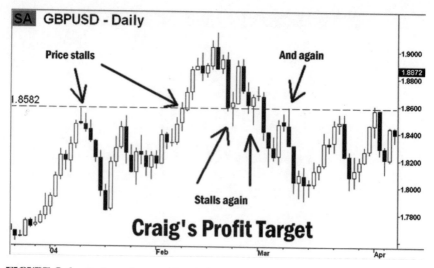

FIGURE 8.1   Craig makes up his mind.

ME: Did you learn how to do this kind of stuff on your own?

CRAIG: Mostly, yes. And with the help of a mentor and friend.

ME: How soon do you think that I can talk to your trading mentor?

CRAIG: Soon, yes.

ME: Where do I find him?

CRAIG: He'll find you.

ME: I'll just start studying some things about trading, maybe fix up the house a bit, things my wife has been wanting me to do anyway. And I can start trading when I get over this bad experience.

CRAIG: No. Don't take any more trades right now.

ME: Why not?

CRAIG: Because you're a horrible trader.

ME: Thanks a lot.

CRAIG: You bet. Happy to boost your spirits anytime. Listen, I gotta run. Market's gonna blast off here in a few minutes. Get some books. Dig in. See if you can sneak your way onto a Wall Street trading desk. You'll be surprised what you can learn by sitting there for a morning. Then call me back.

ME: Okay.

SNEAKING INTO U.S. NATIONAL BANK

I put on my only suit. I borrowed my neighbor's briefcase. I shined my shoes. I hadn't looked this good for work in at least 10 years. And I was going to need to look my best indeed, because today I was going to become Charlie Flank.

All Gini knew was that I was following up on a job lead from Craig Taylor. Perhaps I could get myself a job on a trading floor. That was everything that she needed to know. I didn't want to tell her I wasn't making any trades; she asked me twice the morning after our talk when I was going to be making some money from full-time trading. Now that we had both committed to my career as a trader, she expected that I would work at it like a full-time job.

But I knew that I should obey Craig's advice. I wanted to trade—after all, my first two trades were brilliant successes, and I had the Amazing Forex software. It was hard enough to explain to Gini that I was going to wait a day or two, let alone try to explain it over and over to myself.

The best way to pass the time, I decided, was to capture another glimpse of a trading floor. Armed with my list of nine Wall Street trading superstars that I had taken from the office, I decided that I had a chance of seeing at least one more trading operation. If I couldn't get on the floor at the first two or three, then I would start begging for a tour. Surely one of the firms would allow tours.

It was Friday April 2, 2004. I took the C train to Wall Street, and at 8:15 A.M., I entered an emotionless granite building that looked as much like a train station as a New York office building, and certainly was older than any of its surrounding firms. I knew that U.S. National Bank had a trading operation here, and because it was located in the heart of Wall Street, I assumed these guys were good. There were other firms on my list that I'd taken from Wakeman on my last day at work; I came to U.S. National first because I wanted to visit Wall Street anyway. If I didn't like it here, or they didn't let me in, I'd have my choice of three or four other firms nearby.

When I thought about it, I realized that being the filing manager at a law firm had paid off in an important way. The Anderson case files were full of names of Wall Street firms and traders; after all, the case was about how much a good trader deserved to be paid, and all I needed to look at was the research compiled by our firm. The research file was a gold mine of information. With more time, I could have stockpiled a ton of names, salaries, addresses, and probably phone numbers of traders. But I'd only had time to take the names of a few firms and individuals.

I knew that if I could investigate just one of these trading operations, I could learn enough to convince Craig I was doing my part to be ready to learn from him or his mentor. Craig had been right when he said that I was a terrible trader. Who would want to work with me unless I at least learned more?

Which was exactly what I was going to do right then at U.S. National Bank.

I took the elevator up 20 floors and exited. There I found a front desk that looked a lot like the one at Ernest Wellington, which protected a large door not much different from the steel one that I had passed through to see Anderson and Craig and 200 other wild traders. I walked confidently up to the desk and offered a professional smile that said, "You are about to let me in the large door." But what I really said was:

ME: I have a file to drop off for Mr. Sutherland.

I knew from the Anderson files that Mr. Sutherland was an executive who worked on the trading floor. My ingenious plan would now unfold like the napkin on a fancy place setting, or some other thing that unfolds very classy-like and easily, without any problems from the police or building security.

BORED RECEPTIONIST: Your name. Your firm.
ME: Charlie Flank, with Wakeman, Butterman, and Bailey.

I was lying a lot more these days, and getting pretty good at it, or the people I was talking to were just getting dumber. Either way, the Bored Receptionist was going to escort me through the trading door any moment. I could feel it.

She didn't even verify my credentials. What a pushover! After I signed a guest registry, she stuck a name tag on me that said VISITOR and CHARLIE FLANK, and then she unlocked the large door and let me through.

Next time I was just going to tell her to print me off a name badge and put me on the payroll! This was easy! I had assumed that Craig had been a genius for installing himself at a trading desk at Ernest Wellington. Not so! I could probably get myself onto five or six other trading floors in the next week. If sneaking onto trading floors could pay money, I could make a living at it for sure. I was the James Bond of sneaking into Wall Street firms!

Before I could complete my fantasy, the receptionist led me onto a much smaller trading floor than the one I had seen at Ernest Wellington. Maybe half as large. Probably 60 or 70 people in this room. But it wasn't the size of the space that seemed odd. Here everyone spoke in hushed voices or not at all. I saw no sports sections from the *Daily News*. No messy desks. Hardly any computers! While every desk had a coffee cup and a large phone with colorful buttons, not every desk had a computer monitor. While there had been three or four screens per desk at Ernest Wellington, I could count on my hands the number in this room. Dark green carpet covered the floor and stopped at each cherry-wood paneled wall. There were windows on the western and northern walls, but most of the curtains were drawn and the office was lit mostly by floor and table lamps. This looked more like an expensive steakhouse than a trading operation.

Perhaps I'd come to the wrong place. Apparently I had walked into a gathering of men (no women in sight) who didn't care what might happen in the markets that day. I'd soon find out I was right.

I suspected that the average age of the traders here was at least 45 years. Some of them appeared older than that, maybe as old as 60 or 70. Not one of them wore anything but a blue or grey suit, with the coat still on. At Ernest Wellington, I'd seen a trader wearing Bermuda shorts and a Hawaiian shirt. That person would seem very out of place on this floor.

Each of these men had a spacious work area that was separated from the others; they were sitting at their own wooden desks and some of them even had visitor's chairs in front of them. Some of them had small televisions on a side table. Only a few of them were tuned on, all of them showing CNBC. Melissa Francis was reporting from her luxury box above the New York Mercantile Exchange.

If anyone here traded for a living, he would have a hard time proving it to me. Surely I had stopped at the wrong floor, for retired traders. These were the stables where they put out the old men to pasture and told them to watch some news, visit with old friends, make a few phone calls, and have a cup of coffee. Perhaps the Federal Reserve was about to make another interest rate announcement. That would explain the hush-hush environment and the focus on the few television monitors.

I also decided that since I had gone to the trouble of sneaking onto the trading floor, I deserved to know why in the world no one here seemed to be trading. But I didn't know who to ask. At Ernest Wellington, with everyone screaming, it seemed natural to talk with the first person I saw. But here I was intimidated. No one seemed alive, let alone happy to see a visitor. Since the receptionist had left me alone, I didn't have a tour guide. I considered walking out and moving on to the next firm.

Thank goodness, someone spoke to me first.

"Son, you look a mite lost. Who ya lookin for?"

The wrinkled face of a man at least 80 years of age smiled broadly at me. "Not too many of us here, I'm sure I can give you a hand."

"What's everyone waiting for?" I asked him. "It's quiet in here."

He just looked back at me like my head was on fire. "Well, boy, it's quiet in here every day. This ain't no two-bit operation up in Midtown. You're standing where John Pierpont Morgan himself used to stand, or at least nearby."

John Pierpont Morgan? Was that long for J. P. Morgan, the famous banker from 10 million years ago?

"Wow," I replied, hoping to appear as impressed as he obviously wished I would be.

"Well, then, if you're waiting for someone, come on over here and you can sit down."

He guided me to a desk where a man not much younger—but much bigger—than he was sitting. He towered over the desk in his chair; he was probably six and a half feet tall and had massive hands that made the mechanical pencil in his hand look like a toothpick. He was playing solitaire with a worn deck of cards with the other hand, in between using the pencil to write notes on large sheets of graph paper in front of him. The desks on either side were empty. It was clear this guy was a loner. I gathered up some courage and sat myself down in one of the guest chairs in front of him. The other old man waddled off so weakly I wondered if he could find his desk.

"Good morning," he offered without looking up. "I don't recognize you. Come here to gamble this morning? You new around here?"

I shook my head, but he wasn't looking at me. I replied: "Gambling's not really my thing. I'm just here to drop off some documents."

He looked up. "Not dropping anything off on me, I hope."

"Of course not." I held out my hand to him. "Harry Banes."

He grunted. "Looks like today you're Charlie Flank."

I looked down at my name tag. "Oh, that," I replied. "That's who I was when I checked in at the front desk."

He furrowed his brow and looked at me oddly.

"I sneaked in here because I want to be a trader. That's the honest truth. But I feel like I just took a trip to another planet."

Ah, the truth. Telling it gave me the feeling of seeing an old friend. Well, at least an old friend that I had sold up the river.

He laughed, grinned, and stretched back in his chair and put the pencil behind his ear. He spoke to me, but he spoke so loudly I suddenly felt very conspicuous. Not wanting to draw attention to myself, I sunk a bit deeper into the chair. He boomed: "Sounds like something I would have done forty years ago," he told me. And then he pointed across to the television a few desks away. Melissa Francis was gone, replaced by a group of talking heads who were saying things I couldn't understand. The old man continued: "You picked the right day to come in here. NFP [Non-Farm Payroll report] is out in two minutes. You're gonna to see this place blow up like a rock concert."

"Really?"

He chortled and the pencil fell out of his ear. I stood up to get it for him but his arms were so long he could reach down for it on his own. He offered his hand to me and we shook, my hand disappearing into his. With a closer look at him, I realized that although he appeared old, he had a spark and energy that told me there were a lot of years left in him.

"Is this place really going to blow up?" I asked again.

"No, Charlie," he answered. "It's not. It's not going to hardly blow air." He looked around him. "Half these guys don't even know what day of the week it is."

"Oh, my name is Harry. Sorry for the confusion." I tore off the name tag sticker, then said, "You mentioned that the NFP was coming out in a few minutes."

"Yep."

I didn't know what that meant. Was this a report like the FOMC minutes? I wished that I could be sitting next to Craig Simpson right now, to see what he would be doing. This guy wasn't paying any attention to the television any longer. He had returned to marking up his charts, continually breaking the lead in the pencil. This frustrated him and finally he threw the pencil in the trash can next to his desk.

"Gotta pen?"

I gave him mine.

"You don't seem to be too concerned about the NFP," I observed.

This impressed him. He wanted to be noticed for not paying attention. "I'm working on my charts this morning, like I do every first Friday. Listen, I'll give you a tip: You don't trade the day of the report—you make longer term bets after it's out. Most of the young guys in this city are going to trade their brains out for the first hour after the report is out. They would sell their own mothers to get this number before it's released. But they don't have to sit on the edge of their seats like they do. They can just wait to see what the number is, then make a rational plan."

"From the other trading floor I've seen, rational behavior is in short supply. It was chaotic."

He smiled. He was pleased that I understood him.

I stood up and looked down at his charts. There were X's and O's all across his graph paper. It looked like a financial chart that I would see on TV, only instead of lines going up or down, there were X's and O's. He could see that I was interested.

"Point and figure charts, my friend. No one pays any attention anymore. But I still plot them by hand. Wait, here comes the number."

The gentleman with the television closest to us turned up the volume on his set and for a brief moment, most of the heads in the room turned to look. The shot moved to some massive trading floor somewhere, with a reporter smack dab in the middle of the room:

RICK SANTELLI: Three-hundred-eight thousand!

It was as if Zeus has called down to his people. And he had told them that he was coming to kill the trader who acted the most like a human being. And that sent everyone on the television screen into a frenzy. The sound turned back down on the television, but all around the reporter, the place blew up. Traders screamed at each other, throwing hand signals to each other so quickly it was totally impossible to decipher anything. This is probably what it looked like over at Ernest Wellington. How I wished I could be there right then!

It was obvious to the old man in front of me that I had no idea what was going on. From the reaction in this room, I decided that no one here really traded, but that they were all retired. We had lawyers like that back at Wakeman—old men who would shuffle around, tell dirty jokes, and go home at 2:00 P.M. every day.

While Craig at Ernest Wellington was furiously trading, along with all the people around him, this man and his associates appeared not to belong on a trading floor at all. I got the feeling they had seen a lot of these reports, and they no longer held the same interest. He said: "Charlie, what just came out is the March jobs number. It tracks how many new jobs were created in the United States."

"Okay. It looks like the people on television really care about it."

"Right. Just like I said. Guys on Wall Street would chop off their feet to get just one of these numbers early. Today we got a good number. A great number for short-term traders. Way off expectations. You can bet that a lot of guys and gals on the street are buying U.S. dollars right now. They're betting that today the dollar will go way up because of the number. But what really matters isn't what happens in the next five minutes. What matters is what happens by the end of the day and then next week."

"But you aren't going to trade today?"

"Hello no."

"When will you trade?"

He enjoyed this question. "I'll answer you without giving you the information you want. Do you have access to charts?"

"Currency charts?"

"Sure. Currency charts."

I nodded. "Yes, at home."

"Learn how to use them. But don't look at the short-term charts. That's what the hooligans are focused on right now. You need to watch the longer term charts."

He had just called Craig Taylor a hooligan, just because he liked to short-term trade. He seemed wise and friendly but totally ignorant of how much money could be made from the short-term trading that Craig did. Maybe I could ask a few more questions and then bail out of here.

"What's the difference between short-term and long-term?" I asked.

"The young guys are all looking at the five-minute charts, or God help them, the one-minute charts, or lower. The tick charts even. Maniacs. I am looking at the daily and weekly charts here."

"Should I look at those, too?"

"Sure. Do that. And add in the four-hour charts. Can you do that?"

"Absolutely," I answered.

Even though everyone here seemed out of touch with the high-tech form of trading, I was at least happy that he was talking to me, and also aware that if I had studied some before I had met him, I could be asking him lots of intelligent questions about the market. Right now, I was positively unable to comprehend anything more advanced than his instructions to look at the long-term charts. Other than that, he was speaking a foreign language. I knew that everyone on Wall Street (except the men at the Rest Home for Old Guy Traders) was making trades. I knew that we had just gotten a March Jobs Number, or "NFP."

"You said that everyone who trades in the short term would be buying dollars, trading currency. What about stocks?"

"Stocks aren't traded here on the same floor as currencies, usually. Here we can trade whatever we want. The equities floor would be separate from the currency floor in most places. But to answer your question, stocks could make a nice move upward today. Stock market likes a strong economy."

I was confused on so many levels. For sure, my brain had melted and was now draining out my ears.

He could tell I did not understand much of this and that I was totally captivated by the chaos on the television. He smiled. "You are a total rookie, aren't you?"

I nodded. "With a capital R," I answered.

He looked down at his charts and looked up at me. Then he looked down and up again, trying to decide what he was going to spend his time on.

"I'd love to help you kid," he said, "but I've gotta get myself ready for Monday. It's nine A.M. and I'm leaving at noon, and I got twenty-five other charts to work on. It's not like I was expecting you. Was I expecting you?"

"No."

"Right. You need to read a book about this stuff."

I was willing to read *War and Peace* backward if it meant I could better understand what was happening around me.

"What book?"

He shook his head. I guessed that I had asked just a few too many questions in too short of a time. "I don't know," he told me. "I started in the mailroom a thousand years ago and learned this stuff by sitting at a desk and asking a guy questions, like you're trying to do with me. Come back on Monday and you can bother me some more. My name's Samuel Wilson." He stood up, shook my hand again, and that was the sign that it was time for me to go.

"Thank you, Mr. Wilson. I will do that. I really appreciate this."

He grinned and now looked happy that he had helped me.

Although he couldn't answer any more questions, I didn't see why I couldn't stick around and watch what happened next. He didn't mind, and he even said that he'd make sure no one bothered me. I sneaked over to a nearby desk that was closer to the CBNC television, and settled in for a little while. This made me really, really happy. Even if I couldn't learn much about the new methods of trading from this old man, he at least would cover for me while I watched some television to see more of the reaction in the market.

And I wasn't going to leave here empty-handed.

From just a few moments on this trading floor, I knew about one more economic event that needed my attention: the NFP. I had a lot of studying to do. It occurred to me, as I saw everyone working furiously on television, that all those people knew what they were doing. They saw that jobs report come out, and then they were ready to react. Like tigers pouncing on their prey. Or bullies on a playground trying to get a piece of a fight. They had been waiting for someone to announce the number, and then they knew what trades to take.

Even the man next to me, who was plotting away on his charts, had a system that he was working on. He wasn't reacting immediately to the news, but he had said that he was going to base some of his trading decisions on this report—just not immediately after it was released.

With so much happening at that moment, I decided not to bother any other traders, but instead make some observations.

Even though I was sure these old men had been successful at some point in their lives, I decided that the real trading life for me would resemble the life of an Ernest Wellington trader. I could see myself with a computer at home, several monitors, the sports section open next to me, television tuned into CNBC in the background. That was more like it, and much more like my personality. The computer was going to be the most difficult part.

I couldn't believe how long I had lasted at the law firm with barely enough skill to answer my e-mail, pecking on the keyboard one letter at a time. They probably should have fired me long before they did, on the basis of my technological incompetence alone. It was positively going to be the case that when I started trading for a living, I would receive some kind of formal training on computers. In the meantime, I could get my wife and kids to help me a bit. Maybe I could pay Scott, or at least offer to pay him, to tutor me.

But first, I was going to have to get a whole lot smarter than I was now about the basics: the language of trading. I would have to read enough so that I could at least ask basic questions that could help me start learning the advanced stuff that everyone I was watching on television—and Craig—knew already.

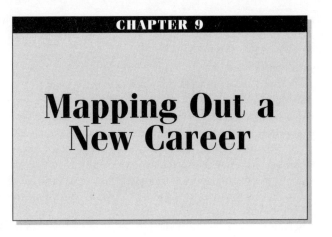

CHAPTER 9

Mapping Out a New Career

I showed up at the Barnes & Noble in Rockefeller Center an hour later. Just around the corner I'd also find Teuschers, the Swiss Chocolatier. If I arrived home with chocolates in one hand and 1,000 new books in the other, Gini would focus on the chocolates and not on how much I'd spent. And I planned on spending a lot of money on books that day—I was going to stock myself with books about trading, then hole myself up at home during the day and study my brains out.

It wasn't hard to find a clerk who was interested in talking to someone about something other than travel guides to New York City, and he walked me through the investing section one book at a time. I found books on economics, on options, on forex, on day-trading stocks—you name it, I found it. The clerk also recommended a few books that were just stories about traders. Although these books were less relevant, I bought them anyway. As far as I can remember, that day I bought books on day-trading stocks and futures and commodities, books on economic indicators, books on technical analysis (reading charts), and books that taught me about the currency market specifically. Then there were some books on the psychology of trading, or stories about traders. While they seemed interesting, I knew that I'd be just passing the time by reading them and that they would be a waste of time. Those would be my reward for making profitable trades. I could only read those after I'd studied all the other books at least twice.

I am sure that I bought at least 20 books. I had so many of them that I could not carry them by myself and had to arrange for them to be delivered to my house. They were more than happy to oblige, so I grabbed just one of the books—the book about day-trading forex—and I left the store, hopped on the subway, and headed home.

By the time the subway reached my stop in Queens, I was so wrapped up in the book that I never got off. I stayed on all the way to the end of the line, and although by then I realized what was happening, I stayed on anyway. From what I could tell, the currency market was the most liquid market on the planet, and trillions of dollars a day changed hands (or computer screens) in trading. The book was written for the guy trading currency at home, which was perfect for me—and it had systems, it had tools, it even had advice about how to keep a log of my trades. I had placed a total of three trades in my entire life but I was determined that it wasn't going to be long before I was trading on a daily basis.

When I arrived home, I had two things waiting for me: a frustrated wife and a box full of books sitting on the porch so heavy that we could hardly move it. Gini was wondering how on earth I could justify buying all those books when I had just lost my job. It was funny, because I hadn't thought about my lost job all day long.

Once I ate dinner with my family and put the kids to bed, I rushed to the computer and fired up the charting program. That was the first thing I wanted to see: the charts. Mr. Wilson had told me to look at the longer term charts. So that is what I did (see Figure 9.1).

The daily chart told me nearly everything that I cared to know about Craig's trade. Just the day before, on the first day of April, his trade had

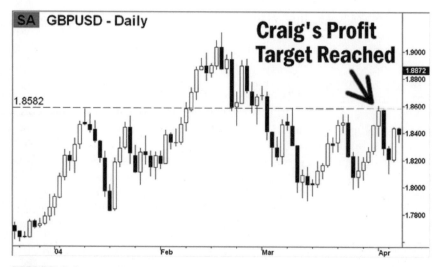

FIGURE 9.1 Harry looks at a long-term chart.

closed at his profit target of 1.8600. But I needed to see a chart closer up that would show what had happened today. So, against the wishes of old man Wilson, I switched over to a 15-minute chart.

From my book on technical analysis, I learned that each of the candles I looked at represented the movement of price in a designated period of time. On a 15-minute chart, each candle showed how far the price moved in, well, 15 minutes. Dark candles meant that price had gone down. Light candles meant that price had gone up. Easy enough (see Figure 9.2).

Looking at the chart, I realized that the GBP/USD had moved its entire distance for the day—200 pips—in the first 15 minutes after the report was released. Then it rose back up 100 pips, and then it fell back down 100 pips. What a wild ride! Surely a lot of money could be made in a very short period of time. That's where the money was! In the short-term trading, just like Craig Taylor was doing. If I could react fast enough, I realized, I could get in on the first move of a currency pair after the Non-Farm Payroll report (ah, the NFP!), or the FOMC (Federal Open Market Committee) interest rate decision, and then ride it for a quick profit. And what if I traded more than just one currency pair?

While I knew I had made a mistake when I traded after the FOMC interest rate decision, I now understood that it was more a mistake of how long it took me to enter the trade and for long how I stayed in. It had nothing to do with whether I bought or sold. There were fast profits—even easy profits—to be made when these two reports were released. How many more reports were there? When did they come out? Would Craig show me how to trade them? I felt badly for Mr. Wilson. That old man was sitting around

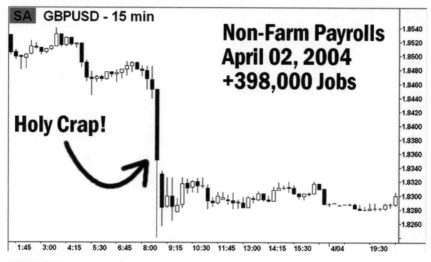

FIGURE 9.2   A wild ride.

waiting for days to trade, while Craig was enjoying freshly baked pips after just a few minutes of trading! How on earth was Mr. Wilson going to make money by sitting around and not even reacting at all to the economic report?

I dove back into the books. I finished the first book that evening, and then spent the rest of the evening wading through the others. I had four or five open at a time, and I was sucking in as much information as possible. Although I was learning a lot from them, and the terminology was coming quickly, I couldn't get the idea about trading after the economic reports out of my head. From the books, I was learning lists of important economic reports. Here are the ones that seemed to cause the most movement:

- Non-Farm Payroll
- Consumer Price Index
- Trade Balance
- FOMC Interest Rate Decision and Minutes

There were other economic reports listed, but these were supposedly some of the most important ones.

Together with my new-found understanding of economic reports, I had the Amazing Forex software, and I was sure that I could make that expensive tool work for me in this system. It seemed perfectly designed to help me make a decision about what trade to take after an economic report.

By scouting around online, I also taught myself about leverage, or margin. I learned that forex dealers were willing to offer 100:1, or even 200:1 margin. This meant with an initial investment of $1,000, I could command a $100,000 position, or even more, in the currency markets. What got my juices flowing about this was that, apparently, I could keep my small trading account, and once I started learning to trade like Craig, I could still make a lot of money on a daily basis. Trading for a living from home was now making sense to me. The only reason I had lost so much so fast was that I had left my trades open while I was doing other things. If I had been paying attention and trading in the short term, I could have cleaned up.

The math I was doing in my head was shocking. My forex dealer offered 400:1 margin. That meant that I could put up $100 in margin, and command a $400,000 position. That would be worth $40 per pip! I'd have $400 in margin left over still. Just like the woman from the forex dealer had told me on the phone—every time the price moved against me by 1 pip, or $40, that would be deducted from my available leftover margin. So, I could allow an economic report trade to move against me 10 pips before I needed to get out. That was fine, I realized—the market only moved in one direction after these reports! I could just be ready to go in the direction of the movement after the report, and then bank some quick profits.

I'd seen the GBP/USD move 200 pips in just a few moments. If I just got 50 of those pips for every economic report, at $40 each, that was $2,000 in gains. Every day! It was no wonder that those Wall Street guys were making so much money. They were trading position sizes of probably $10 million at a time. That would be . . . $1,000 per pip. At 50 pips a day, they were easily making hundreds of thousands of dollars per week.

That was when I knew it was my time to shine. I could not wait to start trading again. I had broken down my wife by losing my job. I had raised her hopes high on the plans to become a trader, and now I had to prove myself. She was giving me another chance to make right the bad trade and the loss of $1,200. I decided that I never wanted to talk about that loss again. I was going to focus on the future! What gain could come from miserably dissecting the past?

So I mentally stepped into a phone booth and changed myself into Harry Banes: Supertrader. This was my destiny. I was going to earn back every cent that I had lost. I might even earn it back on one trade.

I told all this to my wife the next morning.

She was supportive. "You got a nice severance check, and I know it wasn't easy to get that. Maybe we should put that money in the trading account instead of the bank. You can earn more trading it than we can in interest."

"That is not a bad idea," I agreed. "The severance alone is not going to get us very far." I did some calculations in my mind. With a $6,000 account, I could use $3,000 for margin, and I'd be able to command a $1.2 million position, which would be worth $120 per pip. Now we were talking about serious money. More than enough to live on. On a daily diet of 50 pips off economic reports, I could expect to make $5,000 per day. This was nearly too great to comprehend. I was going to be rich. It occurred to me that so many people in life never took advantage of their opportunities. The $6,000 severance money was a fantastic opportunity.

Because I'd recently lost a big chunk of money, I decided to play it cool. I told Gini, "What I'll do is get the trading account back up to a thousand dollars, and then we can put the six thousand in. That way I can get my new trading plan off the ground, try it out, talk with Craig again. That will be perfect. By the time I talk to him, I'll have lots of good questions, and he can help me maximize the severance money."

Gini believed this was a good idea. "How are we going to get by in the meantime?"

I had a plan for this. "I think we should take my retirement money out of the Wakeman 401(k) plan. And we can live on that for at least six months."

I had between $15,000 and $20,000, if I was remembering correctly, in a retirement account. We had promised each other that we would never touch it except for an absolute emergency. Now seemed like an appropriate time.

"Do you think you should trade with that money too?" she asked.

This didn't feel right to me. Not at all. The severance money felt like a gift, like a $20 bill that I'd found on the street. But the retirement savings seemed completely different. That money had been set aside for a long time, had been growing slowly and steadily, and I'd taken less pay home every two weeks just so we could put more money toward retirement.

"No, I don't think so. That money was meant for something else. Only in a total emergency would I consider taking that money out."

"Okay," she agreed. "That money could keep us going for more than six months, if we scale down a bit. We can get by with less. No more huge spending sprees at the bookstore."

"All right."

"And we can change the way we eat. I bet we could get by for seven or eight months on that money."

"What do you mean by scaling down?" I asked. "Do you mean selling some of our stuff?" This didn't sit right with me. I was positive I would be making a lot of money very soon. She seemed to be taking the safe route. And what's more, she didn't seem bothered by this. It was as if she now considered this to be exciting—even an adventure with her husband, the currency trader.

We had no idea what an adventure it would be.

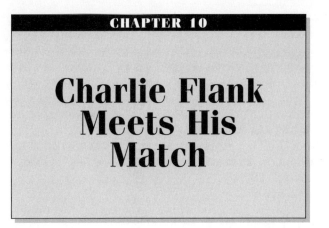

CHAPTER 10

Charlie Flank Meets His Match

That weekend I learned that the words "scaling down" actually referred to selling off all the things that I liked in the house. My wife canceled the expanded cable television subscription. She auctioned off our big screen television on eBay, and replaced it with a tiny 17-inch set that she bought online for $50. She sold my bookcases to a neighbor. Now that my book collection no longer had a home, she visited a used bookstore in her old Brooklyn neighborhood, and just a few days later they came and picked up all the books except for the new ones about trading. She sold the high-end stereo components that she'd given me for Christmas two years earlier. And she sold my tennis racket.

Lest I only tell one side of the story, I'll admit that she also gave up her sewing machine and gave a ton of her older clothes and some of our furniture to a consignment shop down the road. She was boxing up the microwave one afternoon when I called a halt to the entire operation.

"We gotta eat! We've definitely sold enough of our things."

She paused. "I just want to make sure we don't go bankrupt. So far I've raised a lot of money for us."

This made me feel like we were trying to raise funds to buy a kidney for one of our children. "How much?" I asked.

"Five thousand, give or take a few hundred."

I had to admit that it was impressive. I hardly missed the books and actually missed the television far less than I had imagined that I would. The kids missed it terribly, but they would get over it. If I added my wife's ability to sell things to the retirement money (which turned out to be just over

$23,000, which was on the way to our bank account) this brought our savings to $29,000.

"What else?" Gini asked. "What else can we sell, if you don't want to give up the microwave? What about the car?"

I shook my head. "We are not selling the car. You've sold everything you need to sell for now. We have almost $30,000 and that's enough. We'll do all right with that. We can make a budget and work out the numbers. With trading and that money we are going to be all right."

"Are you sure?" I noticed that she was worried. That all this selling of our stuff had more of a reason behind it than she had told me.

"Gini, are you all right?"

She shook her head.

"I promise we're going to be fine. I promise I can do this."

"I've started to worry that maybe trading is a bit more risky than I first thought."

"Why?" Had she talked to someone? Seen something on television?

"Well," she started. "You did lose over a thousand dollars in one day."

Oh. She had seen me. That was the source of her doubt. Hearing this was mildly depressing, but I determined to face it head on.

"I am not going to do that again. I learned my lesson. It wasn't really even my fault—I left the account only because Herbie wanted to chew me out."

"But it's not just that. I do believe you can do better. But my father's best friend lost everything day-trading the stock market. You know Emilio Gonzales, right?"

"The guy who carried mail with your dad?"

She nodded, and continued: "He took out something like fifty thousand dollars of their retirement money and bet it on the stock market. Then when he lost that, he mortgaged their home. Then he lost everything after just two months or something. They lost the home; they had to sell their car; they even sold their furniture on eBay, just to survive."

We were both quiet and uncomfortable for a few moments. I could hear the traffic outside. Some boys were yelling and playing basketball on the court down below the apartment building. A pigeon settled down outside our living room window and cooed. Something tugged at my emotions; I could sense that whatever Emilio Gonzales had done wrong, I could do wrong as well.

I took a deep breath. "I won't do that. I won't use our retirement money to trade. That is only for us to live on. And we might not even have to use it all."

Gini liked this idea. Neither of us wanted to feel negative about trading. After all, it was the only solution we had at this point.

"Maybe you could go talk to Emilio. Learn from what he did wrong."

"I'd rather talk to Craig. He's been successful. I don't know how much I could learn from someone who lost everything."

"When are you going to see him again? When are you going to start trading?" she asked.

"Soon. I want to meet with Craig one more time."

"When is that?"

"I will call him today."

"What about the nice old man at the other bank?"

"Mr. Wilson? At U.S. National? I guess I could call him, too." I didn't remind her that he had invited me to stop by the next day, Monday, to talk some more.

"You guess you'll call him?"

"Okay, I will call him."

But I had no intention of doing so. In the past two days, Mr. Wilson had drifted into the background. The more I thought about it, the more I realized that the traders at U.S. National Bank didn't take advantage of what Craig knew—they were living in the past. No computers! How could a trader succeed without a computer? Everything told me that I wanted to be Ernest Wellington-esque in my trading. On the forefront of information, of technology. This is how the big boys made money. It was how I would make money, too.

While Gini had been selling our possessions, that weekend I had helped watch the kids and read as much as I could on economic indicators. Realizing that Scott was no longer around to help me, I had reread the entire user's manual for my forex trading platform. I'd learned how to effectively use the new charting program. In all, I now had set myself up to be ready to trade the economic reports. I didn't really need Mr. Wilson and decided that it would be best if I didn't bother him again.

Over dinner on Sunday, we continued the conversation. I had one eye on my currency charts the entire time.

"And you're sure that you can do this trading thing," my wife remarked.

"Yes," I promised her. The GBP/USD was moving sideways. Not doing anything. Sunday nights clearly didn't matter in currency trading. Who would trade at this time of day, anyway? I turned back to my wife. "Yes, for sure. Especially with all the tools that are out there right now. It's probably easier to make money than ever before. This operation at Ernest Wellington was first class. Those guys are making a million dollars per year. Craig is going to show me what he does to make that kind of money. And I'm already learning a ton of stuff on my own."

"You are sure you can get Craig to teach you what he does?" This brought to mind the subject of Craig's mentor. I could still meet and learn from the person who taught Craig how to trade. I wondered if he was a trader at Ernest Wellington. I wondered again if it was really Anderson, or someone else I had seen on the trading floor at Ernest. For a moment I considered calling Craig that very evening to see if he could set up a meeting. By now I had learned plenty enough to qualify myself for some advanced mentoring.

This emboldened me even more. "I am sure I can learn what I need to learn. From Craig, from books, from others. I have the names of eight more Wall Street banks and haven't even tried to visit them yet."

The events of the past two weeks had left her understandably unstable in her emotions. What I love about my wife is that even after I'd lost my job and half the trading account, and I had no evidence to prove that I could duplicate the results of a Wall Street trader, Gini was still willing to go along with the entire plan. Surely, the knowledge that Craig made $1 million per year helped to convince her to give the plan a chance.

I wondered what the other currency pairs were doing. I switched pages on my charts. The USD/JPY was moving down fast—my one-minute chart was showing some serious action! Apparently the traders in Asia could get things moving even on a Sunday night! Well, of course it was Monday morning for them, I realized. No wonder. I summoned all my willpower to avoid taking a trade.

HALF A TRILLION

I called Craig the next morning. Having seen the action on Sunday night I could not resist getting back into the game, but I determined to not trade again until I received more instruction from someone who knew more than I did. And from someone like Craig who could teach me to trade the economic news. I had learned more in 30 minutes with Craig than I had from reading any of the books so far. The books were good for learning terminology. But the practical knowledge I could get from a successful trader would take me to the next level.

Which is why I dialed Ernest Wellington's number on Monday morning and asked to speak with Craig Taylor.

He answered immediately.

"Have you started trading again?" was his first question.

"Not yet," I told him, "I took your advice."

"Hallelujah!" he cried. "How I wish I'd taken that advice early on."

"I also plan to put a bit more money into the trading account. That way, I can actually make some real money."

This didn't impress him. "Remember that you don't need a huge trading account to trade successfully. And that trading doesn't have to be your only job. You could do something on the side. Earn some money to put into your trading account."

This was perhaps the dumbest idea I'd ever heard. Of course I didn't say that. Instead: "Anyway, did you trade on Friday?"

"Sure did. Did you watch the market?"

"Yeah, I did. I actually sneaked onto the trading floor at U.S. National Bank."

"Really! Impressive! You did that? Did you meet any of the traders?"

"Yep. They were a boring bunch. Like a funeral home in there. Wood paneling."

"Oh," he said. This seemed to jar his memory. "Those guys. I don't know anyone over there. They are the slow bunch. They take it nice and easy. No short-term trading for them."

"Right. I thought I was going to fall asleep there. Obviously, they need some computers. Maybe they can't afford them."

Craig let out a hearty laugh. "Those guys? Oh, they can afford computers. They could afford to buy every last computer on Wall Street if they wanted."

"Really?"

"Really. They were the most profitable trading floor on Wall Street a couple of years ago."

A slight twinge of regret fell over me as I realized I was supposed to be meeting with Mr. Wilson right now. Maybe I had misread him.

"How profitable?" I asked.

"They had something like half a trillion dollars in assets. Their trading desk probably made two billion dollars in profits last year alone."

"Whoa."

"Right. We did a billion last year. With twice as many traders. You should definitely see if you can get in there again. Did you meet Hank Doorecker?"

"No." Doorecker? I was sure I would have remembered a name like that. "Who's Hank Doorecker?"

"Hank is probably the best trader on the street right now. He's older, has been trading for at least three decades. Only trades currencies. He never gives interviews so you can't learn anything about his methods. You should look him up if you get over there again. He and I have the same mentor. Just years apart."

I now felt really badly that I'd not shown up at U.S. National Bank that morning. There could be a lot of people there worth meeting! Would Mr. Wilson mind if I showed up late? He hadn't specified a time. I now decided that as soon as I hung up with Craig I would race downtown. Hopefully, he would not have already left for the day. Perhaps if he was gone, I could try to meet Mr. Dudley Dooright or whatever his name was. If he was anything like Mr. Wilson, he wasn't going to be busy with trading and would surely have time to talk.

"They trade a lot of currency and bonds futures there," he said, "And if you can get them to show you how they use the long-term charts, it's fascinating."

Clearly, I was a moron. I had missed a huge opportunity by not learning more while I'd been there.

"What about short-term trading? I've been thinking about doing more short-term trading. Like you do."

"That's good too," he answered. "It's really good. You can make money either way."

"That sounds like a contradiction."

"It's not," he shot back. "Not at all. It's a misconception that almost every trader goes through. We think there's one best way to do this. But there are a zillion ways that can work."

But it had seemed that short-term trading had huge opportunities to make money fast. I had already decided it was better for me.

"You know, I did interview there," he said. "They've got an aggressive operation over there. Quiet, catatonic, like they're all sleeping on the job. The reality is that they are wholly unimpressed with anything except making huge sums of money. And behind that stoic impression, they are hungry to be the very best in the business, and they usually are. They go after profits like an animal that stalks its prey for a long time, and then just pounces. And when they pounce, they don't let go."

"Sounds cool."

He laughed and agreed. "There is a story about Hank Doorecker buying up the Swiss Franc against the British Pound in the late 1990s—slowly, methodically, until he held an enormous position on the spot forex market. Rumor is that he actually placed calls to the finance ministers of small countries and talked about how they needed to protect themselves by selling any British government bonds they had and replacing them with Swiss bonds."

"What would that do? How would that help him?"

"Well, I don't have time to get into all of it, but what happened was he started a free fall. In the next year, the Swiss Franc gained over 1,000 points against the Pound. People say he made one hundred million dollars on that trade alone. If you can meet him, it would be awesome to hear the story firsthand."

What Craig was describing seemed slightly dishonest, if not outright illegal. And hugely profitable. I wondered how close I wanted to get to Hank Doorecker. And at the same time I hoped I could meet him. There was so much to learn.

"Do you have traders like that at your firm?" I asked. Maybe I could meet them. Getting to meet and learn from Mr. Wilson or Hank Doorecker seemed more difficult now that I knew how profitable their firm was.

"We have lots of short-term guys. All short-term guys. No one as famous as Doorecker or the other guys at U.S. National."

Because I wanted to short-term trade, I was happy he had brought up the subject.

"Do you think I should use the one-minute chart?" I asked.

His tone of voice dampened, like he had been asked this before and didn't want to talk about it. "I don't know. It depends."

I changed gears. "Did the short-term traders at Ernest Wellington do well on Friday? It was a big move down for the British Pound at least."

"Oh, yes. A lot of us jumped on that fast."

"What did you do?" I asked.

"I sold Pounds, as you can imagine. Sold everything I could for as long as I could that morning. When that report is first released, all the liquidity dries up. Your short-term charts will show the price falling, and that's exactly what it is doing. It's falling hard because there isn't anyone who wants to buy it."

"Supply and demand," I offered.

"Exactly," he continued. "No one wanted to buy Pounds for the first two or three minutes. Then when it had fallen a good 200 points, it rebounded slightly, as traders who were already short going into the report closed their positions by buying back Pounds and selling U.S. Dollars. You can see this happening on a short-term chart, like a five-minute. Even a one-minute, like you were talking about. You can see the price fall fast and then rebound suddenly."

"And the rebound showed some interest in buying the Pound again."

"And that's when I sold it. I sold all of it that I could."

"Where did you get out?" I asked.

"Oh, I was out fifteen minutes later. That was it for me. I didn't trade again that day."

"This sounds much like what you did on the FOMC interest rate decision."

"Yep. I follow a similar method all the time, really. It has worked for me very well."

This was the time when it was appropriate to ask Craig how much he had made.

"How much did you make?"

"Well, I did 100 points. Which was an excellent—a very excellent—NFP day for me."

It was odd. When he spoke about his own gains, it wasn't about the money. It was about the points or pips that he had made. Another flood of questions came to mind. This was either going to be a four-hour phone call or I was simply not going to get all the answers I wanted.

This was exactly the reason that I wanted to meet with him again in person, and his mentor, to learn more about short-term trading. So much easier. The excitement of trading the economic news appealed to me, of course. But the thought that I could make a pile of money in a half hour and be done for the day—that was overwhelming.

"I'm surprised you kept yourself from trading when you saw the Non-Farm Payroll reaction," Craig remarked.

I grinned and said, "I didn't have a computer or a phone with me. I couldn't trade."

"Well, it's all the same anyway. They'll have another Non-Farm Payroll report next month."

"And I'll be ready for that one. Did everyone at your firm trade it like that?" I asked.

"No. One guy got full of himself and started selling the U.S. Dollar against the Yen. He was totally out of his mind, talking about how the reaction to the jobs report was ridiculous and that he had a tip from a big Wall Street trader that the dollar was going to sell off big time, and that the Non-Farm Payroll reaction was a perfect time to take advantage of the idiots who were buying dollars. And then he said that the USD/JPY had to fall at least 200 to 300 points from the high of the day."

"Did he lose a lot of money?"

"Oh, yes," Craig answered. "In fact, he left his trades open and then left for the day. He didn't want to look at the trades any longer."

"He is allowed to do that?" I asked. "Seems like he could get fired for doing that."

"He's got a leash," Craig replied with a chuckle. "He can only lose so much and then the firm closes his trades. He's allowed a certain amount of leeway. They used to call it a Daylight Limit, although around here it's called a Net Asset Value Calculation, and for short it's called Net NAV."

"But shouldn't someone step in and get him out of the trade before it gets worse?" Talking about this guy made me think about my FOMC trade, and how I wished that someone would have stepped in and ended the trade before it got as bad as it did. Imagine if I still had $1,000 instead of $500! I really wanted that money back. It hurt to think about how stupid I had been.

"Good point, Banes. Yes, it would be good if someone could step in and help him. But he's not the kind of person to accept help. Remember, all these guys including me are used to being the best at what we do. We made good grades in school. We played first string. We are meant to be right, to be making money. It's human nature to not want to admit that you're wrong."

"I know exactly how that works," I told him. "That pretty much sums up my disaster trade."

"Well, at least you didn't lose ten million dollars of your company's trading capital on the trade."

Speaking of a firm's trading capital made me think of Sam Wilson. What was he buying or selling today? Had he seen enough on Friday to make his decisions today? Was he trading at all? What about Doorecker? Had he bought or sold?

"That's a ton of money. Ten million dollars lost on a trade. You would think that he would just know better."

"He and his friends. Right. He told his friends he had this hot tip from a famous Wall Street trader—couldn't name him, of course—but it was a sure thing. And those guys all together loaded up even more. Man, they really put themselves in a bad spot. When I saw the buying pressure just shoot upward for the dollar, and I saw the British Pound fall, that was all I needed to know. I sold Pounds and took my profit and I was done. I've had my days of listening to other people and then losing. Those days are over."

"Replaced by calmly following the charts after an economic report is released."

"That sums it up nicely."

"And you learned all this with the help of your friend. Your trading mentor." Perhaps now was the right time for Craig to introduce me to his teacher.

"Winklestein? Oh, you'll meet him. For sure. I told him about you."

"Really?" This was excellent news!

"Winklestein is his name?"

"Yep. Harvey Winklestein." Craig paused, which told me that he was reflecting back on some good times with his teacher. "He is the best teacher of traders in the world. No one like him anywhere else. I think he's interested in helping you. You're lucky. He doesn't work with very many people anymore."

Now it was my turn to pause. How was I going to pay this teacher?

"Craig, I have no way to pay him," I admitted. "It's the embarrassing truth."

He laughed. "Oh, Harvey doesn't want your money up front."

This didn't make a lot of sense. "He wants my money later on?" I asked.

"Sort of. I'll let him describe it to you. When the time is right, you can meet him. I am excited for you."

"Me too." My mind raced: Who was this guy Winklestein? Where was he from? He had trained Craig and Doorecker, so obviously he'd been around for a long time.

"I gotta go in a second. The Institute for Supply Management, or ISM Services report is going to be released in half an hour. But before I hang up, who is this guy you met at U.S. National? What's his name again?"

"Samuel Wilson."

"Never heard of him. What does he trade?"

"Apparently anything he wants. He's been there for 40 years. Said that he started in the mailroom. Worked his way up."

"Now that's the kind of guy Harvey would love. And it looks like those guys over there at U.S. National are hungry for more U.S. Dollars. I see on my terminal that U.S. National is selling the Euro against the U.S. dollar in a big way. They have orders stacked out even higher up than where they had first traded after the report."

"Orders stacked out?"

"Right. Orders to buy U.S. Dollars. Orders to sell the Euro. They can't unload two hundred fifty million Euros on top of someone at the current price, so they offer to sell Euros at a price outside the market. Let's say that the EUR/USD is trading right now at—" he broke off to check his computer screen—"1.2020. That's the bid price it's trading at now. They could probably push though an order for fifty million dollars near that price right now. But if they want to unload a quarter of a billion Euros, then they might have to offer to sell them at 1.2000 or so."

"That means that the buyer gets the Euros at a great price."

"Right. Unless it is going to fall a long, long way."

I imagined this in my mind. Hank Doorecker and Samuel Wilson wanted to sell Euros. They couldn't sell as many as they wanted to sell in one chunk unless they agreed to give the buyer a sweet immediate profit. This would entice a buyer to do the transaction. But if the price then fell hard, the buyer would be left holding Euros at a higher price than they could sell them for. U.S. National would make a huge profit and the buyer would be screwed.

"And other traders accept that offer?" I asked. "Knowing that they are going to get screwed?"

"Sure. All the time. Keep in mind that the other side of the trade—some other major bank or a hedge fund—thinks that it's buying a ton of Euros cheap. Because their computer programs or high-paid analysts tell them that the Euro is going up." This made sense to me. Craig continued: "The Euro is so heavily traded. This type of big transaction happens all the time. For every buyer, there are lots of sellers, and vice versa. For the bigger orders, like I just described, traders might have to put up orders outside the market price, but that's okay. They know what they want to do."

It seemed to me that whatever Samuel Wilson, Hank Doorecker, and U.S. National wanted to do would be a good idea. I asked: "What price are they offering to sell at?"

An idea brewed in the back of my mind. This might be the best idea I'd had yet.

Obviously I couldn't see Craig, but I imagined a wide smile on his face. "I think I know where you're going with this."

"Yes. I want to sell at the same price." I was already logging into my online bank account, and setting up a wire transfer to send $5,000 more to my trading account. That would increase the size of the account to $5,500 total. I decided that if I only had one chance to take advantage of piggybacking on a trade with U.S. National Bank, I was going to take it. When I had completed the wire online, I asked Craig: "What price are they selling at?"

"They have a huge sell order at 1.2200."

"That's nearly 200 points away. And it's upward. Why sell when it is rising? And why not just sell down at 1.2000?"

"They've got their own reasons. I don't know. Listen, I gotta go."

I told him how grateful I was for his time. The wire transfer would hit my trading account within a day, and then I would plug in an order to sell the EUR/USD at the same price as Samuel and the dudes down at the bank.

"You're welcome," he said. "Don't make any trades just yet. Maybe watch that 1.2200 level for a sell trade. But keep the risk down this time. You can get killed on these long-term trades. It could move 100 pips against you before it turns around. Understood?"

I agreed to play it safe.

"And we should have lunch in a couple of weeks," he told me. "When this whole missing Anderson file thing blows over."

Missing file? So they'd fired me over a missing file, just as I had presumed. A file that Herbie had probably misplaced.

"A couple of weeks? You sure we can't meet sooner? I was thinking I could take you to lunch later this week. I checked the economic calendar, nothing's really coming out."

"Well, actually, that's true," he replied. "You did your homework. Okay, call me back in a few days and we'll see if we can hook up, even if it's just for a few minutes. And be on the lookout for Winklestein. He can show up at anytime, anywhere."

I looked forward to the meeting with Harvey. In the mean time, I thought I'd just run downtown and see if I could meet up with Mr. Sam Wilson.

U.S. NATIONAL BANK ALMOST KILLS ME

When I showed up at the front desk on the trading level of U.S. National Bank, the secretary recognized my face but not my name. No matter, it wasn't good news.

"May I help you?" she asked it in a way that let me know clearly that she had no intention of helping me at all. Instead, I had the feeling that she might have already called security. She looked just the way my mom did when she had caught me stealing the pennies from the free penny dish at the convenience store. This was not going to be a happy conversation:

ME: I have an appointment with Samuel Wilson.

SKEPTICAL RECEPTIONIST: Sure you do, Mr., uh, Charles Flank, who no longer works for Wakeman, Butterman, and Bailey. You have a special meeting with, um, Samuel Wilson, who doesn't work here?

ME: [protesting] No, really, I do have an appointment with him. He does work here. My name is Harry Banes.

SKEPTICAL RECEPTIONIST: No, really, you don't have any appointments here, Mr. Banes. There's no Samuel Wilson at U.S. National Bank. Never was. And there's no Harry Banes here, either.

ME: Yes! Yes there is a Harry Banes at U.S. National Bank. And if you double-check, there is a Samuel Wilson here, too.

SKEPTICAL RECEPTIONIST: Should I call Mr. Sutherland and see what he thinks about your appointment with Mr. Wilson?

ME: [looking dumb]

This left me with very little to say. I most certainly did not want to miss any news about how Samuel and Harvey and the rest of the U.S. National Bank trading crew were handling the trade to sell the EUR/USD at 1.2200. When would that trade open? It could happen today, for sure—even though the currency pair would have to move 200 points upward to get to the entry. Why were they selling all the way up there? Craig had said they could get an order sooner than that. Why wait that long? And where was Mr. Wilson? How could I get in there without her calling the police?

Worse than calling the police would be to call Mr. Sutherland. Pissing him off would end my chances forever of seeing the trading floor here, or anywhere else, for that matter. Mr. Wilson was probably waiting for me, expecting me, and I was going to ruin the opportunity if I didn't get in there. So I decided that I would beg.

"I promise. Last time I didn't see Mr. Sutherland. I know. I lied. I lied to you, I lied to my wife earlier last week, I lied to my boss and to some other people that I can't remember right now. But you gotta let me in that door. I swear Mr. Wilson works here."

She had transformed suddenly into the Angry Receptionist. "I've already called security," she told me very matter-of-factly. "Don't you think I know who works here? Don't you think I would have checked first? Now would be a good time to turn around and leave."

I heard a ding and the sound of elevator doors opening, and heavy footsteps behind me.

"Would you please call Mr. Wilson and tell him that I am here? If he says that he doesn't know me, then I will go. You can handcuff me or arrest me. You can just page out to the trading floor, or look up your directory again."

Now I was really hoping that Mr. Wilson did not suffer from any form of senility. I mean, he had looked older than anyone else on the trading floor, and it was possible that he had forgotten all about me. For sure, he would have left my name at the front desk. Wait a minute! He hadn't told them that I was coming! No wonder I was having all this trouble. Certainly he had forgotten about the appointment. Just as I imagined—he was generous and helpful but not very bright.

It was now just one minute before noon and I was positive that I was never going to get in—he would probably not even be at his desk any longer, since he worked shorter days. He was an old man. Needed a nap or whatever.

By then, two security guards were standing by my side and I must have been giving the Angry Receptionist the most pitiful look ever, because she did pick up her phone.

"Judy, there's a psychopath out here in the lobby and he wants to know if we have a Samuel Wilson at the firm." Then a pause.

"No, not a real psychopath. He's just demanding to see a man named Samuel Wilson, says he works on the trading floor." Another pause and I thought my bladder would explode from the tension. I held on, knowing that I only needed a few more seconds before she'd realize her mistake, I could use the restroom, and then I'd be whooshed through the giant mahogany doors, where I'd find a happy Mr. Wilson ready to instruct me in the ways of secretive, rich, master traders who would take me in as their own and raise me up to be the greatest trader who ever lived.

Or not.

I felt a hand grip my right arm. Then another grabbed my left elbow. They were huge, meaty hands that could crush a man's dream of going onto the trading floor at U.S. National Bank. I looked to my left and right— within 10 feet there were windows on either side. We were 20 floors above ground. I wondered from which side they were going to throw me out. This is not how I had planned to die, but it was possible that I was going to leave this world never having seen more than one Non-Farm Payroll jobs report. And with a planned order to gain glorious, innumerable pips from a sell trade on the Euro!

PRIEST: Dearly beloved, we gather here this grey and cloudy morning to celebrate the life of Harold Banes.

No, wait. That wasn't it.

PRIEST: Dear friends, Mr. Governor, Senators, Members of Congress, Mr. Sutherland, Mr. Taylor, Mr. Wilson, and Mr. Herbie Johnson: We meet this sorry, rainy morning to mourn the pitiful life of Harry Banes, destined to be the greatest trader who ever lived, et cetera, and stuff like that.

[weeping]

PRIEST: Our only consolation is that the Angry Receptionist at U.S. National Bank was fired yesterday for not knowing the names of the traders at the firm.

[more weeping]

The hands gripped tighter on my arms.

"There is *no* Samuel Wilson at the firm."

She was now Angry *and* Happy Receptionist, as if she at once took great pleasure in the fact that I would die a sorry heap of human flesh at the corner of Broad and Wall Streets below; and at the same time had been deeply offended at my insistence that she did not know the names of the people that she worked for.

"Goodbye, Mr. Banes."

Oh, double-crap. My entire plan was now totally backfiring. I did the only thing that I could, as the grip on my elbow tightened and I started to move backward against my will. My feet were dragging on the floor as I was pulled into the elevator. I called out:

ME: [yelling] I am Charlie Flank, too! Mr. Wilson, it's me, Charlie Flank, and Harry Banes! We are here to see you!

She hung up her phone and turned back to her work. Of course, she could claim no hand in my murder, especially now that she was not paying attention to the situation. The World Wrestling Federation had nothing on these guys who were now pressing the buttons for the first floor, while holding on to me tightly, as if I could get away once locked inside the elevator. Thankfully, I had not been thrown from a window. But would the police be waiting for me outside? Would I have to call my wife to bail me out? How much of my severance package would now disappear in legal fees?

On the first floor, the doors to the elevator parted, and they pushed me out. Then they walked me out to the main doors and shoved me onto the sidewalk on Wall Street. I fell down. People just walked over me, or kicked me. Luckily, no one tripped. My head popped up, and I could see the New York Stock Exchange down the street. I put my head back down.

I was never going to be a trader, I told myself.

"Sure you are going to be a trader," a familiar voice called down to me. I lifted my head and saw an old, wrinkled hand offered to help me.

I looked up. It was Samuel Wilson.

"Harry Banes?" He grinned. "Charlie Flank?" An even wider grin. "Is that you?"

I did not smile back. I wasn't angry either. Just totally relieved that he was there. I looked up into his eyes.

"Help!" was all I could say. My eyes started to well up with tears. Why hadn't he told them I was coming to see him that day? Why did I have to struggle so much just to get ahead? I imagined that my trading platform had self-generated a Euro trade and that it was now opening, that I was now selling EUR/USD at 1.2200, and it was just racing upward in a climb that would suck up all the remaining funds in my trading account. My wife would leave me, take all the furniture except my favorite reclining chair, which would then break, then the last lightbulb in our apartment would burn out, and I would sit in the dark until I died.

"No, Harry," he told me, stretching his hand out again. "That is not going to happen. You are going to be a great trader. Perhaps the best ever. I promise that."

How did he know what I was thinking?

How had he shown up at just the right moment?

Samuel Wilson knew who I was!

And he wanted to help me! In that moment I handed myself completely over to him, to do his bidding, to learn whatever he had to teach me. He was my friend in the darkest moment and that was enough; it was plenty enough to know that he wasn't going to leave me to die an embarrassing death on the street that symbolized all my unrealized hopes. That he would stand up for me when I couldn't stand up for myself. That he would appear at the exact moment when I was letting go of all of my impossible dreams. And then I realized, with a shudder of adrenaline that raced from the tip of my head, through my entire body, and down to my feet: This man wasn't who I thought he was. This wasn't Samuel Wilson.

This was Harvey Winklestein.

CHAPTER 11

Coming Clean

Harvey's grip was strong. He pulled me up from the sidewalk with one arm.

"What are you doing lying around here?"

"I thought this is where all the future currency trading superstars got their start," I replied, dusting myself off.

He chuckled. "You're more right than you might think."

When he led me back through the doors and into the elevator, I was skeptical. "Do you think they will let me back in? They were not very happy."

"I am sure they weren't."

"Why didn't you let them know I was coming?"

He paused. Looked me straight in the eyes: "You weren't honest the last time you were here. You also didn't keep your promise to visit again." He stopped. All I could hear was the sound of the elevator moving up. The truth stung me. "You needed a lesson."

"I got the lesson."

Then he placed both hands on my shoulders and turned me to him. It felt like he could pick me up right off the floor. "This is the lesson, Harry: Don't ever lie to me. Or to anyone else. Ever. Lying will kill you in trading."

I looked him back in the eye. "I promise. I promise to be honest from this point forward. About everything."

With that, he said, "Good," and we stepped off into the reception area of the trading floor. The secretary was not happy to see me again, but she did smile when she saw Harvey. "Hi, Harvey," she chirped. "He's with you, I suppose?"

He nodded. "Thanks, Valerie. He's now okay here anytime. No more calling security." She nodded back. I could tell that she wished that security had thrown me out the window. When we sat down at his desk, I noticed that most of the traders had left for the day.

"Where is everyone?" I asked.

"Gone. They're done for now. They can go home and get the same information about their trades as they can get at the office. We're not filling client orders here or anything."

"How would that make a difference?"

"Well, if we were at a major Wall Street desk, clients would be calling here and asking for us to quote a price on Sterling or Euros or Yen. And we'd give them a price and so on. They can call all day long."

"What do you do here that is so different?"

"We trade the firm's capital."

"Does anyone quote prices for clients here?"

"Yes. But they're on a different floor. Here, we are all prop traders. Proprietary. We trade for the firm, to make the firm money. Well, I don't. But everyone else here does."

"What do you do here?"

"Whatever I want. I look at my long-term charts. I make some trades. But this is just a desk that I'm allowed to use whenever I want."

"For conversations like this?"

He shook his head. "You're the first trader that I've brought here."

I squinted my eyes at him. "I got here myself."

He laughed. "You didn't do anything yet that I didn't already know about. You got in the first day because of me. Just like you are here now."

I wondered how he knew all this. For now it did not matter, but I made a mental note to interview him about how he knew so much about me. It was like he could read my mind. But first I had lots of questions. "You were going to talk with me about honesty," I told him.

"Yes. Let's get right into that. This is one of the most important laws of trading: *Traders must always be honest.*"

HOW HONESTY RELATES TO TRADING

ME: You said that honesty is one of the most important laws of trading. Why? Why aren't we talking about the trades you are taking? I think I heard you are about to take a long-term position on the EUR/USD. Why don't we start by talking about that trade? Shouldn't I dive right in?

HARVEY: You already dove in. You dove in when you took totally irresponsible trades. That was diving in. We don't want to do that. To build on the analogy about diving, I want to teach you to test the water first. To make sure that there isn't a riptide. To prevent you from drowning.

ME: Walk before I run.

HARVEY: More like prevent you from diving into shallow water. That's what you were doing before.

ME: So how does honesty fit in with all this?

HARVEY: It's the first step. It's actually one of the most important lessons. I have three most important lessons, each of them equally critical to your progression as a trader.

ME: I'm ready. For anything you say.

HARVEY: Okay. How many times have you lied in the past month?

ME: [silence]

HARVEY: All right, I'll repeat the question in a different way. In the past month, did you ever lie to Herb Johnson? Or anyone at the office?

ME: Yes.

HARVEY: How many times?

ME: I'm not sure that I know how to answer that. It wasn't that many.

HARVEY: That is not an acceptable answer. You'll have to do better than that.

ME: Okay. This is not very comfortable for me. I thought I was going to be asking you all the questions.

HARVEY: We'll mostly learn by me asking you questions. That's because everything you need to learn is already inside you—I am just going to pull it out of you. Like an infected tooth, or a burst appendix.

ME: How pleasant.

HARVEY: So what's the answer? How many times did you lie at work?

ME: At least ten times. At least. I lied about where I was. I lied about Anderson wanting to give me a job. I lied to an attorney about who I was talking to on the phone. I lied to cover myself a few times.

HARVEY: Is that all? Just the spoken lies?

ME: Just the spoken ones? What does that mean?

HARVEY: It means that you can lie by your actions, too. Not just your words. This is important. So important, that what I told you in the elevator is true. Don't ever lie to me again. Or anyone. I'll cut off your training and we'll see how you do. I don't have time to mess around.

ME: But what do you mean when you say that I can lie through my actions?

HARVEY: I mean that you can steal time from your employer. Did you ever do that?

ME: Steal time? Gosh, it seems to me that anyone working in a law firm is there to steal time.

Harvey: That's funny, but it still avoids the question. Did you steal time? Did you trade while at work?

Me: Yes. I did. But—

Harvey: That's stealing time unless you do it on your break. Did you trade only during your breaks?

Me: No. Not only during my breaks. I did it on the clock.

Harvey: Anything else?

Me: Well, when you talk about it like this, I've been stealing time from the law firm for a long time. For ten years. I probably stole an hour a day for ten years. At least that much.

Harvey: How?

Me: By taking an extra few moments on a break here and there. By taking my time as I walked around. Walking the long way to get to a partner's office. Filing something twice so that it would double the time it took to do one thing, so I didn't have to get on with the next big project. Gosh, now that I think of it, I wasn't honest at work at all.

Harvey: How about your wife?

Me: Yes. I have lied to her. Yes.

Harvey: Anyone else?

Me: Probably yes. Well, definitely yes. Sure. I haven't been very honest in the past few weeks. I lied to Valerie at your front desk. I lied my way onto the trading floor.

Harvey: It's good that you are admitting all of this. Now I want you to go outside the door here and apologize to Valerie. I will be here when you get back.

MAKING AMENDS

Apologize to Valerie? What was that all about? How was that going to make me a better trader? I hoped that he didn't intend for me to show up at Wakeman and find Herb Johnson, just so I could pull mini-Napoleon out of a partner meeting so that he could listen to me offer a lame apology that I didn't even truly want to give.

But when I apologized to Valerie, her face brightened. "Really?" she said.

"Really. I mean it." And I did. The saying of the apology created some of the sincerity. The speaking of the words also cleansed me a bit. I stood a bit taller and felt a bit happier. When I returned to Harvey, I said so.

"That's no surprise. That's good. You don't need the burden of an angry young lady who works the reception area. She would give you problems forever. You have to cast all that aside, all the negativity you have stored up inside."

I did not ask him about apologies that I would owe to my former employer. That was something I didn't want to do and I am sure I would not get the words out of my mouth before I was escorted out of the building. But apologizing to my wife? That was something I would do as soon as I got home. I needed all the help I could get, and I couldn't expect to have her help if I could not be honest with her.

"Now," he said, "you've earned your first lesson about why I am taking a trade. Remember you were asking about my reasons for wanting to sell the EUR after it rose upward?"

"Of course. I actually wanted to put on the same trade—when I found out you and Hank were planning to sell the Euro, I decided that I wanted to be part of it. I did not want to miss out on the opportunity to make money."

"No one wants to miss out on money. It's a huge problem for many new traders—they cannot resist following the idea of another person because they don't want to miss out. But you should know that I don't actually have that Euro trade that you're talking about. I don't necessarily want to sell the EUR/USD at 1.2200. It's not something that I am going to do for sure. This is the danger in jumping in on a trade because you hear about someone else taking it. You take it, but in the end, that other person might not, and then what do you have? A trade with no backup, no planning, no rationale other than you didn't want to miss out."

I gulped. That was not good. I was now planning to place an order to take a trade that I thought had substantial backup. But I was on my own. No Harvey, no U.S. National Bank standing behind the order. Suddenly, I felt dumber than ever. I was going to lose my trading account any moment now with plans like this. I could feel it. All the money I put in there was going to go up in flames. I needed to stop trading.

"But Craig said—"

"Craig was looking at his order screen and saw Hank Doorecker test the waters. An order 200 pips above the current market price is way too far off to leave out there. We do actually want to sell in the near future, but we wanted to see how much enthusiasm was out there for it. It's not like someone else was going to trade that far out of the market."

"So really, why did you do it?"

"We want to sell. We do. That is for sure. But we want to only sell after it's gone up a bit. Hank has a theory that he has tested for many years that if he puts an order out there, way out there, that it will tempt people to bid. I don't agree. It is so far away that it is really just showing them our cards. I like to hold my ideas closer than that."

"How so?" I was now feeling better. At least Harvey really did want to make a trade on the Euro. I just didn't know where. So the idea wasn't so far-fetched, after all. And I might still be able to piggyback on the trade. That is, if I could now find out what the trade would actually be.

"I want to see the price rise, then I'll make up my mind. I don't have to do anything sudden or immediate."

"You sound really uninterested in trading. Like, if you do or you don't, it doesn't matter. If you don't trade, you won't make any money."

He grinned. "I was hoping you would get around to that." He leaned closer to me but did not lower his voice: "Harry, if you do trade, you won't make any money."

This hurt. But he did not back off.

"Are you upset about that? I can see that you are. It's natural. I used to work with a lot more traders. The one thing that everyone asks me is, how are they supposed to make any money when I am telling them to be patient and not trade, or to be patient and look at the long-term charts? They say that if they don't trade, they can't make any pips and if they can't make any pips, they don't make any money. But the reality is that until that point, all they have proven is that if they do trade, they lose money."

I could not dispute it. He wasn't telling me this because he hated me. He was telling me this because he wanted to help me. And he was right.

"I agree that you're right. I have proven that when I trade, I lose money."

"Yes you have. One thousand dollars in the toilet on one trade. That was a huge amount of your account. You will learn more about money management over time, but the basic premise is this: you have to understand that taking more trades does not mean you will be making more money. Especially for a new trader."

"How do you know about my trade?"

He smiled. "Your forex dealer? The guy who started it?"

"Yes? What about him?"

He smiled again, this time much wider.

"You know him?" I asked. Then I said it again, this time more sure: "You know him. You probably worked with him five hundred years ago when you were trading the Florentine Peso against the German Potato."

"Not quite. But yes. I did work with him years ago. He's an old friend. I haven't seen your account statements but he did tell me about the loss."

So this is how Harvey knew so much about me. He knew everyone in the business.

"Back to business, Harry," he told me. "Does it make sense that if you make more trades right now, you don't necessarily make more money?"

"That makes sense."

"Why? Explain to me why it makes sense. I want to hear it from you."

I stopped and thought about it for a moment. Just thinking about this, I could sense that what he was teaching me was true. "You're saying, if I understand you correctly, that a beginning trader has no idea why he is taking trades. He is making trades to, well . . . just to make trades. It's terrible to realize this, you know. I am feeling pretty stupid now."

"Tell me why you feel stupid."

"I feel dumb because I just wanted to be like Craig. I thought that if I traded the short-term charts, that is where the action would be. That is where all the movement would be, right after a major economic report. And I sort of just assumed that, because it was moving a lot, I could capture a bunch of it. But I have no idea how to do that. I was using software, or hearing rumors about trades that other people take. I wasn't basing my trades on any kind of analysis."

"And?"

"And what?"

"Harry," he started. "That's an excellent start, but there is more to it. You're correct that new traders have no idea why they are buying or selling. They are usually buying because they bought software that teaches them that they don't have to think for themselves, or because price is shooting upward, or because they heard a rumor that someone else was doing it. The rumor trades are the worst because you can't even confirm that it is true, and you have no idea if the rumored trade is actually for real. And you can't talk to the trader to find out if he actually takes the trade you heard about. But there is more than that.

"When you said that you are not basing your trades on any kind of analysis, what did you mean?"

I told him that I didn't really know what I meant. But I knew it was true.

"A solid, honest answer. But it's no good," he replied. "You gotta do better than that."

I thought for a moment. "I meant to say that I've now started to assume that a good trader is going to have to do some type of his own analysis before he takes a trade. Some kind of a plan. Some kind of a checklist of things to look for."

"Excellent!" Harvey cried out. No one paid any attention or turned to look at us. Apparently, he was known to scream like this.

"A checklist," I continued, "would guide me through the process of making sure that I am following something that works. So if I took a trade, and I am just making this up, but it is sounding really good, that means that I am implementing a system."

"Right! Right again!" he exclaimed. "That means you are implementing a system. And if you have a system that you are following, it doesn't really matter if the trade is a winner or a loser, as long as you understand that over time the system is going to return profits. The goal is to make money, right?"

"Right!"

"The goal is not to make trades. Can you see the confusion with people? They want to make trades, just like a gambler wants to pull on the slots, or a dope head wants to get high. They are doing it for the sake of getting the rush. They are not serious about making money. Can you imagine if a brand-new lawyer at Wakeman wanted to step into the courtroom and represent the largest corporation in the world, on his first day on the job?"

"Yes, I can imagine exactly what Herb Johnson would say."

"He would throw him out onto the street. A new attorney doesn't earn the right to step into a role that important until he proves that he can be trusted with that much authority. And a new trader is no different. Until you can prove that you don't have to trade, you are not going to ever do this successfully."

"Prove that I don't have to trade. It makes sense now, but it's nearly melting my brain to think like this."

"It's melting your brain because you are thinking about two things at once. You are thinking about supporting your family. And you are thinking about making good trades. If you combine those two concepts, you get a zero equity balance in your trading account. Why?"

"You're asking me?"

"Yep. Why is that true? Why is it the case that a trader who is trying to pay the bills is going to be far more likely to lose his account?"

This didn't make sense to me. Wasn't it good to be hungry for profits? Couldn't a need to make money drive a trader to do better, not worse? I told him this.

"You are defending the concept because you are living in this very situation," he told me.

That could be true. I didn't argue with it. He continued.

"You want to believe that a new forex trader who needs to support his family is going to be driven to be the best. But that's an image you've conjured up in your head. A new forex trader is more likely, because he has to feed his family or pay his electric bill, to make a bunch of dumb trades."

"Because he's got to make money, and how else is he going to make money unless he trades?"

"Right! Right again!"

"That makes sense now. And a new trader, like me, has maybe seen other people do this on television, or someone like Craig. And we think that trading profitably is just the act of pushing some buttons. We expect it to be easier or simple or . . ."

"Or what?"

"I don't know. I guess we expect it to be less like a job."

"Bingo. You've got it. You understand it perfectly now. Trading is just a job, like filing stuff away at some windbag Midtown law firm founded by

Thomas Jefferson or something. And traders don't want to hear that trading is going to be like a job. They want it to be sexy. They want to imagine that they can just sit down at the computer at any time of day, and the forex market will be there ready to offer them golden pips served by a butler. They don't work for it. They think all they have to do is want it."

"Saying it is like a job makes it sound awful."

"You're right. It does burst the image. Does it change your mind about whether you want to do it?"

I shook my head. "Of course not! I want to do it more than ever. It's okay if it's like a job. I am fine with that. It still seems like a better job at least. Better because I don't have to have people yelling at me. Better because I can set my own hours. Better because it will pay more over time. Better because I can see my family more often."

"Harry! Harry!" He reached out and grabbed me by the cheeks. "You don't understand! You are about to try to be successful at one of the most difficult jobs on the planet. You want to be a trader! You know how many people can do this and make money at it? Hardly anyone! And you know what? The people who do well at this don't necessarily get to see their family more often. They might have people yelling at them. They might have horrible hours. And at the start, it pays worse than picking up garbage."

He was now staring down at me and didn't look happy.

"Yes?"

"I thought we were making progress. But we'll have to talk again tomorrow."

I was devastated. Where had I gone wrong? If trading was going to be more difficult, give me less family time, not make me any money right now (because I wasn't going to be trading), and would involve people yelling at me with longer hours, then what in the world was I thinking? Why not just back out now? I had gone from superhappy and on top of the world, to depressed that I could never succeed at doing this for a living, and even if I could, I wouldn't like it anyway!

Harvey broke me out of my thoughts. "Stop sulking, kiddo. You're not out of the woods yet. I got more bad news for you. And we're going to get the bad news tomorrow. I want to get it all out of the way."

I straightened up. "All right," I agreed. "I am ready for whatever you want to teach me. I am a bit confused, but I can take it. I want to do this."

"Despite what I just told you?"

"Yes, despite the fact that you just burst the bubble and made trading sound like a job as a filing manager."

"Good. That is good, Banes," he replied. "This conversation has done a good job over the years at busting through the myths. But it usually takes longer. And usually creates way more depression. So we're going to speed things up, like I said. We're going to get the bad news out of the way."

"What's the bad news?"

"I am going to take you to a hedge fund tomorrow. It's a firm that is running two billion dollars in other people's money."

This didn't sound bad at all. It sounded downright fantastic!

"You might think it's going to be fantastic," he said to me, reading my mind. "But you're going to see that it's pretty dumpy."

CHAPTER 12

Looks Can
Be Deceiving

In a plain-looking 25-story building, in a so-so looking part of no-man's land, on the border between Midtown and Chinatown, we stood at a receptionist's desk that appeared to be just a door set on top of two sawhorses. The receptionist had a computer, but it was running so badly that I could hear it clanking around. And instead of a fancy flat-screen monitor, he had a huge clunky monstrosity that looked like it belonged in a dump. There wasn't any sign or notice of where we were. Either this was a superprivate hedge fund or it was doing so badly that it didn't want any attention.

What kind of hedge fund was this? While we waited in the reception area I thought I'd find out what kind of fly-by-night operation had dumpy computers and ratty carpet.

"What kind of place is this, Harvey?" I spoke in a low voice so I wouldn't embarrass him or myself. We were waiting for the chief trader or something and I didn't want to be caught talking trash about his trashy office.

"You'll find out in a moment."

And that's when the owner of the place, or the chief trader, or what-ever, walked into the room. He was looking dumpier than everyone and everything else in the place. He wore a suit that was at least 700 years old, and his shirt was frayed at the cuffs. His hair stuck up straight in the back, where he had fallen at his desk or something. Although he had a bright smile, I kind of felt sorry for him. He held out his hand and I wondered if it was clean enough to shake. I did anyway.

"Harry Banes, meet George Sisler," Harvey said. I winced. The man had a strong handshake and wasn't afraid to use it.

"Thanks for meeting with me," I offered. I hoped we could get this over with quickly and then we could go see the $2 billion hedge fund that Harvey had talked about.

We walked through a (not surprisingly) old door and out onto what was apparently George's trading floor. It was a scattered group of more old doors sitting on top of sawhorses, sitting on top of old carpet. The computer screens looked newer, but the 20 or so traders were all wearing either older suits (even the young guys) or casual clothes. The other thing that looked remarkably different was that there were an equal number of men and women here or perhaps even more women than men. All the traders that I saw had the same things on their screen: an Excel spreadsheet up with a bunch of columns stretching into eternity, a set of prices flashing quotes for several currencies, and charts. The place wasn't quiet, but it wasn't a playground either. I could tell that I was standing in the midst of a focused crowd.

I figured that we would sit down inside George's office for a chat, but what I didn't understand at first was that the entire room had no private office. It was just one room, sitting high enough that we had an excellent view out the windows of a Chinese restaurant, an overflowing dumpster, and a parking lot with cars stacked on top of each other Manhattan style. Inside the room, beside the desks, there was a broken 30-inch television and a watercooler. This was one classy place!

Because George had no office, we sat down at his desk, which was in no way distinguishable from any of the other desks. It wasn't bigger; it didn't have more screens; it was not in a prominent place (like the center) of the room. But it was spotless. There wasn't one piece of paper floating anywhere. Nothing out of place. It felt very strange to be sitting down for a meeting about this guy's business, while everyone else was easily within hearing range.

Despite all my impressions of the place, Harvey seemed delighted to be here. This appeared to be something of a reunion between him and a former student (who apparently needed some help). From the moment we had entered the office, Harvey was scanning the room, grinning and happy and altogether way too jolly about everything he saw. Walking in between desks, he was shaking hands with people he knew, bending down to look at their screens, asking about trades, and basically acting like he was the Mayor of Piptown.

"Harry," he told me as he finally came over to sit down next to us, "isn't this a great place? Now, Harry, this is how to run two billion dollars."

I was speechless. George wasn't. He said: "Three billion."

Harvey lighted up. "Howdy do! Wow! Fantastic, George. Not a surprise. Are you up 50 percent for the year?"

"Yes. We are. We have really been hitting it good for the past four months."

It was possible that Harvey would now explode into shards of happiness. I imagine his head flying off his body, but still smiling and still commenting about how cool this place was. At the same time, I was having trouble keeping my own head attached to my body. Had I heard right? Was this George Sisler guy really managing three billion dollars? Could he not afford some nicer stuff? This was nothing like what I saw at Ernest Wellington, or other major banks, or on business television.

I could tell that there was going to be a lesson here for me and that, like everything else Harvey had told me so far, it would overturn some mistaken assumptions about the business of trading.

Harvey spoke and broke me out of my daze: "Still hitting singles?"

George nodded. "Yep. Still hitting them."

And then Harvey looked at me. "It's time for you to ask questions, Harry. Ask George anything you want."

I had lots of questions. But most of them I thought would be insulting or at least inappropriate.

"Go ahead," Harvey said, responding to my thoughts. "Ask him anything. George already knows you're wondering why his office looks like a dump."

I INTERVIEW GEORGE

George didn't have much time for me. But in the time we talked, I learned a ton about how a hedge fund works, and about what I was going to need to do to be successful.

ME: Harvey was right. I am wondering about your office.

GEORGE: It's not that spiffy, I know. But we do get the job done.

ME: If you are managing so much money for other people, why not upgrade just a bit? For clients?

GEORGE: You can imagine that you're not the first person to ask. But the answer is that I am no longer impressed by wealth, or really a show of wealth. I have come to believe in the obvious truth that showing off wealth is not the same thing as being wealthy. Material possessions are to be used in the process of building wealth. But showing off wealth or trying to look better than other hedge fund managers—that's not what this place is all about.

ME: What is this place all about?

GEORGE: The accumulation of wealth. We want to earn the most amount of money with the least amount of risk, while spending the least amount of money on overhead.

ME: Sounds okay with me. But why can't you also accumulate some desks? Normal chairs? Don't your clients expect to see someone who appears, well . . .

GEORGE: More successful?

ME: Right. I didn't mean for it to sound bad.

GEORGE: It doesn't sound bad at all. You see, my clients expect to make the most amount of money possible. So I don't charge them a management fee. Most hedge funds will charge a fee of 2 percent of total assets under management, plus about 20 percent per year of the profits. What's 2 percent of three billion dollars?

ME: Um . . .

HARVEY: He is a math genius.

ME: Um . . .

GEORGE: It's sixty million dollars.

ME: [silence]

HARVEY: [silence]

GEORGE: This year we'll walk away from 60 million dollars in possible management fees that we could just pay out to ourselves in this office. Instead of putting that sixty million dollars in our own pockets, we'll reinvest it, we'll put it to work. That sixty million by the end of next year might be worth eighty million. And guess what? We get a cut of the profits. So if we do well, we get paid well. Do you see how charging a management fee like 2 percent would reward us even if we were not performing well?

ME: [silence]

HARVEY: George, I think he's still thinking about the sixty million dollars.

GEORGE: Ha! I don't blame him. My wife thinks about it all the time. But, think, Harry. Think about it for a moment. If you invest your money with me, do you want me to be rewarded if we succeed, or if we fail?

ME: If you succeed. If you fail, I want to take my money elsewhere.

GEORGE: Right! And if we fail and still take 2 percent of your money every year, that seems ridiculous. Completely at odds with what is obviously a true principle: A money manager should only be compensated if he earns money for his clients.

ME: That does make sense. So how much money do you earn when you succeed?

GEORGE: We charge the standard 20 percent of profits. This year, we've made a billion dollars. We had a big win when we bought a chain of supermarkets in the Midwest, and then sold them to a larger chain. Right there that deal was five hundred million dollars. If we stopped trading right now, we'd take in an incentive fee, at the end of the year, of about two hundred million dollars.

ME: Do you mostly buy companies? Then sell them?

GEORGE: No. The supermarket deal was dropped in our lap—we have a guy here who trades for us, and he was a grocery analyst at a major Wall Street firm. He liked what he saw in this Midwestern chain. We manage some money for the CEO of a major U.S. chain, and we told him that we were going to bid for the business. We had no intention of keeping it for a long time, but we realized we could get a great deal on it and then resell it later after we trimmed it up a bit. First he told us that he wasn't interested, and six months after we bought it, he told us that he was, and we sold it to him at a major markup.

ME: And this was a one-time-only type of deal?

GEORGE: Yes, that's a good way to put it. A deal too good to pass up. We generally trade a lot of currency and foreign stocks and bonds. We don't do much in the United States, really. We see the growth overseas and that's where wc are focused.

ME: There aren't very many traders here.

GEORGE: Right. I hate managing people. These people manage themselves. We hardly ever hire. When we do, I offer a million dollars as a signing bonus and we don't have a lot of trouble getting the people we want. This is totally and completely a performance-based business. Each of these traders manages as much of the capital as they can justify to the rest of the team. Each one is an expert in one area—Mickey Cochrane over there borrows money in Japan and buys British, Brazilian, Australian, and New Zealand bonds. He's making a killing for us right now and it looks like it's going to keep on moving.

ME: He borrows money in Japan?

GEORGE: Right. This is what is called the *carry trade*. Ever heard of it?

ME: No. I don't think so.

GEORGE: I'll describe it to you. I hope that it blows your mind like it did mine the first time I heard about it—and keep in mind, I was a year out of Goldman Sachs and should have already known about it. Are you ready?

ME: Ready.

GEORGE: How can a person or a company borrow at low interest rates?

ME: Good credit.

GEORGE: What else?

ME: From a bank offering a competitive rate.

GEORGE: Excellent. Perfect. What would you say if I told you that right now, I can borrow a hundred million dollars from a Japanese bank at 1 percent interest?

ME: I would say you should buy yourself a new television and some couches.

GEORGE: Very good! Probably true. But what else?

ME: I would say that you should look for a way to earn more than 1 percent on your money, since you are going to have to pay back the principal and the interest.

GEORGE: Brilliant! That is correct. Well, guess what? We can go to our brokerage firms—Bear Sterns, Goldman Sachs, for example—and deposit the money. They will let us leverage that money a few times over. So we can invest with three hundred million dollars. That's called investing with leverage.

ME: Sounds even better now.

GEORGE: And if we go out and buy a basket—or a collection—of foreign bonds that earn a combined average of 7 percent, then we are earning 7 percent on three hundred million.

ME: But you only have to pay interest on one hundred million!

GEORGE: Bingo! Give the man a banana. You're right on target. We borrow, and then we invest with leverage.

ME: So you are, in essence, earning 21 percent on that money annually, minus the 1 percent interest on the loan.

GEORGE: Right. That is exactly right. Now it gets more complicated, of course. Mickey has to move money around, and has to open and close trades to get into the best collection of bonds and so forth. And we pay fees and commissions on the trades we take. But that's the basic strategy.

ME: Very cool. I want to do that. Can I borrow from a Japanese bank?

GEORGE: Theoretically, yes. But practically, probably not. You probably can't get the trade going right, unless you have a few million dollars. Do you?

ME: Very no. Definitely no. I wish.

GEORGE: Well, if you're working with Harvey, you're going to have that much. Eventually. Don't rush it. Let it come to you. And I'm sure that if you think about it long enough, you'll find a way to do a trade like this. It's got to be possible in the retail forex world, by playing the swap rates off each other or something. In fact, we should talk about that again. Right now I have to go, but tell Harvey—he's over there talking to Mindy Swanson—that you should stop by in a couple of weeks and that you're going to tell me about how to do the carry trade on a retail platform.

ME: But—
GEORGE: I gotta take this call.

And with that, the discussion was over. George had a phone appointment that he had to take, and he just stood up and gripped my hand like he was going to fling me out the window.

MINDY TEACHES ME HER ONE-PIP WAYS

Harvey had been chatting it up with a young woman on the other side of the room, and he called me over.

"Harry, this is Mindy. She only trades currency."

"Great! I was just talking to George about the carry trade."

Mindy smiled. "That's long term. I'm all short term. I am in and out all day long."

"In what way?" I asked.

"Look at my screen," she said, pointing to the quotes in front of her. She had at least seven currency pairs open at once, and they were flashing quickly enough to make it very confusing if I stared at it for long. I was used to seeing the currency pairs quoted like this:

1.8500/1.8504

But on her screen, the quotes appeared with just the last two digits, leaving out the "1.85" part.

With only the last two digits below the rest of the quote, I had a hard time telling where the currency pair was really trading.

"Notice anything different between my screen and your screen at home?"

"Yeah, like how the quotes are displayed."

She winked at me. "Not quite. Look again. What's the spread?"

I looked again. The EUR/USD was trading at 1.2103 bid, 1.2104 ask. The spread was just 1 pip! On my retail platform at home, the spread was 4 pips on the same pair. I told her that.

"Right. That's why most short-term bank traders think that trading currency from home is a fool's game. Because the spreads are so high. It's why Harvey is probably going to teach you to look at the longer term charts."

Harvey nodded. "Exactly."

"But why can't I trade short term even with a 4-pip spread? It seems that I can build a system to still make money."

She nodded. "I'm not saying that it's impossible. I am just saying that the fees would be outrageous. Let's do an example." She found a piece of paper and started doing some math. "Let's say that you are going for 20 pips on every trade, when you trade from home. And that you trade twice a day, and that you trade two hundred times per year. To make it simple."

"All right."

"And every time you trade, you are trading with one standard size lot. How much is that?"

"A standard lot is one hundred thousand dollars in currency."

"Right. And that's ten dollars every time it moves 1 pip. So how much are you paying the dealer every time you trade?"

"Forty bucks."

"Now multiply that times two trades every day, two hundred times per year. That's four hundred trades. Times forty dollars."

"That's sixteen thousand dollars. I pay the spread on the winners and losers. So I'm going to pay that much no matter what."

She nodded, satisfied that I was getting the picture. "That's your money. If you reduce the spread, you make more money. Consider it another way: 4 pips, your spread, is 25 percent of 20 pips. If you are going for 20 pips on your trades, you are losing 25 percent of your gains to the dealer. You could be getting 3 more pips on every trade if you traded here. Get it? It's not just the dollar amounts we're talking about. We're talking about losing 25 percent of your gains. If you lower the spread by just 2 pips—you make 10 percent more every year."

"I never considered any of this."

She was happy to hear that. "I'm glad I could teach you something. We belong to the church of frugality here at Sisler and Company. We spend our time not only getting the best return but also cutting costs. It's about accumulation of wealth—we build it a bit at a time."

"So how do you trade? You mentioned that you were in and out all day long."

"Well, Harry," she started. "Now imagine that you have a 1-pip spread on the EUR/USD. You already know that the pair can move up and down all day long. Or just up. Or just down."

"Right."

"Its average daily range is 130. This means that it is going to move that many pips on average. But in between, it's going to move a bit up, a bit down, and so forth. I just grab 1 pip at a time out of the market, all day long."

"How many pips can you get?"

"My daily goal is 40. I can do that three or four days every week."

"Do you trade a standard lot?"

She laughed. "No. I trade Tens."

"Tens?"

"As in ten million. Ten-million-dollar positions. On the EUR, that's one thousand dollars per pip."

She was making forty thousand dollars a day. Two hundred thousand dollars every week. Ten million dollars a year. Holy crap.

I realized that she was glancing at her screen and setting up another trade, so I decided that I would give her some space. Harvey and I thanked her for her time and we left.

Out on the street below, we found some hot dogs. Harvey paid even though I insisted that I owed it to him.

"You've done so much already," I protested.

"Well, you're going to pay me back," he replied. "Don't you worry about that. You'll pay me back. Not now, but later. And we're not going to talk about that right now. For now, you just have to follow some simple instructions, and we'll go from there."

"Okay, I agree. But I do have some questions."

He ordered another hot dog. He was eating like a machine. Two bites, and the next dog was gone.

I started: "I didn't want to mention this upstairs, but Mindy is only making ten million dollars a year for the firm. Now I don't want to seem unimpressed, but when they are managing three billion dollars, doesn't she have to contribute more to the firm?"

"That's a good question, Harry. And I suspect that George is going to be talking to Mindy about that very soon. She's been there six months, and I am sure she's already made at least half her yearly goal, or more. But you're correct in thinking that it's just not enough. When she was trading at a bank on the West Coast, that amount of money was brilliant. It made her a superstar. But she is going to have to step up a notch if she wants to work with George."

"So why did he hire her?"

"Because she is a brilliant goal setter. She goes for 40 pips and she gets it, day in and day out. Over and over again. George likes consistency. He would rather have her making ten million per year almost automatically, than have some guy there that has a 50 percent chance of either making or losing one hundred million."

"That does make sense. Predictability in the returns."

"And a lack of volatility in the performance. He wants to show his clients that he can return year in and year out. Mindy's trading style doesn't have to change for any reason, ever. As volume and liquidity grows, she can increase the size of her positions and even make more. At the bank, she was trading one- and five-million-dollar positions. She is already trading about the most she can with the system she is using."

"And she is probably hoping that she can increase the size of her trades to the point where she is returning something more substantial."

"Right. And George will give her the chance to prove it. What's your next question?"

"Where were the accountants? They are managing three billion dollars but they don't have any accountants. Or other staff."

"It's all outsourced. All the reporting, the reconciliation, all of it, he signs off on it but it is done by a third party. He doesn't even pay his own bills there. They just trade. That is all they do. Nothing to put them off focus."

"That makes sense. Can you tell me again what they are doing with an office here on the border of Chinatown, with a bunch of old furniture? I am sorry, but to me it still leaves a bad impression."

He nodded. "I can't disagree completely. I wouldn't want to work there. But there is a story behind this. Let's take a walk and look for an Italian soda. And I will tell you the story of George Sisler."

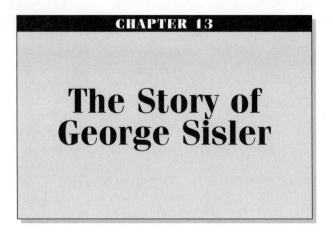

CHAPTER 13

The Story of George Sisler

H arvey knew his way around the SoHo/Chinatown border, and led me through some alleys and backstreets until we emerged on Mulberry Street, which was just about all that was left of a neighborhood that once had been home to tens of thousands of Italians. From Mulberry, we turned left onto Grand Street, where we found Di Palo Fine Foods. This is where, he said, we could find the very best soft drink in the world.

Harvey bought us a half-pound of mixed olives, some prosciutto (Italian ham), and two cans of *Aranciata*, which he believed to be the nectar of the gods and that was essentially a lightly sweetened orange soda. And yes, it was the very best soft drink in the world. As we ate the olives and the ham, Harvey told me the story of George Sisler's hedge fund.

"George managed a group of traders for a major European bank about 10 years ago. He had been a rising star in the commodities trading desk, and they promoted him to run a separate, outside-the-office proprietary trading operation in New York. It was a team of currency traders, just seven or eight, and they were essentially running a little hedge fund inside the bank, with the bank's money. It wasn't really a hedge fund, but it operated like one. They made their own trading decisions, the traders were paid a portion of their gains, and their entire mission was to produce spectacular returns on the bank's own money."

"How much money did they have?"

"At least five hundred million. It was a good deal of money at the time and George was young. He knew how to trade but he really didn't know how to manage traders. You'll find that out in a moment. But first I want to tell you about the office they had."

"Was it a dump, just like George's office now?" I asked.

"Definitely not. This office was the height of technology at the time. They had satellite dishes bringing in news from foreign countries. They had direct data connections all over the world that were costing tens of thousands of dollars per month. They had a famous decorator set up the office—it was amazing—the furniture and art in the office alone were worth millions. They were perched in three thousand square feet near the top of a forty-story tower in downtown Wall Street, with a floor-to-ceiling view of the Statue of Liberty."

I could picture it in my head. This seemed the ideal hedge fund office layout. "So they were set up with a perfect environment."

"Perfect for a fund with a track record of 30 years, maybe. But not a bunch of hotshot kids just out of Harvard. They demanded all this stuff and they got it. And George led the charge for all of these toys—and had written into his contract that he would only work in that particular office building with that specific view of Lady Liberty."

"Why?"

"He was positive that the European bank would do it, first of all. They were late to the currency prop trading idea, and wanted to play catch-up. They feared they would miss out on huge profits if they delayed any longer. So they gave in. On top of all of this, they guaranteed George a half-million dollars per year in salary and each of his traders a quarter of a million. So they were making giant money from the very start."

"I can see where this is going," I replied.

Harvey was eating olives so fast that I could hardly grab one out of the plastic dish in front of us. They were good and I determined that if I could keep putting olives in front of Harvey, he'd keep teaching me. And the faster I learned, the sooner I could be trading and making money. I still wanted to know more about the sell trade on the EUR/USD at 1.2200, especially now that I'd seen the pair rising upward in George's office. He continued.

"They were doing well for the first six months. Really well. Probably up 20 percent for the year. So good that they started to get a bit cocky about their trading. They were all young, and although they'd had some great success early in their careers, they really hadn't had enough failure to teach them to protect their gains."

"Wouldn't they have some sort of system at a bank for making sure they couldn't trade too much?"

"Most banks have automated systems for that now, yes. But at that time, George's bank had what they called a *daylight limit*, or a maximum drawdown for the day. So if a trader lost, say, two hundred thousand dollars for the day, he'd be asked to close his open positions and shut down until the next day."

"I remember Craig Taylor talking about this. How was the Daylight Limit determined?"

"Usually, as some percentage of capital lost," he continued, looking a bit sad at the empty dish in front of him. "No more olives. I think we need to correct that." He stood up, and this time, he ordered a full pound of them and returned smiling. Then he started again: "The team bought and sold as individuals usually. But as they worked on during their first year, they started to take on a lot of similar positions. Meaning, one guy would buy Sterling—the British Pound—then the next guy would do the same thing, on down the line, until they were all pretty deep into the same currency— against the U.S. Dollar, against the Swiss Franc, the German Mark, and so on. Long Sterling against everyone in a big way didn't leave them much room for a correction."

"But they had their risk limits."

"Individually, yes. But remember, they were earning money—big money—for just making trades. Imagine going from a base salary of sixty or seventy thousand, to a base of four times that amount. Just for coming into work every day, they were minting money. They were hungry for more—but their financial comfort sort of lulled them into believing that any profit they made on top of the salary was just gravy. Something that was not as important to protect."

"I get it," I told him. "Because they were taken care of already, it didn't seem like a big deal if they didn't make any extra."

"Right. That's exactly right. I think George fell into this as well. He bought a bigger house, enrolled his young daughter in a superexclusive nursery school that cost something like twenty thousand bucks a year. He bought a Porsche for himself and a Mercedes for his wife. It got to the point that he was going to need the end-of-year bonus to make ends meet."

"You mean, he couldn't live off the five hundred thousand?"

"Right. He was raising his lifestyle faster than his income."

"This doesn't sound like it has a happy ending."

"Really? This is the part I like the best," he answered. "I like it because what happened next drilled a lesson home for him that he never forgot."

"And what did happen next?"

"Those long Sterling positions—they started to add onto them as the currency weakened. It did not have to fall very much for the trades to start losing a lot of money. They had piled position on top of position until they were losing twenty or thirty thousand dollars for every pip it fell against them."

"Did they reach the Daylight Limit?"

He shook his head and frowned. "Nope. That's what I was going to tell you earlier. George never instituted that system with his group. He could have, but he didn't. And it wasn't imposed from the outside."

"So they held onto the losing positions?"

"Yes. They did. They were all in this together, you see—and none of them wanted to blink first. Especially George. He should have shut the whole thing down when they went to breakeven for the year—when they lost one hundred million, they were back down to the same amount they had started with. They had lost all the profit for the year."

"And he didn't shut it off?"

"No, he didn't. He kept it open—remember, if he closed the trades he would lock in a zero gain so far that year, and that would lock in a zero bonus. Holding on, to George, was the only way he saw that he could save the profit."

"But he didn't have the profit any longer!"

"Exactly!" Harvey yelled. "Exactly, my boy! You are solidly dead on point. He didn't have the darned profit any longer! He was holding onto the trade, hoping it would come back—so that he could save something that he had already lost. He had several options. But for now, let's just say that he and everyone in that office were holding onto the trade when they knew they shouldn't."

"Wasn't he worried about getting fired?"

"Harry, he had a lot of autonomy. The bank was headquartered in Switzerland. He had negotiated a lot of freedom. He had locked up the firm's capital for a year, meaning they had an agreement that he would have at least a year to produce returns and then they would review the success of the fund. And breakeven wasn't going to get him fired. So he wasn't worried about his job. He was seriously concerned about his pay. That became the first and most important priority."

"Did the trade turn around?"

"It did for a little while. It came back and they were up by about 10 percent for the year—so they had only lost half their profits and could have still been okay. But they all decided, under George's lack of leadership, that they wanted to ride it out. That they were sure they made the right decision and they weren't going to back down. Truth is, most of those guys were in the same financial position as George—they had overextended themselves and only a bonus could get them out."

The solution here seemed really obvious to me. "Why not close the trades and climb back with better ones?"

"Because that would make sense. It would require a brain. Here's the deal, Harry. Traders who only think about the money are bound to blow up because they are less likely to close their losing positions. They don't want

to lose money. Or they feel that they can't lose money. They have to win because they need the money to pay bills, or buy new cars, or prove that they
were right. Trading attracts some pretty egotistical people. That's true for
George and it's true for you, and it's true for most people who watch late-
night television and buy trading software. They want to be right. They believe they should be right. So they let their losers run."

"I have heard the statement that traders should let their winners run
and they should cut their losses short."

Harvey winked. "Yep. That's true. Even more true is that if you don't
cut your losers, you can't have any winners."

"How so?"

"It's like you said, Harry," he continued. The olives were gone but the
story continued. "Because they had tied up their capital in the losing position, they couldn't take any more trades. So they were locked into a bad
spot."

"What did they do?"

"They started to hedge the position."

"What does that mean?"

"Using their relationships with banks, they actually traded the other
side of the position."

"They sold Pounds?"

"Right. About one hundred points lower than they had bought it, they
started to sell it. Meaning, with separate liquidity providers, they opened
the opposite position. This means that they were now locked into a one-
hundred-point loss."

"What good would that do?"

"First, it prevented them from having to be wrong. Closing the trade
completely would mean they had to admit they were wrong. And they
didn't want, above all else, to close the position and then see the trade go in
their favor. Think about it! They were afraid of losing money that they
hadn't earned! They were afraid of missing out on a move that hadn't happened and had become less and less likely. By the time they hedged the losing position with another set of trades, they had way overextended
themselves on their capital, they had removed the chance of opening new
trades, and they were locked into a sure loss."

"This sounds so unlike George."

"Unlike the George you met today. But totally like the George you
would have met back then."

I scratched my head. "When did you come in?"

"Not yet. By this time, I knew about George and his positions. I was
helping the trader who took the other side of his hedged positions. He was
on the sales side of trading, and was in the business of providing liquidity
for funds and for some midsize manufacturing companies. I was helping

him learn not only how to quote Pounds but how to know when he should offset the positions to reduce his risk, or to actually take the other side of the trade and build a position for the bank. He's still working at that same desk now and makes a huge amount of money."

"Can we visit him?"

"Yes. Sure. We'll do that next week perhaps."

"Great! I appreciate that. What happened next to George?"

"He held onto this losing position for three months. By then, three traders had quit and he couldn't hire more because he'd have to show them his terrible trades. He started to get depressed. He came into the office every day, and they were watching the same position, over and over. Looking for a time to get out of one side, and keep the other. Sterling fell, but they were in a buy and a sell at the same time, so that didn't help. Then it rose back up, but they didn't know if it had bottomed out, so they stayed in. These were professional traders making a lot of money, and they were basically sitting on their rumps for months, watching something go nowhere. Can you picture that?"

"It's hard for me. I imagined that professional traders would be, well, more professional. Or better."

He chuckled, "Harry, that is the single greatest myth about bank traders. That they know more, or have access to special information, or more profitable systems." He was looking around for more food. When he didn't find any, he continued: "And maybe they do have access to all of that stuff. Maybe. But they don't have access to more discipline. And discipline is all that matters."

"You're saying that access to better information, or inside information even, doesn't make a difference." That didn't make sense to me, and I told him so.

"Well, let's say that George and his team of traders really had a great system for getting into the Sterling. That's why they bought it. But without a Daylight Limit, or a cutoff point, what good is the system? What good is the system, or the special inside information, if you don't have the discipline to implement it according to the rules?"

"So you're saying this is about money management."

"Sure! Of course! But it's more than that. It's about agreeing to a set of principles that will guide you as a trader, and then never violating those rules. That's all that matters. I've been training traders for many, many years—more years than you would believe. They have all been professionals. The one great distinction between the winners and the losers is self-discipline. That's why George, at the end of the year, shut down the entire operation."

"How much did he lose?"

"They lost 27 percent of the starting capital. On December 26, George closed all the positions and waited for them to settle—it takes three business days. That ended the year with the loss. Then he packed up his office and left."

"Where did he go? Had he been fired?"

"No, Harry, he wasn't fired. Not by the bank, anyway. They would have happily let him go at least another year. But he fired himself. He had lost his confidence. He had gone from up 20 percent to down 27 percent. It was a staggering amount of money to lose. He couldn't stop thinking that he'd been looking at a profit of one hundred million dollars but then couldn't hang on to it. That he had violated his rules when he hedged the position. That he had played dead and let a losing position run for months and months without confronting it. These are basic principles that he had learned a long time before."

"And without the discipline to implement those principles, he didn't feel able to trade."

"Exactly, Harry. Perfectly right."

"So he fired himself from trading."

"Yep."

"But you helped him? You're the reason he's trading again today?"

Harry shook his head. "I helped him, yes. But I only brought out of George what he already had inside himself. And that's what I'm going to do with you."

With that, he stood up and I knew today's instruction was over.

"Harry, do remember that George asked you to look into a way to do the carry trade on the retail platform? That's your homework for the next week. I want you to look into that. I don't know if it is even possible."

"What are we going to work on tomorrow? What about the buy trade on the EUR/USD? Is there any chance that it will still happen? Do you think that 1.2200 is a good entry?"

"Harry, I do think that 1.2200 is looking better and better. If you can justify taking the trade on your own analysis, then I agree that you should take it. Otherwise you should avoid it. But remember, if you take it, you are going to have to prove to me that you justified it in some way. And I'm going to be hard on you about it."

"I agree. And tomorrow?"

"Tomorrow I am going to Hong Kong, to celebrate the one-year anniversary of working with a hedge fund manager. Then I am traveling to see some prospective students until we meet again next week."

"All right. I am grateful for everything I've learned so far."

"I know you are. But you aren't out of the woods just yet. Remember what I told you: No trading. You can only take the EUR/USD trade if you can justify it to me."

"Agreed."

"Harry, remember what happened to George. Okay? You got me?"

"I understand."

"You can lose a lot of money very quickly if you start screwing around."

"I understand that, too," I said, laughing. "I am not going to trade. I have a lot to think about."

And I meant what I said when I promised not to trade. As he walked away, moving down the sidewalk of Grand Street and then up Mulberry, I had a peaceful feeling that came from knowing that for right now, I didn't have to trade, but instead I could work on figuring out the interest rate carry trade, I could write down my notes about my visit to the Sisler hedge fund, and I could hold on to my trading capital until the time was right.

But I broke my promise. I did take a trade.

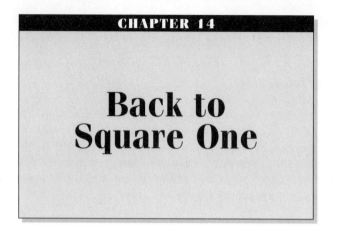

CHAPTER 14

Back to
Square One

My wife was excited for me, but she was anxious that I start making money. It was hard to argue with her about that. If I didn't make money, then we were going to have to dip farther and farther into savings. We did have the money from selling off all our cool stuff and the savings/severance, which meant we had $30,000. I had put $5,000 of that into my trading account. Gini didn't mind at all, especially considering that I was planning a trade with the supervision of a bank trader and it seemed more reliable this time.

It shouldn't have seemed like trading was urgently necessary, but when she spoke, it was impossible to remain patient. I had what might be the chance of a lifetime for a currency trader—to follow an order and pick up on the momentum created by a major bank.

"The longer you take to start trading, the less in savings we are going to have," she said that evening. "And if you start making more good trades, we can keep more in savings, and maybe even have more to use for trading down the road."

"That is true." Although her words conflicted with what I had promised Harvey, she was my wife first. I wasn't married to Harvey. I didn't have to put a roof over Harvey's head. I didn't have to buy him food or school supplies. So I decided that I would take a look at the charts.

The first chart I opened was the four-hour chart for the EUR/USD (see Figure 14.1). Harvey told me that I could trade it if I could justify it, and that's what I intended to do. To miss out on a trade that he and Hank Doorecker had planned—it was too much to resist. Perhaps his admoni-

FIGURE 14.1 Four-hour chart for the EUR/USD.

tion not to trade had been a test: to see if I could adequately justify a trade on the EUR/USD. Just to see if I was really listening.

I saw nothing. There wasn't anything here I could work with. Zero. What in the world were they looking at over at U.S. National Bank? What was so inviting about selling the Euro? I could see that it had tanked on Friday after the jobs report. I could see that it had now risen back up a bit. Big fat hairy deal! That didn't give me any trade ideas. I couldn't justify selling it now or at 1.2200, for that matter. What was going to happen at 1.2200? Harvey had said that bank traders didn't necessarily have access to better information. Well, apparently they did!

That's when the phone rang. It was Craig Taylor.

"Harry, I hear you've met with Harvey. That's the word on the street."

It was good to hear his voice. Not only did I need to thank him for setting me up with Harvey, but I needed help on this trade.

I told him how much I had learned already and how much I appreciated the introduction. Then I told him I was stuck. "I can't figure out where they go with this trade idea," I admitted. "Harvey told me that I could trade it if I could justify it, and I sure do want to trade it."

"What are you looking at?" he asked.

"The four-hour chart," I replied. "I have been explicitly commanded not to look at short-term charts."

"That's good. You're working from one of Harvey's favorite time frames. So you've made a good start. What else do you have on the chart?"

"Nothing."

"No indicators at all? No trendlines?"

I admitted that although I had read about all those things, I'd not found the time to implement them. "Well, Harry," Craig began. "You first of all shouldn't start with the idea of trying to figure out what Harvey is thinking. That's not going to work. If you are going to justify this trade, you are going to have to come up with some type of analysis of your own."

"I have no idea where to start. I know what a trendline is, but I'm not sure what to do with them."

"I gotta run, Harry. You can figure this out. But doing some testing and experimenting on your own is going to make a huge difference."

FORCING MYSELF TO DO SOME LINES

I sat in front of my computer screen for at least 20 minutes before making a move. Determined to not give in, I prepared myself to sit there until I at least drew some lines or plotted some indicators on my chart. I finally decided that I would at least draw a line at the entry price of 1.2200. I would start there. That was my goal: the number that I wanted to justify. After I drew the line, my chart looked like the one in Figure 14.2.

At least I had a starting point now. I could see where I was planning to buy. Was it wrong of me to be back doing this trade? Although I was doing my own research here, I couldn't take credit for the original idea. It oc-

FIGURE 14.2 Harry's entry price.

curred to me then that Harvey wanted me not only to explain why the trade was reasonable, but also to start developing my own ideas. Harvey had other traders to work with. He wouldn't be available forever to keep feeding me trading ideas that I would go home and justify. Part of what I wanted to do that night was to figure out how to plan these trades on my own.

The books I'd read had a lot to say about indicators—moving averages, oscillators, and so forth. It seemed rational that I would jump into some of those. So I added a 200-period moving average as a dotted line. The moving average was just what it sounded like: an average of the price over a certain period of time—in this case 200 periods of four hours each. Once plotted, I saw that it hovered above the current price and seemed to have stopped the currency pair from rising earlier in the month of April. Perhaps the average would stop it again and that was a good justification for the trade. But how could I say that price was going to hit the 200 moving average again? And that it would fall back? That was stretching things a bit.

The books also talked about oscillators. These were indicators that supposedly showed when a currency pair would be overbought (and ready for a move down) or oversold (and ready for a move back upward). I flipped open to a page in one of the books that talked about the stochastic. That seemed popular enough! So I added that, too, with the standard settings of 14, 3, 3. This time I was getting closer. The stochastic was rising and nearing the top. Could it be as simple as that? That I could sell the pair every time the oscillator reached the top? And buy every time it reached the bottom? Perhaps. But there was no way that Harvey was basing his entire trading system on something that simple.

The MACD, or moving average convergence-divergence, was an indicator of momentum. It was basically a way to follow a trend, built from moving averages. Perhaps that would provide an extra clue. One of the books talked about adding a second or third indicator to confirm what I was seeing on the first. That seemed reasonable—getting some backup. Actually, it sounded more than reasonable. It was perfectly clear to me that any successful trader wasn't going to base his entire strategy off one indicator. No wonder that I had felt uncomfortable with the stochastic alone. Or with just the moving average. So I added the MACD, with the standard settings of 26, 12, and 9. I didn't really know what those meant, but who cared? I was trying to justify a trade, not write a book report on Gerald Appel, the creator of the indicator.

It told me nothing at all. I could hardly understand what it meant in the first place. Now I had a hill-and-valley shaped thingy in the middle of the MACD and some lines crossing above and below. The lines were underneath and the hilly shape was sort of flat. Ho-hum. This was worthless. I'd really rather see the indicator with the hills going down or the lines going down as soon as the EUR/USD price hit 1.2200. Maybe Harvey and Hank

Doorecker had a computer program that could predict that the MACD would be topping out or heading for a move downward once it got to their special entry price.

What if I could also find that at the same time the price was hitting the 200 moving average and that the Stochastic Oscillator (a measure of when a currency pair had moved too far in either direction) was overbought? Now I was getting someplace. Still not sure that I had enough to justify the trade, I decided that I would add some other indicators.

The next one that I added was a Fibonacci retracement. I drew a line from the highest recent point the pair had reached, all the way to the lowest point it had reached. This then produced a series of numbers in between the high and the low, where, according to one of the books in front of me, price was expected to encounter resistance, or selling pressure. The 50 percent level of the retracement that I drew was right at 1.2182. Now we were onto something! Perhaps Harvey was watching for price to rise up to this level, where it was more likely to fail and go no further. I liked this. If I could show that the Stochastic was overbought, that the price was nearly hitting the Fibonacci retracement level—I might be able to justify taking the trade.

I had plotted a lot of stuff on my charts at that point. Well, that's an understatement. My chart looked as if a book on technical analysis had exploded all over the place (see Figure 14.3).

By this time, I had been working for four hours and my family was asleep. I hadn't even heard my wife put the kids to bed. This process had consumed me and I was really getting into it. Another candle was forming

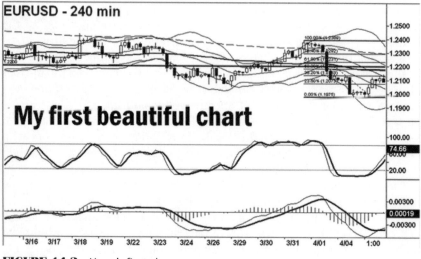

FIGURE 14.3 Harry's first chart.

but it wasn't going anywhere. Price was stalling at the 1.2100 mark and not going anywhere. I was exhausted. I hoped that I didn't have to show Harvey my chart before I took the trade, because I intended to sell the EUR/USD just like he was going to do, and I had my justification.

My wife stumbled in a few moments later and, rubbing her eyes, looked at my chart.

"That looks complicated," she remarked.

"It does," I admitted. "I'm not sure I know what all that means. But I think it is telling me that the Euro is going to be a good sell trade when it gets to 1.2200."

"That's the trade that your friend Harvey is going to take?"

"Yes. That's right."

"Why don't you take it now?" she asked.

She had just risen from bed so I could understand why she was confused. "The price has to rise another 100 points before I can sell it," I told her. "We're going to sell it at 1.2200."

"If you know it's going to 1.2200," she replied, "why don't you buy it now?"

Then she walked back into the bedroom. I wasn't sure if she had been sleepwalking or if she really meant what she said. But it made sense! She was right! If Harvey was so sure that the pair was going up and then was going to be a good sell, then why not make some money on the way up, and then on the way down again? Wow! That was brilliant.

I looked at the chart more carefully. Price seemed to be drawn like a magnet to the 200 moving average—it was surely on its way up there all over again. And the stochastic was showing that it was trending upward and not overbought yet. It had more room to go! And the MACD, like I had seen earlier, was rising, with the hill on the top side forming just now. And price was moving up toward that 50 percent retracement level.

For the next 30 minutes, I added a few more indicators that seemed to be all telling me the same thing—it was rising upward and I was going to be able to buy it on the way up. So I opened my trading platform. I had $5,500. If I traded long now, I stood to make 100 pips. If I traded $1,000,000 in currency, that would be $100 per pip, for a gain of $10,000. That would be a huge gain and bring back way more than I needed to pay for a month of bills. It would redeem just about everything I had done before I started making stupid decisions. I clicked on my trading platform, entered and double-checked the numbers, and took the buy trade.

At 12:35 A.M., I bought at 1.2098. It cost me $2,500 in margin to make the trade.

I did not place a stop loss or a take profit order. I just pulled myself up from the computer table and stumbled into the bedroom and fell asleep. I didn't even get out of my clothes.

THE NEXT MORNING: FLAMES FOR BREAKFAST

The next morning as I was gulping down a glass of carrot juice, I realized that I could have been a tad bit zealous about trading the Euro. I can remember a splash of carrot juice running down the front of my Wakeman, Butterman, and Bailey "20th Anniversary" T-shirt. I can also recall my son tugging on my shirt sleeve, asking when he would could play on the "tomputer" that day. I also can clearly hear my wife's voice asking me if I took her advice and took the trade upward. And I will never forget what the chart looked like when I walked calmly to the computer, started up the charting program, selected the EUR/USD, and then choked. It looked like Figure 14.4).

Oh, crap.

This wasn't going to look good. Not to Harvey. I suddenly realized that no matter how much research I'd done about selling the Euro, I'd bought it on pure speculation. Once again, I had fallen into the trap of believing I could game the system. Thinking that I knew more than I really did, I had managed to get a second margin call. I was down to $2,500 in my account. I had lost more than half the account!

Even worse, I realized that I had made the right decision. Looking at the chart (Figure 14.5), I found that I had actually made a trade that eventually would have been profitable—if I had not traded such a large lot size, the trade would still be open at 8:00 A.M., with some smooth, tasty profit

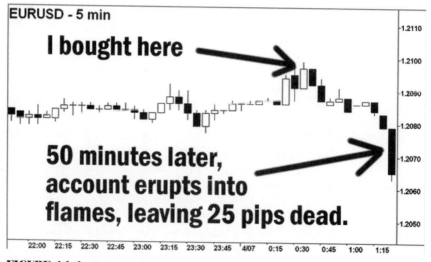

FIGURE 14.4   Harry chokes.

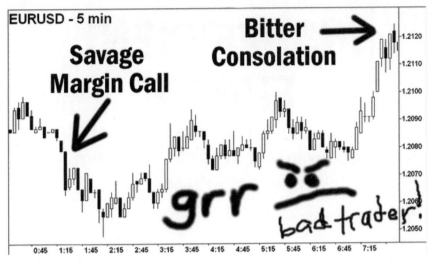

FIGURE 14.5   Harry's bad timing.

waiting for me. Sure it had fallen right after I'd bought it. But then it just climbed right back up!

No way! That was not fair! I had certainly picked the right direction. I had made a good choice. But my timing was off. My trade size was too big. My amateurish analysis had created a spark that led to a full trading account conflagration. With half my trading account in ashes, what was I going to tell my wife? I now understood that I'd made the right decision and I could engage in some redemptive revenge trading. If I could get back the money I'd lost, I wouldn't have to say anything about it at all. So what if I'd lost half the account so far! I could gain it back by just understanding my error and correcting it.

I'd read about this in the trading books. When a trader makes a bad decision, he should admit it readily and not stubbornly grip incorrect assumptions about the market. Better to gulp down some pride, reverse the trade, make back the losses and move onward.

I clicked on the order button to buy $1,000,000 worth of currency—just as I had done the night before. Figure 14.6 shows the response.

Insufficient funds! I didn't even have enough money to execute a standard lot trade!

I needed $2,500 in order to do a standard lot, and that's all I had in my account—which would leave nothing for available margin. That meant I had to reduce the size of my trade. Which I did. I traded a half standard lot, or $500,000 worth of currency, for $50 per pip. I bought the EUR/USD at a price of 1.2119 at 8:05 A.M. on April 7, 2004. It cost me $1,250 in margin to make the trade.

FIGURE 14.6   Harry is denied.

    This wasn't far from where I'd bought before, but at least now I knew it was going up. At least I understood what I'd done wrong and could make it right. I felt a sense of righteous retribution against the market for having treated me so poorly. Everything I did in these few moments was done with pure emotion.

    I didn't move. I couldn't hear my wife or kids or phone or anything in the background. It was me against the market and nothing was going to get in the way.

    At 8:10 the pair was trading 11 pips lower, at 1.2104, and I had lost $550.

    At 8:15 the pair was trading 17 pips lower, at 1.2098, and I had lost $850.

    These amounts were staggering to watch. How could I watch this much money go by? If I'd watched this happen the night before, I would have closed the trade early and not withstood the damage. Should I do that now? I asked myself. Should I close it? If I closed it and it simply went in my direction, then what? I'd lose more money and be even farther in the hole. The only solution was to hold on tight.

    Between 8:20 and 8:40, I got some delicious deliverance from the savage fall—the pair traded up to 1.2107 and was closing the gap on my loss. I knew I'd made the right decision and took a break to use the bathroom. My family was gone, probably to the park or something. It didn't matter. I'd have good news for my wife when she returned with the kids.

    When I returned from the bathroom, I'd been margin-called.

    I felt and heard a thumping sound in my head.

    Whump!

    I rubbed my forehead. A beastly headache was forming in the back of my head, which was the section of my brain probably used for storing numbers, such as the amount of money I just lost.

Whump!

Now what? I had lost $1,250. I only had another $1,250 left. This was all I had left from what had been a $5,500 account just a few hours earlier. Why hadn't I stopped? Why couldn't I have at least taken some of that money out when I had the chance?

My wife's iPod sat on the desk in front of me. Cradled in its connector thingy to the computer, its silky white face mocked me. The navigation wheel looked like a giant mouth, laughing openly at my predicament.

There was nothing much left to lose. If I lost it all now it didn't matter. What was $1,250 at this point? What did it really mean? Not much anymore. If I lost it, I couldn't feel much worse than I felt right now. If I gained back even $125, I would have doubled my account from this point and at least would have the satisfaction of not having given up. Clearly, the EUR/USD had never intended on going all the way up to 1.2200. Switching to the four-hour chart, I noticed that the stochastic had never reached the overbought area but was starting to turn downward.

It was never going to get to Harvey's number of 1.2200! Instead of rising up that high, it became exhausted near to his number and would turn downward for at least 50 to 100 pips. So I sold. After waiting for one more five-minute candle to close lower and prove that I was making the right decision, I sold at 1.2082 (see Figure 14.7). I could only afford to sell $200,000 worth of currency, for $20 per pip, and it cost me $500 in margin.

It only fell 3 pips lower. It never even covered the spread. Not for one second was it profitable. It only took about 37 pips before I got a margin call.

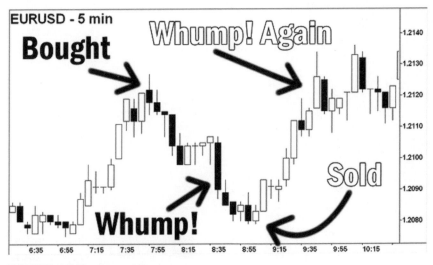

FIGURE 14.7 Harry sells.

Whump!

Whump!

Whump!

I stared at the $500 in my "available equity" column until 10:15 A.M., when my wife returned with the kids.

She banged open the door, called out to tell me she was home, and then cheerily yelled over to me: "So, Harry, how did that trade work out last night?"

Then I threw up.

CHAPTER 15

Breakfast with Harvey

Harvey Winklestein was going to kill me.

It was only four hours later—or 48 five-minute candles, or 16 fifteen-minute candles. He sat in front of me at the Utopia Diner on the West Side, on Amsterdam not far from Lincoln Center. They had great Mexican omelets, but I didn't order one. I couldn't eat. I could hardly stand up. Harvey had returned early from, or never gone to, his reunion party in Hong Kong. In fact, he had called me not more than 15 minutes into my nap that morning. I had been lying down on the king-size bed at home, wrapped in blankets and protected by an outer shell of pillows, hoping that Harvey would not find me there. Perhaps he would simply forget about me and leave me to suffocate in a swamp of my own shame. I could cast away my absurd plot to become a currency trader. On the phone, he'd told me that we should meet so he could say goodbye. By trading, I'd transgressed to the point where I lost all credibility as a student. How could he believe me from now on?

"Harry, before I leave you, I am going to teach you one last lesson. Then I am going to hop over to Hong Kong and try my best to celebrate with old friends."

What could I say? Nothing. So I remained silent.

"I am going to teach you the lesson of the pip auction game."

I nodded.

He called over to a man and a woman who were sitting across from us. "Sir? Ma'am?"

They peered over at us. This was New York. You didn't just call over to people and start a conversation. But they seemed to be from out of town. Harvey continued: "You having the Mexican omelet?" he asked.

"Yessir," the young man answered, with a Southern accent that revealed that he was not only from out of town, but he was also probably going to play whatever game Harvey had planned.

Harvey spoke: "You in town from Georgia?"

The young woman's eyes brightened. "Why, yes! How did y'all guess that?"

"Just a lucky guess," Harvey replied, but I knew it had nothing to do with luck. He continued: "I'd like to know if I could have a moment of your time." He paused. "Just a moment."

"What for?" the young man answered. "We're due for a show in half an hour."

This didn't seem to bother Harvey at all. "You folks will get to the show on time for sure. Promise. Scoot over here for a moment and you can help me teach this man a lesson here."

The young man and woman looked at each other, down at their food, and then back at Harvey. They shrugged. Apparently, they didn't have a lot of experience in refusing a request from an older person. They stood up and came over to our table. Harvey asked them to sit across from each other, with the young woman next to him and the young man beside me.

"This is the hundred-dollar auction game," he began. "It's a wagering game, but no one's going to be harmed in the playing of this game. I'm not going to take any money from you at all, and you're not going to lose anything yourself."

They nodded. I could see that they were now thinking of how great it would be to go home and tell their family and friends about this crazy old man they'd met in New York City. I imagined that when this was all over they would want to take pictures together with Harvey and me, and we'd send them off to enjoy whatever boring Broadway show, for which they had paid way too much for tickets.

"Here are the rules: To get this money, all y'all have to do is bid on it. Highest bidder gets the money. Sitting right here. The entire one hundred bucks. Loser still has to pay his last and final bid, but gets nothing."

They looked again at each other, and shrugged. One asked, "So if I bid less than $100, but I'm the winner, I still get the money?"

"Right. The other player still pays his last bid. And gets nothin'. Like fishin' all day and comin' up with an old tire."

The young man raised his eyebrows. You could see he was already mentally spending the money he hadn't yet won. He said: "Then I bid $1." He clearly believed that he was far smarter than his new wife or girlfriend. He was going to pay the least amount possible for this money.

No sooner had he spoke than his wife cut in. "I bid $2."

There was a brief pause, and I noticed that other people in the restaurant were beginning to look over in our direction. The bidding continued, and I was amazed at how fast it was going, and how excited each player was becoming—

"$5."

"$8."

"$12."

"$16!"cried the young man, and then I looked up and noticed that a small collection of people had now surrounded us, including our waitress, a line cook, and enough other people to make me feel claustrophobic. On this last bid, there was some clapping, and everyone was obviously interested in the outcome of this game.

The bidding had now progressed to the point where each player was intent on winning. I couldn't disagree with the bidding, because it seemed obvious that even at $99, the $100 was worth buying. You would be getting a discount of just a buck, but heck, that wasn't so bad.

And the bidding did get there. Within just a moment or two, with the bidding at only $59, the young woman yelled, "$99!" And a cry went up in the diner, and we all assumed we had found our winner. But we hadn't.

Our small crowd was laughing and congratulating the young woman (for being the first one to $99), when her husband (recently married, we discovered later, from Athens, Georgia, neither ever having journeyed past the state line until this trip), who appeared just one notch above frustrated, announced what seemed completely ridiculous: "$100!"

Everyone fell silent. "Wazzamadder witch you?" came a call from the line cook. He was speaking for all of us. Everyone looked perplexed.

The wife looked even more determined now. The husband spoke in a way that showed some intense emotions had started to brew underneath the surface. He said: "I ain't losin' my money. You can pay $99, I'll pay $100, and at least I'll break even."

Then, we all realized that in the heat of the bidding, that the young man, and the rest of us, had forgotten the rules of the game: the winner would pay his or her last (winning) bid for the $100, but the loser would still have to pay. And receive nothing! All of the sudden, as everyone began to realize this, we all became tense.

Now the game wasn't about getting $100 at a discount. It was about not losing a ton of money.

All of us secretly wanted the game to stop now, for we now understood what was about to happen. "Stop bidding," said the line cook. "Neither of yous can't win now." He walked away, slapping a dish rag against a booth. A busboy cleared away the couple's unfinished meals but they didn't mind at all. Breakfast no longer concerned either of them.

Harvey delighted in this. Apparently, he felt no regret for damaging (maybe permanently) the marriage of this handsome couple from the South. He now had feverish, bulging eyes that spoke volumes about his pleasure at getting the better of these two people, for having coaxed them into doing something that they would regret. This wasn't like Harvey at all—not the generous and kind man I had met in the past couple of days.

The young husband was now sweating, breathing hard, and increasingly angry.

His wife, now also angry, raised her bid to $102.

There were sighs from the back of the crowd, and I placed my hand on the $100. "Guys," I said, "let's just stop here. Harvey won't make you pay this. He's just trying to prove a point." I turned to Harvey. "I understand what you're trying to teach me," I told him. "We can stop this now. They're going to miss their show."

Before Harvey could open his mouth to reply, the wife pounded the table and then shoved my hand aside, and shouted an obscenity at me that I'd rather not repeat. Southern hospitality indeed!

"$115!" She had bid before her husband had raised his!

I gulped. They were doing the unimaginable. They were now going to pay a total of $215 for the right for only one of them to have $100. Outrageous!

But it wasn't over.

"$116."

An obscenity.

"$117!"

"$120," replied the young man. I wondered if this would become violent. The wife slammed her fist down on the table. She cried out, "$150!"

And with that, the husband shouted another obscenity and stated that his wife was a lunatic for bidding that much. And it was their wedding gift money!

Harvey, if he was willing to do this to a newly married couple, was probably going to finish this entire scene by killing me and feeding me to the hungry Southerners. He looked at the couple: "Are we done? Is that all the bidding?"

This was the type of moment when one of the two people pulls out a chainsaw and starts to cut everyone in the restaurant into little pieces. With all the anger in the atmosphere, something like that wouldn't seem so out of place.

Harvey then notified the couple that he intended to collect. He asked them for $270. They started digging into their pockets. I was sure that they didn't actually have this much cash on them. At this point their anger at each other was bound to turn into hurt and worry.

My head was spinning. The losses in my trading account from that morning had faded away. The situation here transfixed me. Then Harvey spoke: "Jimmy? Marianne?" They looked up. So entirely stunned from the game, they didn't ask how Harvey knew their names. But it freaked me out that he knew them by name.

They both looked up at Harvey. The husband was still fishing in his pockets and the wife had her hand in her purse.

"You're going to be late for the show. Let me walk you outside," he said. And with that, they quickly gathered up their belongings. He put his arms around them, escorted them outside onto Amsterdam Avenue, where through the window I could see him chatting with them. They started to laugh. He handed the $100 to the husband, who initially refused, and then Harvey leaned in and whispered something in his ear. Whatever he said did the trick and soon the couple was happily trotting down the street on their way to the show. When Harvey sat back down, the rest of the crowd had dissipated and we were alone in the booth. He said: "Did you see, Harry," he started, "did you see what just happened there?"

I had to admit that the only thing that I had seen were two stupid people overpaying for currency. I told him so.

"Okay. Does that apply to trading?"

I thought for a moment. This depressed me. I didn't want to think about my losses from that morning. "I am sure that it does," I replied. "I am sure that there is a lesson in here for me. I honestly don't want to talk about it, though." I paused. The truth struck me then: Harvey would soon leave and I would never trade successfully. Soon I would return to work at some crap law firm if anyone would still take me. My eyes welled up with tears.

"Harvey, I am not sure I can talk about this. I lost almost all of our savings today."

He eyed me sternly: "I already know that." Not an ounce of sympathy from a man who had just given $100 to some complete strangers. "I know that. Tell me something I don't know, or let me finish."

I didn't let him finish. I stood up and walked out of the restaurant.

With a step outside the restaurant, he gripped my shoulder and spun me around. He was very, very angry. His eyes were on fire. Then he began to speak.

THE INTERVENTION

HARVEY: Now, Harry. Answer the question. How was that game like trading currency.

ME: [silence]

HARVEY: You don't have to answer, then. You can just sit around for the rest of your life and hide from your own mistakes. If you take a nap after your horrible mistakes, then you can sleep through the part where you're supposed to learn something. You can just keep on making mistakes and avoiding the consequences. Running out of the diner is just an excuse to avoid confrontation with your worst self. If you go home and nap again, you might never wake up. Sure, you won't sleep forever in the bed. But you'll be a walking zombie. This experience will scar you forever, and you'll never take responsibility for your financial future.

ME: Harvey, I don't have any money left to trade with. I lost five thousand dollars in a matter of minutes today. There is no way that my wife is going to forgive me for that. I don't have a financial future. I gave all the possible trading capital that I have to my currency dealer. Sure, we have some additional savings, but I can't use that now. I can't be trusted with that money. We need that money to live on. I can't believe how fast I let it go. It disappeared so fast. I can't even talk about it.

HARVEY: Harry, sit here on the curb and talk to me for just a few moments.

ME: [silence]

HARVEY: That's better. That's the reasonable Harry Banes that I know.

ME: [silence]

HARVEY: Maybe that was the last trading you'll ever do. That's a possibility. But I gotta talk to you about this. You've got to come to terms with what happened.

ME: Okay. I'm willing to do that. I am willing to listen.

HARVEY: First of all, let's look at what just happened in the restaurant. How was that like currency trading?

ME: I suppose that this morning I engaged in the dollar auction game.

HARVEY: Or the pip auction game.

ME: Right. The pip auction game.

HARVEY: Did you notice that Jimmy and Marianne started off thinking about how much money they were going to win? They were thinking about how they could outsmart the other person and get a discount for a $100 bill. They wanted to spend the least amount of money for the greatest amount of money, and they put very little thought into their bidding.

ME: That sounds familiar. It sounds like what I did today. Just with my trading account. I didn't want to end up a loser, so I kept trading, hoping that I could end up a winner, no matter how much I lost along the way.

HARVEY: Right! Perfecto! This is the next lesson. When you trade like you did this morning, you are chasing after money, no matter what the cost. It was only important to you that you did not have to look like a loser.

Any amount of gain would be acceptable. Remember how just a short time into the dollar auction game, Jimmy and Marianne lost sight of the money that they wanted to gain? Then they started to worry only about not being the loser.

ME: Yes, I did notice that. I realized that they didn't want to look bad. Each one didn't want to be the one that had to pay something for nothing. This morning, when I was trading, I would have been happy to earn back anything at all. When I had $1,250 left, all I wanted back was another $1,250. It was like I was trading to make up for my previous trade. No focus at all on whether the next trade was truly a good idea. Just totally wanting to make back what I lost.

HARVEY: Any trader can fall into this trap. I call it the pip auction game. Even bank traders can fall into this. Every trade you take is simply an opportunity to bid for pips! You make a bid—

ME: In the form of margin.

HARVEY: No, not really. You think that's what you're risking, but it's not. What are you really risking when you take a trade?

ME: I'm risking a loss. The loss of capital if the trade doesn't work out.

HARVEY: And what was your risk threshold today?

ME: I didn't have one.

HARVEY: So your risk was infinite.

ME: Yes.

HARVEY: And your profit potential? What was your profit target on these trades?

ME: Well, for some of them it was determined, and for others I didn't have a profit target.

HARVEY: So you were willing to bid your entire trading account for the chance to win an indefinite amount.

ME: That sounds horrible.

HARVEY: And it sounds like the truth.

ME: I remember what you said about George Sisler and his first experience managing money. I don't want to compare myself to a successful trader like George, but this does sound familiar. At a point, he stopped knowing what he was in the trade for—and he kept the trade open just to not lose. He was, for a while, willing to lose an infinite sum of money in order to win an indefinite profit.

HARVEY: You remember George now! But you did not remember him this morning.

ME: I did forget George completely.

HARVEY: That's because it happened to George! Now we're getting someplace. When you become a great trader, these lessons will not be far off in your mind. You'll remember what you did this morning much more clearly than what happened to George.

ME: I am not sure I am ever going to become a great trader. I don't think I'm ever going to trade again.

HARVEY: Oh, you'll trade again.

ME: I don't have any money to trade with.

HARVEY: Yes, you do.

ME: I am not going to touch that money. I have to live off that money while I find a job!

HARVEY: Yes, you have to live off that money. You do have to find a job. Those things are true. But it doesn't mean that you won't ever trade again. Look at George. See how he's doing. He lost over $100 million in his bad trading experiences. Can you top that story?

ME: Not really.

HARVEY: Exactly. You still haven't even started out. You had your first big loss. You can still do this.

ME: But you told me that you weren't going to continue to work with me. If I were you, I wouldn't.

HARVEY: I said that because you lost a lot of trust with me. And it still might be true. There are some important things that you are going to have to do. And if you do them, then we can work together again. But it won't be easy. And this is where 50 percent of all the people I work with totally give up.

ME: I don't want to give up.

OMELET AND HUMBLE PIE

"What is your first concern, above everything else?" Harvey asked.

We were back inside the diner and I was eating a Mexican omelet. It tasted just as good as it was supposed to. If Harvey hadn't stopped me on the street, I am sure that a lot of bad things would have happened—it's not inconceivable that my marriage would have ended over this. It didn't (more on that later). It's probable that I would still be working for someone else today. Which I am not doing. It's possible that I would have done something drastic. I didn't.

Instead, we were inside the Utopia Restaurant and I was experiencing a frontal pipotomy, a not-so-delicate surgery to remove all of my ridiculous assumptions about how to become a successful trader. Already this discussion had freed me from some of the weight of what I had done to my trading account: I realized that other traders, even superprofitable ones, had experienced similar lapses of trading sanity. Even George Sisler recovered well enough to eventually run a multibillion-dollar hedge fund.

With Harvey's help (if he would still work with me), I could see myself doing better one day. Not making the same mistakes. Perhaps even managing money. But that was far off. Now, instead of thinking of the next trade, or imagining that I could follow along with Harvey's or Hank's or Craig's or anyone else's trading, I concentrated on how I would change my thinking first. I told this to Harvey.

"My first concern," I said, "Is that I change my way of thinking. That I change my mind-set. I have let myself be guided by my greed, or my emotions. I don't want that anymore."

"You want discipline."

"Yes. I do. I don't ever want to find myself in the same position I was in today. Ever again."

"I have a secret for you, then," he told me. And he leaned in closer. Then he said: "There is no secret."

He sat back and waited for my response.

I didn't offer one, so he started again: "There is no secret to obtaining discipline. There are ways you can increase your self-discipline. But there is no secret formula."

"But there has to be a way for me to do something about my lack of discipline. I need something. Anything. What did the other traders you worked with do? It's not like George woke up one day, said, 'Well, I'm never holding onto a trade that long again,' and then was over and done with it."

Harvey simply looked back at me for a moment or two. "Really?" he then asked. "That's not how it went for George Sisler? Why don't you tell me what happened with George? If he didn't wake up one day and make a decision to change for the better, then what did he do?"

I didn't have an answer. "I don't know," I admitted. "I just figured that you would have some sort of action plan for a guy in my position. With my problems."

"I have an action plan, Harry," he replied. "I've got one. But it presupposes that you are fully committed to changing your life. I can't force you to have discipline. I can't live inside your body, or push the buttons on your trading platform, or sit in your house all the time and tell you when to stop trading. I can't force you to exercise, to stop hiding things from your wife, or to never risk losing half your account on a single trade. I can tell you those things but I can't make you do them."

"That does make sense. But where does that leave me?"

"It leaves you with yourself. That's why I don't want to work with you right now. It's why you're going to be on your own for a while. You've earned yourself some downtime. We could have made a huge amount of progress in a very short period, but we're going to back it up. I am going to move on and work with a fellow named Larry Ho, in Topeka, Kansas. He's a commodities trader and he's nearing the absolute destruction of his trading account."

"Please stop him before he does it."

He raised his voice: "Harry! I've just finished telling you that I am not going to be your conscience. You've already got one! I have been working with traders for more years that you would believe. I am not in the business of becoming your mother. If you want to torpedo your trading account, then do it! Do it and get it over with and you can move on with your life! But I am not going to step in and hold your hand. Otherwise I'll never trust you. If you are going to do this, you have to do it on your own. You have to be trustworthy."

"I haven't been worthy of anyone's trust. I get it. I really do understand this time. I still hope that Larry doesn't torpedo his trading account, as you said."

Harvey sighed. "Me too, Harry Banes. Me too."

This gave me an idea. "I want to ask a favor that I don't deserve, Harvey. You can say no if it's not appropriate."

"All right," he answered. "What is it?"

"I want to talk to Larry Ho if he does not savagely destroy his trading account."

The request surprised Harvey. But he answered immediately. "No. Absolutely not."

"Why?"

"The two of you talking together? That would be like having two hurricanes mesh with each other in the Atlantic Ocean before hitting New York City. You would be a terrible influence on each other. Who knows what kind of trade ideas you would come up with."

"What if I spoke to him with you present? Like on the phone?"

He thought for a moment. This suggestion warmed him up to the idea. "Or in person. Then I could cut you off."

"Sure. I can't afford a plane ticket to Topeka."

He had an answer for everything. "But Larry can definitely afford a plane ticket to New York. I'll think about it, Harry. I promise to do that. But first we're going to dive into the next law of trading, and then I am going to leave you for a week."

"I am ready."

MY PERSONAL DAYLIGHT LIMIT

HARVEY: Harry, how much of your account do you think it's okay to lose?
ME: None?
HARVEY: No. That's a lame answer. Of course you're going to have to lose some money in the course of ordinary trading. But how much is too

much? In percentage terms, tell me when you think a trader ought to get out and stop trading.

ME: This is going to come as no surprise, but I have never thought of this before.

HARVEY: Most traders never consider this. But remember when we talked about George Sisler, working at the bank? George had a Daylight Limit, which was supposed to be a loss level at which he would be instructed to stop trading.

ME: I do remember that now. And it would be expressed in terms of a percentage of the trading capital lost. When he reached a certain threshold, it would stop trading. Or he would be forced to stop trading.

HARVEY: I am going to repeat again one of the only advantages that trading in a bank has over someone like you, Harry. It's a forced Daylight Limit. If you had been trading in a bank this morning, you never would have been able to draw down the account so far. Your manager would have known you were drowning in losses and would have cut you off. Your trades would be closed, and you would then go into the conference room and, depending on your boss, you'd get fired, or you'd get some help. But you most certainly would not be allowed, at Ernest Wellington, to keep trading your account into the toilet.

ME: I like that. I know you're not a fan of forced discipline, but—

HARVEY: Right. I hate it. This is why so many bank traders leave the bank, go out on their own, and have all sorts of problems.

ME: Because they no longer have a boss, right? A Daylight Limit that holds them accountable no matter what.

HARVEY: The bank has a systematic way of forcing you to discipline yourself. It's institutionalized self-discipline. The bank is an entity fully concentrated on making the most amount of money possible for the lowest possible investment. These days, they employ risk managers and mathematicians to make sure that they are not over-risking. They're not going to let a trader with even the most spectacular track record go crazy. No way.

ME: All right, then. I've got to organize my life or something so that I can develop the same amount of discipline. I have to say, that it's attractive to have some forced discipline.

HARVEY: But it's the easy way out. Do you see that?

ME: Yes. Because it still depends on someone else to take responsibility for my wins and losses. If I have a supervisor or someone who presses the buttons when I get out of control, then what happens?

HARVEY: When that person is no longer available? You've got it! You've figured this out. You don't want to depend on me. Or your wife or George Sisler or Craig Taylor or anyone else. You want to develop the ability to be a self-directed and responsible trader. It's a big job, but you can do it. And it starts by changing your mind-set.

ME: I am ready to do that.

HARVEY: Good. Now back to the original question. How do you know when you have lost too much? Let's back it up and ask some questions. What do you think a trader should do if he loses 1 percent of his account? If he's trading five thousand dollars and he loses fifty dollars, what should he do?

ME: Umm.

HARVEY: "Umm" is not a satisfactory reply. You get no credit for "Umm."

ME: Well, I don't want to be totally off base here, but I think the trader shouldn't worry about it.

HARVEY: Wrong answer!

ME: I knew it. I knew there was some clever answer you were looking for. I feel like I am working in the law firm again. People asking me questions they already know the answers to.

HARVEY: Try again.

ME: The trader should worry about it.

HARVEY: Better. But why?

ME: Because we're in the job of making money. Sheez, I don't know, Harvey! If you're telling me that I can't lose more than 1 percent of my account on a trade, then I really won't ever be able to trade.

HARVEY: That's not what I'm saying. Think about it differently. Remember when we said that without a Daylight Limit, or a money management program, a good trading system is worthless?

ME: I do remember that. Now I remember. I think I see what you're trying to tell me. You're saying that the maximum possible loss is really dependent on the bigger picture.

HARVEY: And the bigger picture is?

ME: A trading system. If I have a trading system, I know how much that system can lose. I know what it should be losing or winning on a regular basis. I get it! I can understand this now. I wasn't trading with any set system at all, and I had no idea how much was too much to lose. I didn't care, even. How in the world was I going to ever know when to stop with profits or losses? I wasn't.

HARVEY: Make sense now?

ME: Yes. It's way clearer now.

HARVEY: Good. Now, assuming you have a set of rules, a tested system—and we are going to talk about that later—how much is too much to lose?

ME: This time I'll guess—10 percent?

HARVEY: Higher. It's 25 percent. That's the cutoff point.

ME: The cutoff point? For everyone? No matter who it is? Anyone? What about the tested system stuff?

HARVEY: Good questions. Here is what I've found. I have worked with thousands of traders who trade from home. I have found that if they draw down 25 percent of their account, that they are more than 75 percent likely to destroy the rest of the account. It's what I call the *25/75* rule.

ME: So, you're saying, once a trader loses two thousand five hundred dollars of a ten-thousand-dollar account, he's likely to kill the whole thing.

HARVEY: Exactly. He has a 75 percent chance of demolishing the rest of the trading capital.

ME: Why?

HARVEY: Give me some reasons that you were willing to continue to lose today.

ME: Oh! I didn't think about it that way. I was willing to keep losing for all the reasons we talked about—I didn't want to show a loss. I felt that once I'd lost a bunch of the money, it didn't matter if I lost the rest trying to get back some of my money. I was trading on revenge.

HARVEY: Revenge trading is like stacking dynamite underneath your trading capital.

ME: Got it. Understood. I can commit to this. I can promise that I will never let myself lose more than 25 percent of my account. Now that I'm thinking of it, I now understand that if I have this as a rule, I am automatically going to cut myself off earlier than that—I am not going to let it get that far. Because when it gets that far . . . well . . . what would I do? Stop trading, for sure. But then what? Call you?

HARVEY: Heck no!

ME: Right. You don't want to be a part of those situations. You don't want to force me into anything. Instead of calling you, I'd take a break. That's what I would do.

HARVEY: For how long? How would you know you are ready to return to the world of trading?

ME: I don't know. Seems like if I just stopped for an arbitrary period of time, it wouldn't prove anything. I'd have to do something. Like punishment. Or something to ensure that I didn't do it again. Otherwise—

HARVEY: Otherwise, you'd just be planning out the slow bleeding to death of your trading account in chunks of 25 percent.

ME: I don't want to do that. There's got to be something else you want me to say here.

HARVEY: In terms of trading, what is the worst punishment you can think of?

ME: Telling my wife I lost five thousand dollars.

HARVEY: If that was the worst punishment, then you wouldn't have lost it. Right? So that's not the right answer. What do you fear the most?

ME: Going back to my job. Working for someone else.

HARVEY: Right!

ME: Oh, no. I shouldn't have said that.

HARVEY: Yes, you should have said that. Because it's true. You don't want to work for Wakeman, Butterball, and Bonehead ever again. Having to go back there and ask for your job back—

ME: No way. There is no way I am going back there.

HARVEY: You can deliver pizza instead. I'll let you borrow my 1925 Schwinn.

ME: Thanks. But no thanks. I am not going back to the law firm, and I would in fact rather deliver pizza on your old bicycle.

HARVEY: So I've reached the innermost part of your brain where you store your most sensitive buttons. I am pushing the "go back to work for other people" button right now and you don't like it.

ME: No. I want to trade for a living.

HARVEY: You haven't earned the right to trade for a living! Every day, I refuse to work with traders who are even willing to pay me tens of thousands of dollars. You know why? Because they believe that it's their right to trade for a living. But it's not. It's not a right. It's a privilege that you earn through discipline. And I will not work with a trader who is not disciplined. Including you, Harry Banes.

ME: All right.

HARVEY: And you know what is going to happen tomorrow when you go back to Wayfarer, Sunshine, and Doodlebug, or whatever the name of that law firm is? You know what? You are going to think to yourself, "Gosh, Harry, you could be trading the Euro right now, shorting it at 1.2200, but you're not. You're not because you have to earn more money to put into your trading account." That is what you are going to say to yourself.

ME: And I am going to realize that the money I lost trading actually represents something that I have to work for.

HARVEY: It will change the way you think about the money in your trading account.

ME: You're forcing me into this, you know.

HARVEY: No, I'm not. You don't have to go back to work. You can take your remaining savings and you can trade it. You can start trading it right now if you want. You can trade the Euro short with me, you can go see if Craig will talk to you, or if you can get someone else to help you. You don't have to ever do anything that I tell you to do. I am not going to force you. But I will promise you something.

ME: What?

HARVEY: I promise you that if you do this, if you take this first step, that I'll never threaten to stop helping you again. I promise you that you will make a huge step forward in your discipline. And that before you know it, we'll be working together again.

ME: This is really hard for me.

HARVEY: It's hard for me to see you in this spot, too. But I am not going to let you off the hook. So what's your answer?

ME: I'll do it. I will. I will go back to Mr. Johnson tomorrow and I'll ask for my job back. I can't believe that he would ever let me have it back, but I will ask. And if he says no, I'll find something else.

HARVEY: Anything else?

ME: Right. I will deliver pizzas if I have to. But I will earn back the $5,000 that I lost.

HARVEY: Agreed. Assuming you shape up this week, I want you to start on the next law of trading by yourself—it's the law of testing, and I am going to leave you to figure out the details. If you can get that done, then we'll be seeing each other again. Now I have to go.

I SEE HERBIE AGAIN

Harvey left me sitting in the booth with a lot to think about. Mostly, I was thinking about Herbie Johnson tearing my head off and throwing it across the office. I considered checking my passport to make sure it was still valid and then leaving the country, rather than facing Herbie or my wife.

I also realized that losing the $5,000 could have been something totally inconsequential. Without Harvey's help, I probably would have waited a week and deposited more money. I wouldn't have told my wife about the loss. I could see that without Harvey, I would have seriously depleted all our savings very quickly.

So I decided to show my gratitude to Harvey by not wasting any time asking for my job back. I hadn't paid Harvey anything for his time or effort with me, and I had been nothing but a problem to him so far. By following his instructions, at least I showed that I valued and appreciated his help. And I did appreciate the help. Choosing now to ask for my job back, instead of waiting another day, proved my commitment to do the right thing.

And getting a job now was the only right answer to the quandary I faced. I did not want to tell my wife that I needed to trade more of our savings. We had a limited amount of money and I planned to keep it safe for as long as possible. My plan was to regain the losses from that morning, even if it took me two or three months, then start trading again with the money I earned, and this time protect it instead of flushing it away. We didn't have to dip into the savings that way. I had to return to working for other people, I had to face the people who had fired me, and I had to admit that I had carelessly squandered a great opportunity to make a lot of progress in my trading. Honestly acknowledging this missed opportunity was nearly the most difficult thing that I'd ever done.

Traffic was light so I hailed a cab, which got me to the office much more quickly, where I could experience the wrath of Herbie more quickly, and then I could forget about that job and instead go to work delivering pizzas for Bleeker Street Pizza in the West Village. At least I liked their pizza.

I didn't have a plan. Or a good reason that they should hire me back. Maybe I could start off by talking to the office receptionist, and find out if they had hired someone to replace me. By the time I started up the elevator, I planned to first speak to Christy Matthewsen, the office administrator. She'd fire me a second time, or explain to me how very uninterested the firm was in my services, thus saving Herbie Johnson the effort and torment of screaming at me.

Fat chance.

As I exited the elevator on Floor 44, Herbie Johnson was standing right at the reception desk.

"Banes!" he cried. "Just the man I wanted to see. Get in my office. Now."

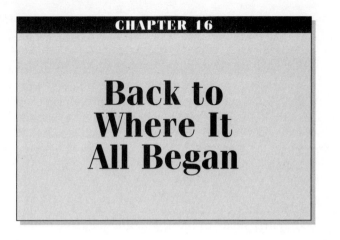

CHAPTER 16

Back to Where It All Began

Herbie didn't look as angry as the last time that we had spoken. In fact, he seemed almost happy to see me. I hadn't ever seen him happy before, so this was a total surprise and I didn't know how to act. Walking back toward his office, with him walking behind me, I had the feeling that I still worked there and that not much had changed.

On the way down the hall, I peered over to the central work area outside the filing room. There were stacks upon stacks of files to be organized, sitting on my old desk. It was more than I'd ever seen before, even more than I had seen after returning from vacation.

"Banes," he told me when he got me into his office and closed the door. "Let's get something out of the way right from the start. Did you know anything about that dirtbag Scott Needleway selling the Anderson files? Did you know anything about that at all?"

"No, definitely not," I told him. "Of course not. If I'd known something about that, I would have fired him myself. Is that what happened to the missing file? Is that why I was fired?"

He nodded. He then said something nasty about Scott that I won't repeat here. He also seemed pleased to find me completely unaware of what had happened. "It's why you were fired, yes. It's why we fired Scott last week, too. He was selling letters and depositions from the file to the business press. We caught him on the phone with a reporter from television. Too bold for his own good at the end. Not too bold after I finished with him. Now I figure that's why you're back. You heard that we caught him and now you want some revenge."

I shook my head. "I haven't heard anything about it until right now, sir. And I certainly don't care to get any revenge. In fact, I came here to apologize."

He grunted. "Apologize? For what?" He motioned for me to sit down in front of his desk, and then he sat on the corner of it, just a few feet from me, much too close for comfort. At least he wasn't yelling.

Then I let him know, with his phone chirping in the background, what a terrible employee I'd been for so many years. I explained that I hadn't always given him an honest hour's work for an honest hour's pay. That I had taken a few hundred extra 15 minutes at the end of lunch. That I had left early and come in late far too many times. That near the end, I had done some trading on company time. That I had lied to him on occasion. And that I was sorry. And then I surprised him and myself by what I said next: "And I want to pay that time back. I owe it to the firm."

I learned later that, in all of his years as a partner in a law firm, he'd never heard a staff member say such a thing. He hadn't ever heard of anything like it at all. And he didn't want to hear it again.

"Don't ever want to hear that again, Banes," he told me. His phone buzzed again. Surprisingly, he didn't reach for it. He hadn't taken his eyes off me for the entire time. He spoke: "In fact, I don't have much time to care about your past indiscretions on the job. I've got seven associates out there right now who I ought to fire for overbilling, but I'm not going to do it because we have more work than we can handle right now. The Anderson case has ten attorneys now and it's a thorn in my side and a mountain of files. And no one around here has time to hire a replacement. We've got stackloads of paper out there for you to file."

I didn't hesitate. "I'd like to come back and help out. I don't know for how long I can stay, maybe a month, maybe two. I've got to earn some money fast, and if you need the help, I need the money."

He didn't mention the severance pay. I didn't either. He grunted: "I don't know how much we were paying you, but if you can start right now, I'm sure we can work it out. How much do you want? How much is this going to cost me?"

His phone rang again. This was the longest period I'd ever seen him do only one thing at one time. He was buckling under the pressure to multitask.

"I can work as a contractor. I can help you find a replacement for me in two months. You can pay me five thousand dollars a month."

"Done," he said, and this time, when the phone rang, he picked it up. "Now get out of here."

I went straight back to my desk and moved the heap of files over to one side, and found my old phone. There was no longer a computer on the desk, and I sort of liked that. I didn't want any distractions. I lifted the receiver and dialed home.

My wife answered on the first ring.

MEANWHILE, BACK IN THE CUBICLE . . .

I explained everything to her. I originally intended to tell her about the trading losses in person, but I didn't want to hold anything back. Better to get all the apologies out at one time and in one place. She was shocked that I had asked for my job back, and she was encouraged that I was willing to earn back the money I'd lost, even though I would have to work at a job I didn't much like. I told her that in the evenings I was going to dedicate myself to figuring out where I went wrong, to developing the right attitude about trading, so that I never made the same mistakes again. She understood. If I hadn't gone back to work, this conversation would have ended a lot differently.

After I hung up, I went straight to work. I got a lot done in the next five hours, staying later than I ordinarily would have. It would take me at least two weeks to catch up with this material alone. But it actually felt good to be working again, to be actively engaged in supporting my family and earning back the money that I had lost. Harvey was right. This was the only course of action that I could take to salvage my trading career. Saving my trading by not trading at all didn't seem to make much sense at first, but now that I was working, I realized how important it had been to protect my account.

At 7:00 P.M., I stopped working for the day. I pulled a piece of blank paper from my desk and wrote on it in capital letters:

YOU MUST PROTECT YOUR ACCOUNT BALANCE

Then I thumbtacked it to the board and headed for the elevators. But I didn't go all the way down. I stopped at the 31st floor, the trading floor of Ernest Wellington & Company. I wrote a note to Craig explaining that I had taken my old job back to earn some money to cover my losses, that I had made a boneheaded trading decision, and that I would like to talk with him when he had a chance. I planned on working through lunch for the coming weeks, but I hoped we could find some time after work. I left the note at the receptionist's desk, and started to leave when a voice called out to me.

"Harry Banes? Is that you?"

It was Anderson.

ANDERSON LOSES HIS MIND

Anderson wanted to talk and I for sure wasn't going to refuse. He led me back onto the trading floor, still staffed with a few people who, he told me, were watching the Asian markets.

"We have people in Japan and other parts of the world, of course," he said, "but we like to keep most of the folks close to home."

"Sounds reasonable."

"Craig tells me you've been doing some trading. How's it coming along?" He found a place for us to sit at two empty workstations. In front of each of us were four flat-panel monitors, and when my elbow bumped the keyboard, the monitors lit up and showed charts, current quotes on the major currencies, and some web pages. Anderson looked over. "Looks like the EUR/USD is trading higher again." I glanced at the quotes.

It was trading at 1.2160. All day it had tried to approach the 1.2200 mark but hadn't been able to reach it.

"Yes, I traded the Euro this morning," I told him. "I lost. I am going to take some time off trading for a week or two."

"Reached a drawdown limit?"

I nodded. I wondered why he was talking to me. He didn't even seem to know that I'd been fired. From what I'd learned about Anderson so far, he wasn't the type of person to engage in idle chat. There had to be a purpose behind this.

"Yes," I admitted. "I lost just about all of my trading capital this morning." Ordinarily a confession like this would make me feel horrible. Instead I felt great. Why lie to him? He didn't have any plans to hire me. I had no reason to impress him.

"We all have those experiences starting out. All of us. I sure did."

He then looked off into the distance and proceeded to tell me a long-winded story about how he had been out of college for six months, then was hired into a major bank, and how he did the working tour, like all the recent graduates, of the different parts of the bank. At the end of his six-month tour, he started working at the equities trading desk. Then he lost a bunch of money, almost got himself fired, and ended up with a story far more boring and far less informational than everything I had already learned.

When he was finished, he patted the desk in front of him. "Harry, if you'd like to come down here after work and talk with some of the traders, that would be fine with me. When you're ready to start trading again, we've can put a computer down here for you and you can access your account from here."

What was he talking about? I wondered. Why had he offered this? Had he lost his mind?

It had to be that he knew Harvey Winklestein, and I was getting the royal treatment because of it. But I thought I had remembered that Harvey hadn't ever met, or didn't know, or didn't like, Anderson. Maybe Craig had talked with him. Certainly I wasn't going to spend all day thinking about it, though. I readily accepted.

"I appreciate the offer. I will usually finish in the late afternoons and maybe in a week or so, when I catch up with some work, I will start coming down here."

"Sounds good. I won't be here tomorrow but if you stop by, I'll have a badge made for you so you can at least get in the door. A computer should be ready for you in a few days. The IT guys are fast. If you have any problems, just call me on my cell," and then he handed me his card. Then he stood up, shook my hand, and looked me in the eye.

"I can see a good budding trader a mile away, Harry," he told me. "I think we might be able to do some business together in the long run. Shake off those losses. Get back on the horse. Don't let the losses get the best of you."

I nodded.

"You can sit around here for a while if you'd like," he added. "I'm going to run now, but you're already logged into Ellen Hansell's computer. If you want to look at some charts, be my guest. The door will lock automatically behind you. Dial 9 to get an outside line."

Then he walked away to check up on some traders a few desks away. He pointed back at me, obviously introducing me to them and making sure they knew I'd be there.

Stunned, I sat motionless for at least five minutes. I didn't know if I should really touch the computer. What if I screwed up and made a trade?

What if he intended for me to trade? Was this some kind of job interview, like Craig had when he sneaked in? Did Anderson want to see what I could do?

I called my wife and told her where I was, and that I was going to check some things out so that when I came home I wouldn't be tempted to open anything up. It would be smart to do my research here, because I wouldn't have access to any of my own trading accounts. That was a good thing.

The first thing I did when I gathered my senses was to open a chart on the EUR/USD. It was the short-term chart, and it only reminded me of the experience I'd had earlier that morning. That's when I realized that I should have been looking at the longer term charts anyway—that's what Harvey wanted me to do in the first place. So I switched over to the four-hour chart again, and drew a horizontal line across the 1.2200 mark. Without any other thoughts, I started to mark on the chart all the points at which the currency pair had hit the 1.2200 level. The chart looked like Figure 16.1.

I started to feel excited. Not to trade, which I knew I couldn't do, but because I finally might have done some actual, real, valuable, not worthless, analysis. And on my own!

Had the 1.2200 price, for some unknown reason, simply been a hard number to break? Was that it? Could it be that simple? I remembered that

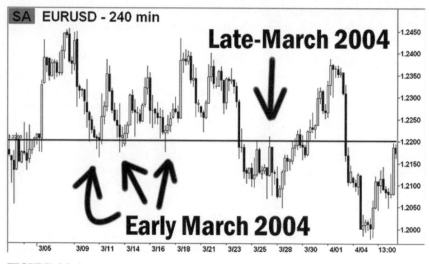

FIGURE 16.1   The currency pair hits 1.2200.

some of the books I'd read had said that sometimes round numbers were good barriers for currencies. I had also read that once a resistance line (a price level above the current price) was broken, it would tend to become support, or a strong floor. This made sense to me. Once a currency pair did all that work to break above a level, some emotional and financial investment would be put toward keeping it above that level.

Likewise, if the currency pair could break below a certain support level, then that level would tend to become strong resistance, or a ceiling. Once again, this immediately made sense to me. And it seemed to be happening on the chart in front of me.

I noticed that three times in early March, the EUR/USD had tried to break below the 1.2200 level. Then on March 24, it finally broke through and closed below 1.2200. And what happened when it tried to rise back above that mark? It couldn't do it. It was stopped cold at least two times that I could see on the chart. Those would have been nice times to sell.

Perfect times, in fact. Just like now?

On March 30, it had broken above and below and shot upward. Then it had smashed through the line on April 2. Did that ruin my support/resistance theory? Was the strength of the 1.2200 number diminished because of that (see Figure 16.2)?

It seemed to me that the line still retained some strength. A four-hour candle had broken the line. But what about the five-minute chart? Maybe it looked like the four-hour candle had an easy time of breaking the level—but it could have bounced on the shorter time frames.

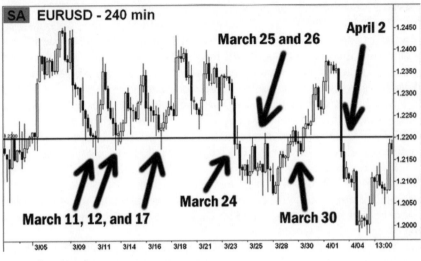

FIGURE 16.2 The strength of 1.2200.

I decided to switch down and look at a shorter time frame chart. It might sound lame to you, but when I saw the five-minute chart, chills ran up my spine (see Figure 16.3).

The five-minute chart showed me exactly what I needed to see: that the 1.2200 level, overall, had retained its strength. Even though a four-hour

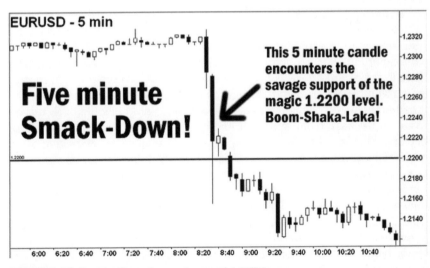

FIGURE 16.3 The five-minute chart and 1.2200.

candle passed through the number, it wasn't as if all the traders had forgotten about the importance of the number. The five-minute candle had briefly traveled lower than 1.2200, but then snapped back upward. This meant that the number could still have importance now, for the present time, and that if the price rose up to hit that level in the next few hours or days, it was very likely to stall and fall back down.

Was this the system that Hank Doorecker had used? All I had on the chart was a simple line. It seemed so sparse, so . . . easy. I imagined that Hank surely looked for supporting information before he traded—a quick horizontal line would never be enough. But maybe it would be enough for me.

I grabbed a Post-it note from the desk and wrote down, "Sell EUR/USD, 1.2200." If I wasn't going to trade it in my own account, at least I could declare my intention to trade it. I had my entry; but what was going to be the cutoff point, at which I knew I'd been wrong? How far did the pair have to go before I would need to jump out?

The farthest I could see that the pair had ever traveled beyond the 1.2200 line before snapping back had been about 40 pips. That was across eight recent examples. I felt comfortable saying that if the price went 50 pips beyond the line, then I had been wrong. So next to the "Sell EUR/USD, 1.2200," I wrote, "Stop: 1.2250." This mean that if the price rose up and shot through the line, I would get out with a loss of 50 pips. But I would have that as a buffer. I had recent history on my side.

It felt good and right to have a cutoff point. At least I wasn't risking a huge amount. This was all fake trading, of course. But just writing it down on a piece of paper helped me feel more responsible. I knew Harvey would approve of the way I was doing this.

But what of a profit target? What would be a profit target?

I looked over all the other examples on the four-hour chart of when the price had been rejected by the 1.2200 mark. The March 11 bounce yielded a maximum of 186 pips before it turned around and returned to the 1.2200 level. The March 12 gave 172 pips, and on the 17th, 234 pips. March 24 produced 30 pips, March 25 did 131 pips, and March 26 gave 153. On March 30, it had bounced off the line and fallen back 40 pips. And going back to that five-minute chart, from April 2, it had hit the support level and then risen back up 20 pips. It had never failed to at least bounce enough to give some profit. The average move was 120 pips. I decided that would be my profit target. Figure 16.4 shows how the Post-it note now read.

I stuck it on the desk in front of me, intending to keep it there as a reminder for the next day. Then I left. This was the best I had felt in a long time. I was working to support my family. And finally, at the very least, I knew that I had discovered the beginnings of a system. It needed more work; I still wanted to test a lot more trades and talk to Craig and Harvey and anyone else who would listen to me. I hoped they would listen to me.

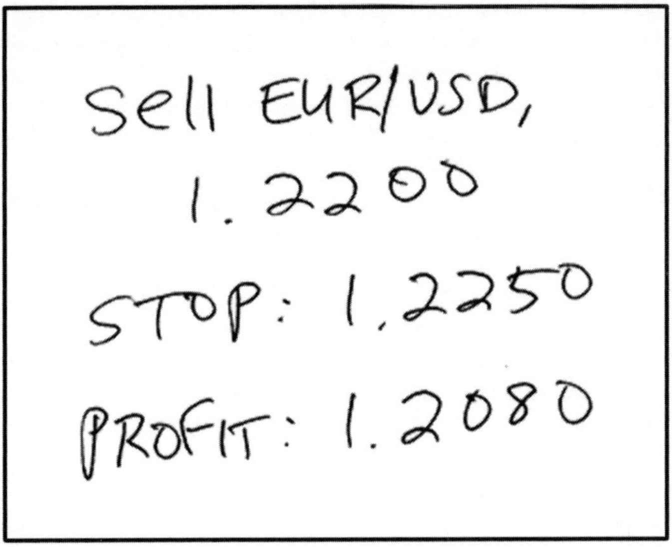

FIGURE 16.4　Harry's reminder.

ON A ROLL

My wife was satisfied that I had returned to work to make right what I had done wrong. She had never felt great about me leaving a stable job in the first place. Now that I was going to earn back the money I had lost and would have instruction not only from Harvey, but maybe from Anderson and the people at Ernest Wellington, we both knew that that I would learn how to trade better—I was on the right track.

The next day I arrived a full hour early for work, filed my way straight through the morning without a break and then skipped lunch to submit a classified ad (to start the search for my replacement). I was working without the help of Scott or interns, but I found that I liked getting things done by myself. I realized that as a manager of the filing system, I had become very lazy.

By 5:00 p.m. I was on a roll. I researched a new computer-based filing management system and took notes on the cost, called the company that sold the program, and left a message, and organized a huge stack of case files that lawyers had probably thought were lost forever. I refiled the depositions, letters, transcripts, and who knows what else from the past four weeks of the Anderson case and found that Scott had made a lot of mistakes, or had clumsily returned things where he shouldn't have, as he was selling off information to the news or to the opposing counsel. I didn't stop to wonder at all where Scott was. He was old news and I was happy that we had left on reasonably good terms.

By 7:00 P.M., I had to pull myself away from work and nearly forgot to visit the 31st floor. As promised, the night security guard had a badge for me when I showed up and it worked perfectly. The floor was just as empty as it had been the day before, with probably 15 people that I could see, sitting at their desks. A few of them were playing cards and the others were surfing the web. None of them were trading.

Near the back corner of the room, only about 20 feet from Craig's desk, a computer was set up where there hadn't been one the day before. The desks to either side were empty, without computers or monitors or phones. A note from Anderson told me that the desk was mine to use, that I should call the tech support guys if I needed to load software onto the machine, and that I should make myself at home.

Next to the note from Anderson was a note from someone named Alistair Martin. It said:

"Harry: sweet trade on the Euro! Thanks for the idea!"

Who was Alistair Martin? I looked up, toward the desk where I'd sat the night before. Then I realized that I'd left my Post-it note on the desk of a currency trader named Ellen Hansell, and that she had taken the trade, probably with Anderson's approval. I immediately punched some keys on the computer (realizing that I had become very comfortable with a computer, without having even noticed it before) and pulled a chart to see where the Euro had traded that day (Figure 16.5).

To say that I amazed myself is an understatement. I shocked myself. For five minutes, I just looked at the chart from several different angles. Was I looking at it correctly? Did I really plan that trade? Had I actually analyzed the charts, picked an entry, a stop, and a profit target? Without blowing up an account? I wondered how much money Alistair Martin had made using my idea. If Alistair was trading one-million-dollar positions, then the 120 pips had made him twelve thousand dollars. If he had traded a five-million-dollar position, then he had made sixty thousand. The numbers amazed me.

I decided that the long-term charts worked better for me, after all. Harvey was right from the beginning, and I never should have looked at the shorter time frames, which only tempted me to jump into quick positions. The short-term charts appealed to my greed. The long-term charts required patience, rewarded analysis, and produced in one trade more profit than any of the short-term trades I'd seen.

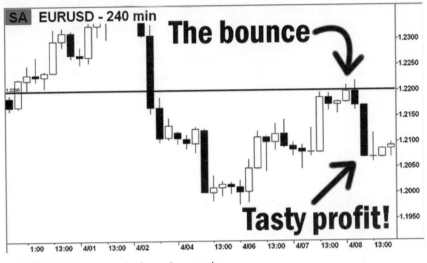

FIGURE 16.5 Harry looks at Euro trades.

I thought of Mindy at George Sisler's hedge fund. It occurred to me that she could benefit from switching to a long-term view, if in fact George was going to require more of her, as Harvey suggested. It made sense to me anyway. Why trade over one hundred times in one day, just to achieve the same profits in one trade by careful study on the long-term charts?

Next I determined that if the system of support and resistance that I'd traded worked before, then it would work again. And if I was tempted to look at a different time frame, I'd select an even longer time frame than the four-hour charts. But first I had some questions.

The first trader I found sitting about twenty feet in front of me was actively engaged in a game of rolling dice against another trader who was obviously working very hard, and not at his desk. Both of them were dressed casually. Neither one was a day over 30 years old. I supposed, from what I learned about traders so far, that their youngish looks and apparent lack of concern for the market had nothing to do with their skills as trader. I started to think that the better the trader, the less the person would actually look like a trader. Or what I expected a trader to look like. Or, more yet, what I expected a trader would be doing. In fact, what did these guys do all day? Why were they even here? I wondered.

"Hi Harry," the first trader said. "Watcha doin?" He spoke with a Canadian accent.

"Hi. I have some questions. If you don't mind. I hope I'm not interrupting anything important."

"Not at all, Mr. Banes," the other answered. "We're just here manning some open positions." This one spoke forcefully with a British accent. His voice had a tone of confidence, and this impressed me. I wanted to speak like that. I wanted to be sure of myself like that, especially when trading. Confidence seemed to play a big role in trading success. After making a mental note to ask Craig or Anderson or Harvey about it, I asked: "Is there any reason that switching from a four-hour chart to a daily chart would make a big difference? As long as I am following the same system?"

The Brit didn't even look up. He shook his head. I think he took me for an amateur (which I could not dispute) and didn't seem to care one way or the other if I got my answer. The Canadian seemed completely willing to help and replied happily: "Not really. What works on the four-hour ought to work on the daily. But you should go back in time and test it to make sure."

That seemed reasonable to me, although I had no idea how I might go about doing such testing. I was going to ask another question, but the Canadian beat me to it: "If you're going to trade from the daily, you're really going for the bigger moves. That's where you can get a big piece of the action, if you can ride along for the swings. A lot of traders here are taking a harder look at the long-term charts for that reason. More profit, less work. And you trade from home, right? Well, it's obviously much easier since you are only going to have to look at the chart once a day. Or at least, you're going to center your planning time around 5:00 P.M. Eastern Time, when the New York session is completely over and the daily candle closes."

Once a day? That made sense. If I planned my support and resistance trades on a daily chart—then I would only really be looking at the charts when the daily candle closed. And now I knew that it closed at 5:00 P.M. I would later learn that in the 24-hour world of currency trading, 5:00 P.M. Eastern Time represented the end of one day and the beginning of the next. At that time, a new day was starting in Asia and a workday was ending in New York. So it made sense if I looked at it from a worldwide standpoint.

I couldn't remember any more questions, so I stood and watched them roll the dice a few times. The Brit chimed in: "Want a piece of the action, Harryboy?"

"Not really. What's at stake here?"

The Canadian laughed. "This game is called 'paycheck,' Harry. He's got me for two paychecks right now. It's a simple game: I roll three times and add up the total. Then Roddy here makes a bet. He bets either that he can beat the total in one roll, in two rolls, or in three rolls. One roll is called a 'one bet,' two rolls a 'two bet,' and three rolls, a 'three bet,' or the 'wussbet,' and you can figure out why we call it that. If he makes a three bet, and he wins, then he owes me nothing and I owe him nothing and I get to roll again. If he loses the three bet, as we call it here at EW, then he pays me half a paycheck. If he makes a 2 bet and wins, he wins half of my next paycheck and gets to roll next. Now he would only make a one bet or a two bet if the numbers say he can win with those, of course. Follow me?"

"Sure. I get it." This was madness. It was 8:00 P.M. on a Thursday night and they were rolling dice to win more money from each other than I would make in two months.

"Now about the one bet," he continued, in his Canadian accent, "That's where it gets interesting. If Roddy wins a one bet, he gets my next paycheck and he gets to roll for the next two turns, no matter if I win or lose. If he loses, he owes me his next paycheck and loses a turn."

I thought: Yes, they're insane. How much money could they possibly have?

I started to leave when the Brit spoke up: "Hey, Banes! How about that trade today? How far you think it can go? You think it can get down to 1.2000? The round numeral, as I like to call it?"

"I don't know," I replied. "My target was 1.2080. Where's it trading now?"

He leaned over to his keyboard and punched it in. "It's still hanging out in the high 2000s. But I think it can make a second drop lower. I'm stayin' in."

"You took the trade?" I asked.

"Yeah, sure I did. I heard all about you. You're working with Harvey, the Winklemeister. Everyone here took the trade. Just about every desk you see here, they all wanted to take the trade—small or large, didn't matter. Some of these guys only trade the crosses, you know, the EUR/JPY, the GBP/CHF, and so on. So they didn't take it. But I did. So did Winnipeg George."

"Does Anderson know you all took it?" I asked.

"Heck yeah," he shot back, obviously thinking I was a moron for not knowing that already. "Anderson knew about it. He signed off on every one of us taking it. It was a fine trade, Harry. You made me some excellent coin today. Cheers!"

"Cheers!" I replied, and then I forgot all my other questions.

What? I thought.

Whump! It hit me on the head as hard as those bad trades had hit. But this time it was a much better whump! It was the whumping that you get in your heart when you are first kissed. Only I had been kissed by sweet, redemptive pippage. Who knows how much money I'd made for these people here? One-million-dollar positions times 10, 20 traders? Or more? Multiplied by a hundred pips or more?

I recollected my brains and then walked back to my temporary trading desk. I didn't try to act nonchalant about it. If I could have skipped back to the desk, I would have done it. My duty now was to find more of these trades. Had it been a one-time-only thing? Had I just been lucky because

Craig had tipped me off to the idea in the first place, and Harvey had confirmed it? Could I repeat this?

I opened up the daily chart for the Euro and went to work.

COULD I DO IT AGAIN?

What surprised me more wasn't that my idea had been used by real Wall Street traders (okay, it was not fully my idea, but it sure felt like it at the time and I needed a boost in confidence), but rather that something as simple as a support/resistance line was powerful enough to create pips. It was a drug to me: I wanted more of it. Did other currency pairs act like this? Could I do the same thing on others? What about those cross currency pairs that Roddy had mentioned, like the EUR/JPY?

The good news was that I didn't need to worry about all that right away. For now, I could focus on the four-hour, and even the daily charts. I could start to understand what Harvey was talking about when he said testing: He was asking me to focus and study one thing. I didn't quite know how to start doing that, but I was determined to try. If I didn't get it right, then I wouldn't see him again.

The moves on the daily chart were much bigger—just like Winnipeg George said—so I would have to plan for wider stop losses and could gain greater profits from those moves as well. That must have been why Harvey was so intent on having me concentrate on the long-term stuff. Greater potential for more reward, for the same effort. Sounded good to me. The four-hour and the daily and the EUR/USD would do just fine for now.

Then I asked myself a series of questions, inspired by Roddy: How far might the Euro fall downward? Where was it likely to stall? Could I find an area, just like 1.2200, only lower? Some area where the currency pair had experienced trouble moving higher or lower?

The four-hour chart was no help at all. I could see some areas that might stall the pair above 1.2200, but not below it. And I needed to find a good stopping point on the downside. So I moved to the daily chart and found something that I really liked (see Figure 16.6).

It definitely appeared that 1.1850 was a meaningful number. On the left-hand part of the chart, back in May and June 2003, the currency pair had struggled to rise above that level. Then in October of the same year, it couldn't break above it at all. Then in November, as it was finally gaining enough strength to pierce the level, it still stalled there for several days, and still surely produced some nice moves back and forth. In all, I found five solid examples of the pair bouncing off that level between May and October 2003.

FIGURE 16.6 The daily chart.

I wanted to choose this level for a profit target. But was this enough research? I looked back at the current chart. How could I know that is where it would stop? The night before, my planning had started with a number that Craig and Harvey had given me, and then I backed into a reason for justifying a trade at that number. But this was entirely different. Would I be willing to write this number down on a Post-it? And leave it on my desk?

More confirmation. I wanted more confirmation. I needed another chart to back me up.

So I looked at the weekly chart, but it was no help at all. It showed that in October 1998, the pair had some trouble with the 1.1850 mark. But had the Euro even existed back then? How could they do charts for a currency pair that didn't exist?

I deleted the weekly chart and wondered what Harvey would do in a situation like this. I decided that first of all, he most certainly would not risk losing money on this trade. So I definitely wasn't going to suggest a buy trade with a stop and a profit target. No way. But would it be appropriate to express my view that I thought the EUR/USD would stop moving down once it hit the 1.1850 mark? Roddy had asked me, after all, where I thought it would fall to. Why not write that down? It was just paper trading, after all. No one was going to get hurt.

So I wrote down: "EUR/USD Stops: 1.1850" on a Post-it, stuck it to my desk, gathered my things together, and left. As I shut the door of the trading floor behind me, I heard Roddy scream out.

Somebody had lost a paycheck.

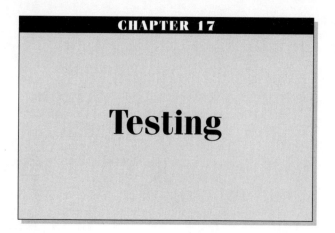

CHAPTER 17

Testing

The next day I learned that I needed to be far more clear about my currency analysis, for when I arrived at Wakeman, Butterman, and Bailey at 7:00 A.M. (over two hours early, because I was intent on starting to pay back stolen time, even if I could never catch up), my voice mail chirped that I had received, and I am not making this up, 37 messages.

I peeked around the corner. Herbie's light was on. He was always in this early, but it couldn't be him. He would leave a note, telling me never to come back. It wasn't like Herbie to leave 37 voice messages, either. This was something entirely different.

The first message said it all. It was Roddy from down on the 31st floor, and it had come in two hours earlier: "Harry, you left a bloody note down here and the traders have all gone mad. They're running around wonderin' if you're buyin' or you're sellin' the Euro at 1.1850. Call down to 31, don't be callin' me. I'm at home and I'm sick of the phone ringin' here just because I saw yer note first. Bugger! Don't leave any more bloody notes!"

The next messages were from all sorts of traders I'd never met and I had no idea how they got my number or why they would care. I was in early, anyway, so I had a couple of hours to sort all this out and then I could return to Wakeman in time to start the day. Although I didn't like the idea of falling behind on the filing, I most certainly didn't like the idea of having our receptionist flooded with phone calls as soon as she got in.

Before I could pick up the phone, my extension rang again. It was Craig. There were loud voices in the background. He must have been surrounded by other traders. He said: "Harry, you had better get down here. I don't know what's gotten into these guys. But they want to talk to you."

"All right," I agreed. How had I become so popular, just from one trade? What in the world was happening? Craig's tone let me know that he wasn't particularly amused that he was the representative secretary who had to track me down. I also rightly assumed that he didn't much like an inexperienced trader like me getting so much attention. When I arrived on the 31st floor, I waved my badge in front of the door, and walked out onto the trading floor. It was loud. It was chaotic. It almost seemed like something had gone terribly wrong. Craig seemed out of place in the midst of it all.

When I found him, I first asked him what in the world had happened. "It's just a bit crazy here right now," he admitted. "There's word that one of our London traders took a huge hit. Massive. Like more than a hundred million dollars."

"A currency trader?"

"Right. So it's sent all the fixed income guys—everyone down here—into a frenzy."

"Why would that affect them?"

It was so loud in the room that we nearly had to shout to hear each other. The upside was that no one recognized me and they weren't paying attention. Business television was covering the story on all the screens above us, and between the comments from the reporters, I heard every sort of vulgarity imaginable.

"This isn't the most stable of trading desks in the world," he told me. "These guys aren't noted for their adherence to Zen spirituality or peaceful living. They are like a bunch of sharks. They smell blood in the water. They sense change. Some of them are already calling headhunters and trying to see if they can move into other jobs on the Street. Some are wondering if there will be cutbacks, and if they will make the cut."

I wondered if Roddy or George were part of the panicking crowd. "I met a guy named Roddy last night. And a guy from Canada named George. Are they in trouble? Are you?"

He shook his head. "Roddy, no way. He's an Asian session expert and has contacts all over the world. He makes prices for some really large companies. Some of them are in London but he doesn't want go back there. Having too much fun here winning everyone's paychecks. He's got nowhere to go but up in all this. He might have a chance for a promotion in all this, as long as he's willing to go back to London. George, he's fine, too. We call him Winnipeg George, because he's from the province of Winnipeg. And George is a great trader. He's been working closely with Roddy for a long time."

"And you?"

"Me? I'm fine. I'm having a great month."

"That's excellent. It almost seems like you don't fit in here with this crowd."

He shrugged in a way that told me he agreed but that this wasn't the time or place to admit it.

"By the way, Harry," he said, "I sold Euros at 1.2200, and I'm still in the trade, too. Why did you tell these guys to make that trade? Anderson told me he gave you a desk but you're not working here. What's going on?"

Now it was my turn to shrug. "I can't explain it. I am sort of shocked that a bunch of bank traders would care at all what I said."

"Ordinarily, they wouldn't. But Anderson really put you on a pedestal."

"Really?"

"Yes, really." There was a hint of jealousy in Craig's voice. "What did you tell him? I thought your trading was going terribly. I told some guys that Harvey was teaching you and they flew threw the roof—that news, combined with Anderson's endorsement, it was too much for them. March wasn't easy on the short-term traders here and some of them got bit, making prices for some clients last month. They wanted to get back on track and they're looking to you now."

"Well," I replied, "first you need to know that I told Anderson that I was a terrible trader and that I'd lost all of my trading capital. That, apparently, was not a big deal to him."

Craig gave me a quizzical look. "It just doesn't make sense."

That stung a bit. Maybe I had drained my trading account. Maybe I had not been a disciplined individual. Those things were true. But I wasn't a complete moron. I was facing my challenges and I had been able to plan a good trade with Harvey's help.

Craig realized what he'd said and tried to backpedal. "Sorry, Harry. I didn't mean it like that. I meant to say that it doesn't make sense that, well," and then he paused. He looked at me square in the eye: "Okay, I probably did mean it like that. And I should not have said it. Your trade was actually really good. We got the entry from Harvey, but you planned the stop loss and the profit target."

"But why would these guys follow someone they've never met?"

"They do it all the time. Every day they're talking to each other, swapping ideas, talking about rumors. That part isn't a surprise. And I know that Anderson can be a great judge of talent. So I'm not completely shocked that he sees potential in you. But to give you space down here? Give you a pass to get in the door? That's a lot of trust for someone he hardly knows. Something seems odd."

"I can't disagree. I'm not sure what to say."

"Coming here today and yesterday, and hearing all these guys talk about your trades, made me remember when I first started here and that I felt like I was on top of the world after one good trade."

I knew where this was going. But I did not interrupt him. He continued: "I've already told you this. But it's like I see some of myself in you. That you have this temptation now to go over the top. To do more of the same. That you can do no wrong. You can get into so much trouble so quickly like that."

I nodded. He was telling me what I needed to hear. Last night I'd been tempted to plan another full trade. But I hadn't. I'd stopped when I realized that I lacked the confidence to plan another trade. Rather than do that, I simply started the next idea—with a number at which the Euro was likely to stop (at least in my opinion). Maybe I was too close to the loss of my entire trading account, but I simply didn't feel like I wanted to go out and conquer the world. I still felt like I wanted to do my work at Wakeman. That I wanted to earn back the trust of my wife. That I wanted to make Harvey proud that I could get my emotions under control. And then, most of all, I wanted to discipline myself so that I could gain the chance to trade again. And trade profitably this time.

I needed to go. I had so much work upstairs and I wasn't getting paid to sit and shoot the bull with a bunch of wild traders. Already, other traders had begun to surround us and were asking me questions. They mostly just wanted to know if I was planning to buy Euros at 1.1850. It only took a few moments to explain that I was simply offering what might be a good profit target on the original trade, if I hadn't already picked a different target. In fact, I sort of wondered why they couldn't come up with their own profit targets. Didn't they know more about trading than I did?

RISKING ERNEST WELLINGTON'S MONEY AGAIN

Work raced by. Friday shot past and the only reason I stopped downstairs was to say good day to Roddy and Winnipeg George, who weren't there anyway. The entire trading floor was empty. I checked the price of the EUR/USD and it was hovering at 1.2100, hardly having moved at all during the entire day. Having opened the charts, I figured I might as well take a look to see if I could justify any type of trade at the 1.1850 level. It didn't mean much just to say that price would probably stop down at that price. If it was going to stop down there, why not buy it for even just a few pips?

I opened up the 4-hour chart again to see the places where 1.1850 had been hit, and then I opened a 15-minute chart to get the finer details of what happened exactly at those times.

The most recent example was November 18, 2003: at 10:15 on that day, the pair rocketed through the 1.1850 mark, never stopping for a breath of air. Perhaps an interest decision had been made that day and it overwhelmed the market. In any case, price flew upward 127 pips beyond the level, and didn't fall back below it for six days. When it fell back through, it fell hard, but I had to believe that I would have exited the trade by then. Taking a loss of 127 pips seemed too great. On a sheet of paper in front of me, I wrote:

November 18, 2003: Loss/127

Then I moved back in time to the next example, from November 16. Price rose upward and came within 5 pips of the mark (to 1.1845) and fell backward 122 pips, almost immediately, which I confirmed with a shorter term chart. It never reached higher than 1.1845 before taking this huge reversal. Did this qualify? I said yes, since I wasn't going to bicker with 5 pips. From now on, I might go ahead and be willing to sell within 5 pips of the line. This seemed perfectly reasonable. Now I added another trade on the piece of paper in front of me: November 16, 2003: Profit/122.

Next I looked back to October 24. Price rose up to a high of 1.1856, and then fell backward immediately. It didn't even stay in the 1.1850 area for more than two 15-minute candles. Then it fell all the way down to 1.1720, or 130 pips, within two days. Another good trade. I wrote: October 24, 2003: Profit/130.

On October 23, price reached as high as 1.1843 but not any higher. Although it would have created an excellent trade, I stayed with my rule of a 5-pip-buffer zone. Staying with the rule meant that I couldn't take this superprofitable trade. But I realized that if I started changing the rules now, I wouldn't have a very good set of results (see Figure 17.1).

On October 10, price reached 1.1845, never went higher, and dropped all the way down to 1.1547 in just seven days, before making its next climb all the way back up to 1.1843 on October 23. This was nearly 300 pips of gain and hardly any risk. I wrote: October 10, 2003: Profit/297.

The next example was October 9, which netted at least 150 pips. I had taken a short trade at 1.1845 to 1.1850. It only went as high as 1.1857. Obviously, this level was important. Maybe as important as the 1.2200 mark.

I then found six more occasions on which the pair had hit that level and reversed. Three times it stretched over the 1.1900 mark before it fell back lower. Once it went as high as 1.1931, not quite 100 pips. Two trades only took 30 pips of profit, if I adhered to the rule of finding the lowest point the pair reached before starting back up to hit the 1.1850 region. All I wanted to know at this point was the maximum number of pips available on each trade.

The total number of trades I found—11:1 loss and 10 profitable trades. If I kept my stop loss at 100 pips, then my average loss would be 100. My average profit across all trades was 171. I realized that this time I had only looked at selling the EUR/USD, never buying it at the 1.1850 level.

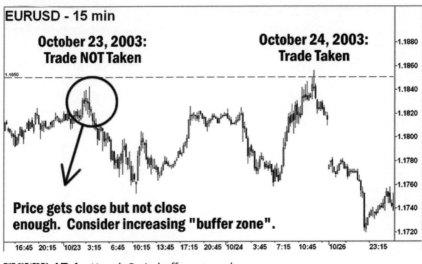

FIGURE 17.1 Harry's 5-pip-buffer zone rule.

I pulled out a Post-it note and wrote:

Short EUR/USD 1.1850 (if rises from underneath)

Stop: 1.1950

Profit: 1.1700

That seemed completely reasonable. But how far did the pair have to fall below the 1.1850 mark, and then rise back up, to create the trade? Maybe I should consider a buy trade at that level. I'd have to talk to Roddy or George, or Craig, if he was interested, to find out if I could reverse the system.

In the meantime, I knew that it would be unsafe to simply plan a buy trade. No Post-it note for this one. I'd have to wait. If I missed it, who cared anyway? I was trading on paper and I was doing this to build up some experience and confidence, without putting money on the line.

Well, not my money at least. Perhaps some of Ernest Wellington's.

This work had taken me over three hours and it seemed like only 15 minutes had passed. This analysis work appealed to me as much or more than trading. I experienced the wonder of discovering new stuff, and none of the pain or emotion of having to commit to a trade or live through it. All my trading up to this point had been impulse driven. But now analysis and study were driving the trade planning.

And I had only scratched the surface. I had a zillion questions:

Could I apply this to any currency pair?

Could I apply this to shorter time frames, if not for trading, then at least to prove the concept of horizontal support and resistance trading?

What about interest rates? George Sisler had wanted me to study up on interest rates. What's more, I'd already seen how an interest rate decision could send the market into a frenzy. How did rates fit into all of this?

I called my wife and told her that I wasn't coming home. I was on a roll.

A WILD WEEKEND

By Saturday morning, I had hit the mother lode of information. At 7:00 A.M., I went home and had breakfast with my family, kissed them all, and returned to Ernest Wellington. My wife was completely supportive, and although she didn't understand what I was talking about, she was happy that I was putting extra time in to figure it all out. We both had a feeling that I was finally taking a rational, methodical approach to trading, so much so that it began to seem more like investing. We liked that.

During the next two days, not only did I research the so-called cross currency pairs, but I had found information on the Internet about interest rates—a lot of information. I was now convinced that George Sisler had given me a huge gift in directing my focus to studying interest rates. I had some ideas about how I could combine what I had learned about horizontal support and resistance with interest rates, but I would have to talk to him first.

Late Sunday afternoon, Roddy and George were the first ones into the office. They came in on Sunday because they worked the Asian hours, and it was already Monday in Asia. They were in good moods and immediately approached me: "Banes, are you makin' bloody trades for the entire office here again?" That was Roddy.

"No, Roddy. Just on your account. You are short a hundred million Polish Zlotys."

He laughed. "Good one!" He slapped me on the back. "Want to start off the week with some paychecks?"

George cut in: "Harry, don't listen to him. We had a bit of a wild weekend."

Who knew what trouble they'd been in. What bars they'd been to, how much they'd drank, what parties they'd gone to. It couldn't hurt to ask. "What kind of a wild weekend?"

"Testing!" Roddy exclaimed.

Testing? Drug testing? Testing for sexually transmitted diseases?

George nodded. They were nearly giddy with excitement. "We've been backtesting a new short-term strategy and we had a breakthrough. We haven't slept for 48 hours."

I nodded. "Neither have I."

"Banes!" Roddy yelled. He actually picked me up and bear-hugged me and screamed: "You've been testing, you bugger! Haven't you!"

I couldn't help but laugh. He was twice my size and had 50 times the energy of a normal human. I admitted to them that I'd been testing and had some breakthroughs of my own, but I needed to talk to people who knew more than I did to confirm what I'd found.

"You can talk to us," George offered, and then pulled two chairs up next to me. Roddy was too excited to sit down and couldn't wait to hear what I'd found.

I decided to share with them my testing of the horizontal support and resistance. They ate it up.

THE LESSON IN BACKTESTING

RODDY: So how many pairs did you look at?

ME: Only five. The EUR/USD first, then the GBP/USD, the GBP/JPY, the EUR/JPY, the USD/CAD, and the EUR/CAD.

WINNIPEG GEORGE: What time frames? Mostly long-term?

ME: Right. All long term. But I did drill down to the shorter time frames to verify stops and profit targets.

WINNIPEG GEORGE: This is really similar to what Roddy and I've been looking at. We call it "short-term trading from the longer term charts."

ME: That's a good name. I kind of feel the same way. I'm just jumping on for some pips on a reversal. Most of the trades aren't open for more than a couple of days. I liked planning them from the four-hour and the daily charts the most, but I have a feeling that this would work on the one-hour charts, too.

RODDY: You've got a good feelin', Banes! It shorely does work on the one-hour! That's me favorite chart!

ME: Why is the one-hour your favorite?

WINNIPEG GEORGE: It's his favorite because he doesn't have the attention span to look at anything longer term than that.

RODDY: Not true! I can look at the fifteen-minute chart all day long!

WINNIPEG GEORGE: That's shorter term.

RODDY: Oh. Right you are!

ME: I did a lot of work to analyze this stuff. I looked at twenty trades on each of the pairs, and kept notes on all of them.

WINNIPEG GEORGE: Your notes are all over the place. You wrote all of this down by hand?

ME: Yep. I guess there is an easier or better way, but I started rolling along and couldn't stop myself.

WINNIPEG GEORGE: You need to start keeping this information in spreadsheets.

ME: I don't know how to use spreadsheets.

WINNIPEG GEORGE: Well, you can worry about that later, but let me show you an example of why it's so important. I'm opening one of our testing spreadsheets right here. We just type in the entry price, the closing price, and the spreadsheet tallies up the wins and losses. It gives us a final pip count for wins and losses. It tells us how big the average winner is, the average loser. It tells us our win percentage—which is how often we can expect to have a winning trade, based on the information we've already provided.

ME: And you do this for all of your testing?

RODDY: Don't leave home without it! We never test without it. We spreadsheet everything. We have spreadsheets on top of bloody spreadsheets. I can hardly keep track of all of 'em. Banes, did you say that you've only tested twenty trades so far?

ME: Yes! Twenty per currency pair. So I actually finished testing one hundred, in total.

RODDY: One hundred's not enough, boy! You gotta do better than that!

ME: How much better?

WINNIPEG GEORGE: Well, we spent the entire weekend testing. We got through about a thousand trades.

ME: [silence]

RODDY: Yeah, Harry. Did you do a thousand trades? I think not!

ME: How did you get that many done?

WINNIPEG GEORGE: We sat on the couch with our laptops—one of us with charts and the other one with spreadsheets. We had food brought in, and we watched basketball, baseball, and cartoons, and only took breaks to go to the bathroom. We didn't shower, answer the phone, or interact with humankind in any way. It was complete focus.

ME: And you tested the same system, over and over again?

WINNIPEG GEORGE: We actually did five hundred trades each on two variations of the same system. The main system we tested was a combination of the CCI [Commodity Channel Index] oscillator with long-term support and resistance. The second variation, that we tested simultaneously, was to look at Fibonacci retracements for exits, instead of using set profit targets.

ME: How did you do that?

GEORGE: It would take too long to describe here, but let's just say that we found a few fib retracement levels that we really liked. Using the fib exits, we increased our average profit by 20 percent.

ME: Are you ready to start trading it?

RODDY: I am! I'm divin' in this afternoon.

GEORGE: That's a bit of an ongoing discussion. I'd like to actually watch it for a week without opening any trades. We've been putting the pieces of this together for a long, long time. We have been testing every weekend for about seven months now. We've changed strategies and rules a million times but now we think we've found something that we can live with for the long term.

ME: And what are you trading in the meantime? I mean, you still have to make trades.

GEORGE: Oh, we do a lot of price making for clients. Remember, that's actually our first job, to quote prices for clients. You already know how that works, I'm sure.

ME: Yes. A manufacturer or a hedge fund might call the bank and say that they want to buy some British Pounds. And you've got to give them a price.

GEORGE: Right. That's what we do all day. We generate profit for the bank by the difference between pricing. Sometimes we offset the trade by selling or buying on the spot market. Sometimes we keep the trade if we think it will be profitable for us.

ME: So how does this new system fit in?

RODDY: Don't say a word, Winnie!

ME: Winnie?

RODDY: That's the name I've got for George. Winnie! He's from Winnie-peg, Canada. So that's his nickname.

ME: I think I've got a lot of work ahead of me. One hundred trades isn't going to be enough.

GEORGE: But don't feel like you can't start paper trading, like you've been doing. You make a lot of sense with the levels you've chosen for trades so far. The 1.1850 level is something that we're looking at, too.

ME: For a buy or a sell?

GEORGE: For a buy. The pair has stayed above that level for some time now, and we think the tables are turned. What used to be resistance is now support. We're going to happily buy Euros at that price. All we can. What are you going to do next? Which pair are you going to test?

ME: All of them. But first I need to talk to George Sisler again.

GEORGE: Sisler? The hedge fund guy? You're going to talk to him?

ME: Yes. If I can. I met him last week and he wanted me to do some research into interest rates—which I've done. But now I have more questions than answers.

GEORGE: Mind if I come with you?

ME: I don't mind at all. I'm not sure he'll actually meet with me. But I am going to try.

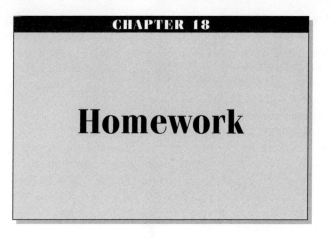

CHAPTER 18

Homework

I doubted that George Sisler would talk to me without Harvey. Anyone running a zillion-dollar hedge fund wasn't going to just waste his time on someone like me. Perhaps Harvey had told George that I had taken harebrained trades and lost my account, in which case a meeting with George would even be less likely.

So I was surprised when George took my call the next day. I called him as soon as I arrived at Wakeman at 7:00 A.M., and he picked up the phone.

"George Sisler."

I had anticipated a secretary or a receptionist. I paused to collect my thoughts, and in that small amount of time, George hung up the phone. Obviously, he was very busy. I called and this time he answered again: "George Sisler. Who is this?"

"It's Harry Banes. The guy that—"

"Harry! Did you do your interest rate homework?"

"I did. I did a lot of work. But I have some questions before I can continue."

"I'll see you at lunch," he told me, and then he hung up.

I worked my brains out that morning so that I could spare a couple of hours for lunch. It had been a personal goal of mine to not leave for lunch at all in the next few weeks, so that I could pay back time lost at the firm. But a meeting with George Sisler took precedence over that for now. At lunchtime, I hopped in a cab and hoped that I wasn't making a mistake by showing up without Harvey.

It didn't seem to matter. George saw me right away. The office wasn't any different from the last time I'd seen it. Just as dumpy as before. This time I had a new appreciation for it. I started to wonder what George's house looked like. Did he live in his car, or under a bridge?

I would soon find out. But first he had questions for me. Lots of questions.

"What did you find?" he asked.

"You specifically asked me to find out if I could figure out a way to take the carry trade on a retail platform," I answered. "That was my focus. I stayed up all night on Friday and did a ton of research on it."

"And? You found that it's impossible." This was a statement of fact, meant to encourage me to move on to the next point. So he was not so mildly shocked when I announced: "Oh, it's very possible. Just not in the exact same way that you do it."

His eyes brightened. "Really? Now I want to hear more."

I pulled out my notebook and flipped open to the tab I'd marked "Interest Rates—Retail Carry Trade." Then I began: "You talked about borrowing cheap money and then investing in high-interest currencies. I sat down for at least two hours and learned why that works. It makes perfect sense to me. A high-rated borrower has, in effect, a huge pool of capital to draw from. I realized that a wise investor should always look to borrow at the lowest rates and invest for the highest rates possible, combined with a reasonable expectation of return. I hadn't ever considered that, not because it doesn't make sense, but rather because it's just not something I would have thought about."

George smiled. "And now that you thought about it, what did you learn?"

"I learned that carry traders don't just invest in currencies. They also invest in U.S. stocks, bonds from around the world, real estate, they even purchase entire companies with the borrowed money. There is a whole lot of borrowed Yen out there. But I will get to that point later. I am sure I am not telling you anything that you don't already know."

He nodded. "Probably true. But I have thirty minutes and I want to hear it all again."

I looked down over my notes. There was no possible way for me to get through everything in half an hour. But I plodded onward: "Once I had an understanding of why it worked, and believe me, it took me a while to figure it out, I realized that I could try to apply the same principles in my currency trading. I called my currency dealer and asked about interest rates. It turns out that retail currency platforms charge and pay out interest in the same way that a bank would charge or pay interest. Only retail platforms call it a *swap rate*, and the interest is calculated at the end of every currency trading day—in other words, at five P.M. eastern time."

"How much are they charging or paying out?"

"Well, for my research here, I used the British Pound versus the Japanese Yen, the GBP/JPY. Because interest rates in Japan are at zero, and rates in the United Kingdom are at 4 percent—and, I might add, expected to keep rising—when I buy one standard lot of the GBP/JPY cross pair in my trading account, which is $100,000 worth of currency, I get paid about $20 every day in interest."

"What kind of leverage do they give you?"

"That's my next point. I have 400:1 leverage with my dealer, which I know sounds ridiculous. It's a ton of leverage. But the leverage is almost irrelevant," I told him, "and this is where it gets exciting. I hope I haven't gone totally wrong with this research, because I think I stumbled onto something really amazing.

"Let's say that I open an account with Universal Currency Brokers. I put $100,000 in the account. I don't have that much money, but let's just say I do. I put up only $10,000 of that money for margin. And because of leverage, they let me buy $4,000,000 worth of GBP/JPY, or forty standard lots. Every day that I hold that currency, I get paid $20 for every standard lot, or $800. Just for holding onto the currency pair in a buy position. This sounds too good to be true, but I called around that night to at least 20 currency dealers. I found that almost all of them are paying interest in those amounts. Almost all of them. I hope I'm okay so far."

George nodded. He looked at his watch. I could tell that I had captured his interest. He said: "I ordered in some sandwiches but I'm losing my appetite while you talk to me about money."

"Me, too. I can eat later."

"Good. So far, this is fine research you've done. This is slightly different than the way it works for us, but it's perfect so far."

"I'm happy to hear that. If the research was faulty up to this point, I'd have nothing left to say. But here's what comes next: I thought, it sounds too easy to just buy the GBP/JPY each day and try to earn $800. Why? Because the currency pair might fall, instead of rise. You know, if some news comes out, or if there is a terrorist act, the currency pair is going to bounce around. And for each standard lot traded, a pip is worth about nine dollars. Say it drops 100 pips, and I've traded 40 standard. If the pair falls 100 pips in one day, I would lose 100 times nine dollars times forty—that's 100 pips, times nine dollars per standard lot, times forty standard lots traded. That's a lot of money. Way more than I would be earning from the interest."

"It's just not worth the risk then," he added.

"Right. It would be ridiculous. But, if I could find good levels at which to buy the currency pair, and hold on, then I would be in good shape. Really good shape. Not only could I earn interest, but I would be earning pip gains, too. This would be far better than taking the same type of trade with a low-interest-bearing currency. This way, I'm basically paying myself extra for holding onto a trade."

"I like what I'm hearing. But how would you be hedged?" he asked.

"Hedged?"

"Yes. How would you balance out the risk?"

"Well, for one, I would come up with a series of stop loss rules to exit the buy trades. That would limit the downside risk."

He nodded. "That is a start. But is there a way you can use options or futures contracts to hedge yourself, in case of a big, sudden decline?"

"I'm not sure I understand. I've never traded options or futures."

"Well, Harry, you've made a good start here. But if you want to be a world-class trader, you are going to have to go one step further. You have to nearly eliminate your risk. As low as you can get it. Meaning, you want to have the least amount of exposure to losses as possible. And I bet that you can find a way to hedge the trade so that you can hold onto it for a long time, without worrying about having to open and close the trades."

"That sounds good to me. I am not sure that would be possible."

He laughed. "It's definitely possible. We do it here all the time. We do it with options and futures. I'm not sure those financial instruments will be available on your retail trading platforms. But there has got to be a way to make it work."

"If there is, I am dedicated to finding it."

"Very good. Here is what I want you to do. It's not going to be easy, but it will be worth it. I want you to do some very, very deep research into interest rates now. I want you to go way down. Do you know how to use spreadsheets?"

I was embarrassed to explain to him that I didn't.

"All right, then. Find yourself someone who does."

Roddy and George! "I know just the people."

"Good. Now I am going to start you off by giving you some data on a CD," and then he called over to a trader across the room. "Bobby! Bring over the spot rates CD."

"Which one, Mr. Sisler?"

"Sterling, Swiss, and Yen."

"You got it."

Bobby walked over and handed me a compact disc. George nodded to it. "Now, please don't give out that data. It took us a long time to compile. It's got spot rates for more than 20 years back on two cross currency pairs: the GBP/CHF, and the GBP/JPY."

"All right."

"I want you to look up interest rates for the United Kingdom, for Switzerland, and for Japan, going back that far. And then I want you to plot on a graph how interest rates have affected currency rates over time. I know you've already told me that you know that interest rates drive currency values, but now I want you to show me exactly how that is true. Understood?"

"Yes. I understand. When do you want this?"

"A week from today. Monday, April 19. I will see you here at the same time."

"If I get some help on this, can I bring a couple of other people?"

"Of course. Now I gotta run. See you in a week."

POUNDING THE YEN

Winnipeg George and Roddy were excited, to say the very least. After I finished work at 7:00 P.M., I visited with them and explained everything. Apparently, they believed the interest rate information was going to be easy to find. "We can stay here tonight and we'll have all of it by tomorrow morning," Roddy told me.

Up all night? During the week? I was missing a lot of family time, and I was also not going to be in great shape for work the next day, if I didn't get any rest at all. "I don't know. Can we do this on the weekend?" I asked. "If it's really this easy?"

"Sure," answered Winnipeg George. "Meanwhile, we can plan more trades, and you can learn how to use spreadsheets."

"Deal," I said, and with that I decided that for the rest of the week I would split my time between planning more trades and learning to use a spreadsheet.

And over the next few days, both endeavors worked out very well. Learning the spreadsheets was easy. And overall, the trades worked out very, very well. Some of them stayed open for over a month. Some were over nearly as soon as they were opened.

The first trade expressed my desire to benefit from the interest rates differential between the United Kingdom and Japan. So I looked at the GBP/JPY, starting as usual with the four-hour chart. I wanted to find a place to buy. The first thing that I noticed was that this pair tended to move up and down a lot—it seemed to trade inside a range all the time. The next thing that I noticed was that recently, the 193.00 level offered a reasonable amount of support to the pair. In the last part of March, the pair had not been able to rise through the level and stay above it; then a week later it was able to burst through the level, but not fall back down below it. This was a perfect example of resistance becoming support.

Roddy and Winnipeg George had their own views of why the 193.00 level was a good support or resistance zone, and it had something to do with the fact that their CCI oscillator was overbought or oversold every

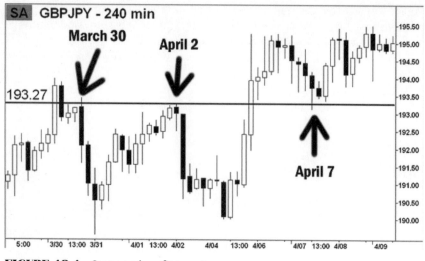

FIGURE 18.1   Stops and profit targets.

time the line was hit. Although I was happy that their tested system was
also confirming the trade, I was ready to write it down and paper-trade it
no matter what. We did agree that although the currency pair had stopped
stone-cold on the 193.27 mark previously, we would wait for it to hit 193.00
even because, according to my new trading partners, this was a currency
pair that tended to obey the round numbers. At this point, I was ready to
talk about stops and profit targets (see Figure 18.1).

Winnipeg George believed that 195.00 represented a perfect exit for
the pair; it would give us a 200 pip target, and it was also the same place
where the currency pair had stalled on three different occasions: first, on
March 18, when the currency pair had fallen to the 195.00 figure and
stopped dead in its tracks before heading lower. Second, on April 6, when
it had finally risen above the 193.00 level. And third on April 8. On each of
these collisions with 195.00, the currency pair had only managed to break
through by 50 pips or so. What I liked the most was that 195.00 had already
played the dual role of support and resistance.

I wrote down:

Long GBP/JPY 193.00, Stop: 192.00, Profit target: 195.00

Roddy and Winnipeg George took the trade for the firm (Figure 18.2).
It was enough for me to watch them with the trade.

This trade opened and closed while George and Roddy were working
the overnight shift—it opened on April 13 at 3:00 in the morning and closed
almost exactly 48 hours later.

FIGURE 18.2 George and Roddy's trade.

I still didn't have any desire to do any trading of my own. The losses from the week before were still fresh in my mind. Maybe I would be ready in a month when Wakeman gave me my first check. Maybe sooner. This was a decision better made with Harvey Winklestein's help, and I hoped to see him again soon.

Harvey's absence certainly didn't keep me from planning more trades, however. Together with Winnipeg George and Roddy, I analyzed and planned for four more trades. Two of them were based on the GBP/USD one-hour chart and each of them netted 40 pips. I was not present to see either of those trades open. Another trade was based on the EUR/USD 15-minute chart and gave us 50 pips. I didn't like the short-term chart as much, but Roddy and Winnipeg George convinced me that I needed to know if the system I was using would work on the short-term charts. It did, and that was enough proof for me. I was still determined not to base my trading plan on the short-term charts.

During this time, we also began to call this trading system the "Winnipeg Special," mostly because Roddy forced us to do so, in honor of Winnipeg George's home province and also because it confused people who asked what we were doing. Roddy thrived on that. Most traders, including Craig, had generally left us alone for the entire week and my trade ideas were no longer the popular flavor. I realized that most traders at EW were interested in the hottest ideas, wherever they could be found. But they didn't focus for very long on any idea in particular. Also, they were engaged in a lot of other stuff, like quoting prices for customers, trading options, futures, and other instruments. My Post-it notes were simply not sexy enough to hold their attention for long.

My focus on learning to trade for myself made up for the lack of interest other EW traders showed in my ideas. With each trade, I grew more confident in my abilities. I had a goal to test 1,000 trades by the weekend and record the results in my spreadsheets, and I was making excellent progress.

Winnipeg George showed me how to build a spreadsheet that would log the entry price, the original stop, the profit target, the largest drawdown during the trade, and the final result in pips. It also showed my overall win percentage and the size of the average win and loss. He said that this information was absolutely critical to my success. I would learn why later.

By Friday I had done over a thousand practice trades and logged them into the spreadsheet. I had been operating all week long on very little sleep and had essentially avoided my family entirely. It was then I realized that I owed George Sisler a ton of research on interest rates, and I had hardly started.

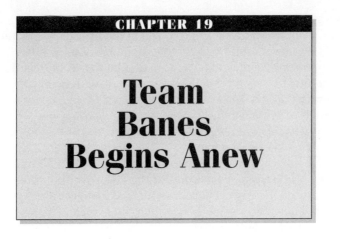

CHAPTER 19

Team
Banes
Begins Anew

Winnipeg George and Roddy were positive that the interest rate re-search was easy to do, and invited me to spend all of Saturday night into Sunday with them, to gather the results. But I had promised my wife that I would attend Sunday morning Mass with her and the kids—something that I rarely did—and I was determined not to let them down. I'm glad that I didn't.

Sunday morning was bright and cheerful and I was happy to spend time with my family. Over breakfast, Gini was excited to hear about the progress I'd made at the law firm, where I had been able to interview several promising candidates for my replacement. I hadn't told her much about Winnipeg George and Roddy, so I explained that they were helping me compile a lot of research. I told her about the trades from that week and what I might be looking for in the weeks to come. She was more interested in hearing that I was finally figuring out how to do my own analysis and less about how much money I was helping George and Roddy make.

"It would only seem fair that Anderson or even George or Roddy would pay you something for the work you've done. You've made them a lot of money."

"Over 300 pips in the last week alone. It's hard for me to believe that I could help plan those trades at all. And they really are paying me back by doing a bunch of research for me today while I spend time with you."

"Maybe. But I still think that if you're helping them make money then you ought to be paid for it. I'm not surprised that you're doing well at it. I knew you could."

Hearing this made the week's hard work worthwhile, and I smiled for the entire walk down to our church, where the priest was standing at the door, greeting the faithful one by one. Father Gonzales pulled me aside when I approached him, and I was sure that he would suggest that I could gain great blessings by attending more regularly with my family. I couldn't disagree with that, but it wasn't what he wanted to say.

"There is a gentleman inside who would like to see you. We had a nice chat about you this morning, Harry," and then he patted me on the back and handed me back to my family.

Inside, I knew exactly who to look for.

Harvey Winklestein was sitting in the last pew and grinned broadly when he saw me. He rose to introduce himself to my wife and children. He had a large paper bag beside him, which, he explained, contained treats and surprises for whoever behaved themselves the best during the services. My wife invited him to our home for dinner and he agreed.

He then told us that he would take a walk around Brooklyn, say hello to an old friend, and then meet us again after our services were over.

I hardly listened to Mass that day. I lost track of where to stand up, sit down, and kneel. Instead I thought of Harvey's wide smile and happy face. Just over a week ago I had decided that I was the worst trader in the world. Harvey had agreed with me, or at least agreed that I was bound to lose all my money if I continued to trade. What a difference a week could make! I hadn't traded at all, but I had proven that I knew how to do my own analysis and testing. I had spreadsheet upon spreadsheet that I wanted to show to Harvey later.

Harvey Winklestein also turned out to be the best dinner guest we had ever known. He read to the children while Gini and I prepared the meal and he finished two helpings of my wife's meatloaf, and then demanded the recipe. When the kids finished and left the table to go play in their bedroom, Harvey was ready to talk about trading.

THE BANES TEAM IS FORMED

Harvey: I wanted to talk to both of you today. From this point on, you are a team in this, and you both need to be involved. This includes you, Gini, even though you will probably not be doing any of the trading.

Gini: I want to be involved. I think I have been included in most of it up to this point. Even if I heard about trades or whatever a few days late, at least I've heard about them.

Me: I do want her to be a part of all of this. I can see how that will help.

Harvey: How?

ME: She needs to be aware of the amount of money we have in the account, the amount of money we have at risk at any given time. This is her money, too, and I am hoping to be ready to trade again soon. But not on my own completely.

HARVEY: This is good to hear. Gini, this means that you are going to have to meet with Harry at least once every day. Preferably before any new trades are open, to talk about what trades are being planned, what trades are already profitable or not, and how much is at risk. There might be times that you both agree to scale down the risk, or scale it up and make a bigger trade. You will know how to do those things as you work together.

ME: I want to show her my spreadsheets, too.

HARVEY: I want to see those as well. Tell me what you learned about testing.

ME: I learned, first of all, that the money management principle you taught me—the 75/25 rule—made so much more sense after I did huge amounts of testing.

HARVEY: Why is that?

ME: Because I had an appreciation for the benefits of a winning system. You taught me never to let my account go below 25 percent. Testing showed me that I could develop a system, test it, and give myself a positive expectancy of gains. By filling up a thousand rows in a spreadsheet, I found that I didn't have to trade on emotion. And that trading on emotion didn't have a positive expectancy.

HARVEY: No, it doesn't. It has a negative expectancy, in fact.

ME: And while I did the testing, I realized that I wanted to only take trades that I could feel confident about. And I couldn't feel confident about trades unless I understood how those trades fit into a larger picture, a bigger overall system. It wouldn't bother me now to lose 100 pips on a trade because I know that first of all, I won't ever risk very much on the trade in the first place, and second of all, that over time I am going to have more winners than losers. And the winners are going to be bigger than the losers, on average.

HARVEY: How much bigger?

ME: It depends. When I tested the daily charts, I tested at least three hundred trades across the GBP/USD, the GBP/JPY, and the EUR/USD. My average winner was 212 pips, and the average loser was 88. So for that time frame, I had a win-to-loss ratio of 2.5.

GINI: What exactly does that mean?

ME: It's good news, because it means that on average, my winning trades are going to be two and a half times larger than my losing trades.

GINI: But what if you lose more than half the time?

Harvey: Great question! Harry, in those three hundred trades, did you tally the wins and the losses?

Me: Sure did. Two hundred thirty-two winners and seventy-eight losers. That means that over the course of a few hundred trades, I am likely to have 77 percent winning trades.

Gini: So this is a good system. A really good one.

Me: Right. But it wasn't the best. I did better on the four-hour chart than any other. I tested over six hundred trades across the same currency pairs. I ended up with an average winner of 267 pips and an average loser of 94. I had a 74 percent win percentage as well.

Harvey: Impressive. Is that the chart you are going to focus on now with live trading?

Me: Yes, as soon as I'm ready. Until then I am going to keep paper trading.

Harvey: Good. We'll talk about that in a moment. For now, I have more questions for the two of you.

Me: Okay.

Gini: All right.

Harvey: Gini, what if Harvey starts trading, let's say, this week, and for the rest of April he only has losses. He has ten trades and all are losers. What should he do?

Gini: I'm not sure what you want me to say. I think I would tell him to keep trading.

Harvey: Why?

Gini: Because over time he is going to make money with the system that he tested.

Harvey: That's right. That's a brilliant answer. But, Harry, what's the other side of that answer? What are we assuming about your trades?

Me: We're assuming that I am only risking very small amounts on each trade, so ten losses really does not damage the account.

Harvey: Perfect! That's the next point to make. If you open another account with five thousand dollars, then I suggest that you trade for just one dollar to three dollars per pip. If you have an average loss of 100 pips, then each time you're only risking a few percentage points of the account. The smaller the trades, the better. That way you can last much longer.

Gini: It's going to be hard to earn a lot of money from trades that small, don't you think? Why not put in more money and take the same percentage risk, but at least have the chance to earn more money?

Harvey: That's not a bad question, but it takes the focus off where it should be. For the next month, Harry should concentrate on taking good trades, checking them with you, continuing his testing, and proving the validity of his system. He is working at Wakeman again so it's not a question of how much money he can make from trading now. It's a question of how much he can make from trading down the road, if he can prove that he can do it now.

GINI: That makes sense. Trade with as little money as possible now, while he is still learning to trade.

ME: And learning to be responsible with the money. If I lose five thousand dollars more, at least we know that I can stay at Wakeman for a while longer. In a way, it's money that we can afford to lose.

HARVEY: There is no such thing as money that you can afford to lose.

GINI: [silence]

ME: [silence]

HARVEY: Do you move into an apartment, and say to each other, well, it's okay if the apartment burns down? We're only going to move into apartments that we can afford to burn down?

ME: No.

HARVEY: Your trading account is your next apartment. It's the Park Slope brownstone you want to buy. Do you want to trade to earn the money to buy the brownstone, and then lose that money? Would that be money that you can afford to lose?

GINI: No way. Harry?

ME: Whoa, I'm sorry! I didn't ever think of it that way. But it's true. If I lost 25 percent of my account now, it would be like losing 25 percent of our future home. That's right. That is exactly why I didn't treat the first account with a lot of respect. I didn't think about what it took me to earn the money in the first place, or what future goals I was throwing away by not being responsible.

HARVEY: I could not agree more. If you can learn to show respect for a one-hundred-dollar account for these reasons, then you can take care of a million-dollar account. The amount of money won't make a difference because you will agree that you will never do anything to damage your dreams.

ME: Agreed. I promise. And Gini will oversee it.

HARVEY: Harry, where do you stand on the emotional scale? How have you felt the past week or so, not trading?

ME: I haven't cared much about it until now. I don't feel compelled to trade on emotion anymore. If I had any desire at all to start making trades this week, it came in just the last day or so because I now have a tested system and I had seen so many examples from that system that I can't really know much more about how it works until I trade it with real money.

HARVEY: All of this is exactly what I wanted to hear. Now we'll get down to the last law of trading: I will hold myself accountable. Harry, your wife is going to hold you accountable, and she is going to make sure that you follow everything that we've said so far. You will need to keep a notebook of your trades. In that notebook, you'll write down your trade plans, including the size of the trade, the entry, the stop, and the limit. You'll write down your thoughts about the trade, and how it compares with other trades you've already taken. You'll include thoughts and a review once the trade is closed. If you can, you should print off a screen shot of the chart from the trade and include that in the notebook as well. Gini will sign off on every closed trade, which means she will have seen exactly what you planned and if you followed through on the plan.

GINI: I like this. I like the idea of being included in the trading.

ME: I like it too. This is going to definitely help me maintain some discipline.

HARVEY: Gini, how do you feel about Harry doing some trading, starting this week?

GINI: As long as we abide by the rules you've laid out, then I am excited to give it another try.

HARVEY: Then let's see what Harry Banes can do. For real this time.

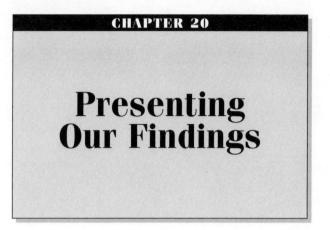

CHAPTER 20

Presenting Our Findings

Roddy wore his oldest suit the next day. This was to show off in front of George Sisler. The fact was that the only thing that could impress George Sisler would be a ton of interest rate data.

And we had it.

Winnipeg George and Roddy had hardly slept on Saturday or Sunday and had produced an astounding amount of information. On that Monday morning I had done some of my own research, finding the time by taking a half day off work. I hadn't seen Roddy or Winnipeg George that morning, so they didn't know what I was going to say. But it would dramatically increase the profits in the system that we were following.

At lunchtime we met in the dark lobby of Sisler & Company, and we were buzzed onto George Sisler's trading floor right on time. I could tell that Roddy and Winnipeg George were unimpressed, to say the least, with the offices. They had heard more about Sisler than I had, and so they'd expected to see a sparsely decorated office, but not a downright ugly one. Later Roddy would tell me that he was going to sign Sisler up for a subscription to *Martha Stewart Living* magazine.

George Sisler had set aside an hour for us, and some of his traders gathered around as well. He explained that they were curious to see what we'd discovered about interest rates, since they had been doing their own research. And then we let Winnipeg George launch into our presentation: "Mr. Sisler, our basic conclusion is that interest rate differentials lead cross currency values by several months if not more. I want to start off by telling you how we approached the project and then, in a roundabout way, let you know how we can use this information in our trading."

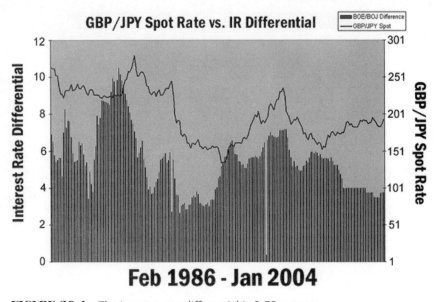

FIGURE 20.1   The interest rate differential is 3.75 percent.

"Sounds fine to me, boys. Let's dig right in."

Winnipeg George opened his laptop and produced a chart. "You can see on the graph here that between February 1986 and January of this year, there have been some wide fluctuations in the difference between the interest rates set by the Bank of England and the Bank of Japan. The dark grey bars in the bottom of the chart represent the numerical difference between these rates. For example, in January 2004, at the far right edge of the chart, the base interest rate set by the Bank of England was 3.75 percent. The Bank of Japan was entering the fourth year of its zero-interest rate policy. So the difference between the rates was 3.75 percent. Does that make sense?" (see Figure 20.1).

Sisler nodded. "Yep. Gotcha so far."

"Now," Winnipeg George continued, "The thin line floating above the grey bars is the spot rate for the GBP/JPY currency pair. And now it becomes quite simple to analyze the chart. Let's start at the far left and work our way forward. We can notice that in 1990, the two central banks diverged farther from each other than they have ever since—the difference between the base rates was over 10 percent in May of that year. But the spot rates kept rising even afterward. In fact, between May and August 1990, the pair rose an additional 2,200 pips, even while the interest rate differential started to actually fall lower" (see Figure 20.2).

"This same dynamic plays out over and over again, all the way up to the present time. The conclusion is that it takes the market time to digest

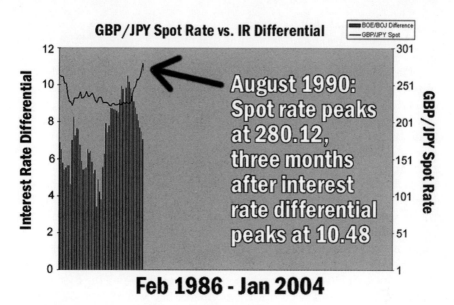

FIGURE 20.2 The interest rate differential drops.

the changes in interest rates, so that it is actually possible to use the interest rate differential to forecast future moves in the spot market." Winnipeg George took a deep breath and waited.

Sisler did not speak.

"Folks, what do you think?" he asked to the traders who had gathered around.

One trader spoke for everyone else. "That is a boatload of data. And it's fantastic." Then he looked at Winnipeg George and posed the question that all of Sisler's traders were dying to ask: "Can I have a copy of that?"

We all laughed. "Of course," replied Winnipeg George. "No problem. We did this for the GBP/USD, the GBP/CAD, and the GBP/CHF, too. You can have all of that."

Sisler then spoke up. "So how does this fit into a system you're already following?"

"Well, sir," replied Roddy, "You see, we don't really have a system that we've been following. These interest rates combined with some of the support and resistance stuff that Harry's been studying, well, we think we've got something good we can follow in the long term."

Sisler nodded. "I like what I see. Very much. Where did the two of you go to school?" he asked.

Winnipeg George answered that he had attended Yale. Roddy had graduated from the London School of Economics. Then Sisler repeated, still looking at the graph: "I like what I see here."

Then it was my turn to speak up.

"I think I've also found something that might be a good addition to this research."

Everyone looked at me, eager to hear what I could add. Suddenly, I realized that they were including me. I was part of their world. It felt strange, and it felt right. I hoped I didn't screw any of this up. I started: "Mr. Sisler asked me a few weeks ago to find a way to produce a carry trade on a retail platform, since that's what I'll be trading on for the foreseeable future. He also said that the purpose of the carry trade is to earn interest at a very low risk. At first I didn't understand how it would be possible, since the standard carry trade done by hedge funds requires lines of credit with Japanese banks, or access to currency options and fancy formulas for figuring the future value of currencies. I can't do any of that. But I did find something on a retail platform that can't be used by a bank or a hedge fund. And it might be even better."

Everyone now sat on the edge of their seat. To them, this was better than a movie. If I had told them I needed them each to sing the theme song from the *Brady Bunch* before I continued, they would have all broken into song.

"What I found is that I don't need options. I don't need futures contracts and I don't need lines of credit with Japanese banks. I can just buy the GBP/JPY in one account, and sell it—or hedge the buy trade—in the other. That way, I would be pip-neutral. I wouldn't earn or lose any pips at all in either account because they would be matched against each other."

"But Harry," began Roddy, "you're gonna get charged interest in the sell-side account."

"Ha!" I cried out. "That's what I thought. I did. But I was wrong. I found three currency dealers that don't charge interest."

"What? That's impossible. The dealer would go bankrupt offsetting the trades and paying the interest themselves."

"That's right. Here's what I found. Today, I asked a sales trader on the floor who his clients were. Not specifically, you know, but just in general. And he named three or four retail dealers that I hadn't ever heard from. He also added that they were always heavy on one side or the other—he noticed that these clients rarely had a balanced or hedged portfolio of currencies. It didn't mean anything to me at the time so I asked what the significance was. He said that these retail currency dealers were probably making fairly reasonable, and hugely profitable, bets that their clients were going to lose all their money."

Winnipeg George's eyes lit up. "So why offset the trades in the first place? They're not getting paid by the spreads. They're betting that most of their clients are going to lose all their accounts—so they trade against their client directly and then take the entire amount of the losses when the trades go badly."

"Right," I answered. "So I knew, naturally, that if they were not offsetting the majority of the positions, that they wouldn't care about interest payments. So I called one of them up and said I was interested in opening a large account, something in the neighborhood of a hundred thousand dollars. And that I preferred not to pay or be charged interest."

"And they agreed?"

I nodded. "The account rep had to check with his manager, but then came back quickly and agreed to do it."

Sisler was now superimpressed. "You could earn a lot of money just in interest alone in a trade like that. Are you going to do it?"

I laughed. "Are you kidding? I've got the paperwork filled out already."

"How can you be sure this will last?" asked one of Sisler's traders.

"I can't," I replied, "but I'm going to make the most of it while it lasts" (see Appendix A).

We sat for a while longer and talked with George. A few of the traders asked if I would let them put some money into the retail carry trade, and I told them I'd talk with them later about it. They didn't want to talk later about it: They wanted to split the profits and go in as soon as possible. These were traders who were used to pouncing on a good idea and bleeding it dry. Sisler was as much impressed with the fact that I'd found a way to game the retail currency trading system as he was with the charts.

I promised that we would test the retail carry trade and let them know soon.

Winnipeg George and Roddy bought me lunch afterward and told me that they were working on something else—something big, something that they couldn't tell anyone else. And that they would share the secret with me at the end of the week.

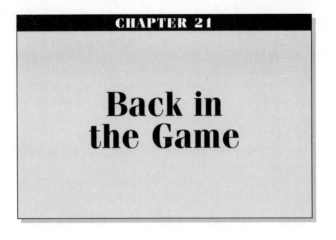

CHAPTER 21

Back in the Game

Now is a good time to bring you up to speed on another trade that Winnipeg George and Roddy and I planned and took. This would be my first live trade since I had blown up my account. Even with Harvey's blessing, I still felt reluctant to take any live trades. I wasn't sure about his insistence that I fund the account with the same amount of money that I had lost—$5,000—and I started to wonder if I could plan live trades as well as I planned the paper trades.

Notwithstanding my doubts, my wife and I funded the account with $5,000 of our savings and on Monday I met up with Roddy and Winnipeg George.

We had been waiting for days for the EUR/USD to fall down to 1.1850. I liked the foundation for the trade—it was based on the EUR/USD line at 1.1850. The week before, on Wednesday morning, Roddy called up to the law firm and started screaming into the phone. He was elated that he'd stayed in his short Euro position (the one from my first Post-it note) all the way from 1.2200, and now it was getting close to 1.1850. He got Winnipeg George on the phone, too, and we talked about what we wanted to do. This was all happening in between the other trades that I've already described.

After just a short discussion, Roddy decided that if the EUR/USD fell within 20 pips of the 1.1850 mark, then he was exiting his sell trade (taking a huge amount of profit) and reversing to go right back in the other direction. Winnipeg George and I wanted to see the pair fall all the way to at least 1.1855 and then buy. By 9:30 A.M., Roddy got his wish when the pair fell as low as 1.1866 and he went long (see Figure 21.1). At the time, I was

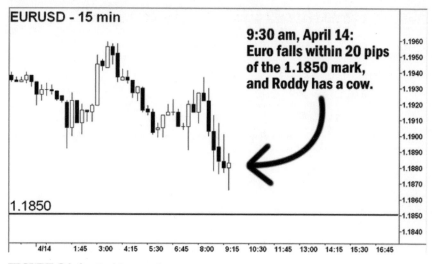

EURUSD - 15 min

9:30 am, April 14:
Euro falls within 20 pips
of the 1.1850 mark,
and Roddy has a cow.

1.1850

FIGURE 21.1   Roddy goes long.

still paper trading and decided that even though I would only be risking fake money on the trade, I didn't like it until it fell further.

We needed a take profit target on the trade and that was relatively simple: Roddy wanted to hold on for 1.2200 and not let go. Planned like this, it would be a complete reversal of the exact trade that he had just exited. Roddy was convinced that until September we were going to see a range-bound market, and he could just keep buying and selling between these levels. He started off with a stop loss of 116 pips, so that he would be protected all the way down to 1.1750, or 100 pips lower than the original entry idea of 1.1850 level.

This made me wonder why he just didn't simply wait for the original entry price in the first place. Anyway, this is what Roddy's trade looked like:

Buy EUR/USD 1.1866, Stop: 1.1750, Target: 1.2200

As I said earlier, Winnipeg George and I stayed out of the trade for the time being. A few other of our trade ideas opened, and I paper-traded those as well. Then came the weekend, the Sunday meeting with Harvey Winklestein, and the Monday meeting with George Sisler. On Tuesday, the EUR/USD fell to 1.1850 and I took my first live trade since blowing up the account. Winnipeg George and I kept the 1.1750 stop loss and 1.2200 profit target that Roddy had used.

Five days later, I was having a cow. In fact, we were all a bit afraid for me—the EUR/USD, which at first had cooperated, had now fallen all the

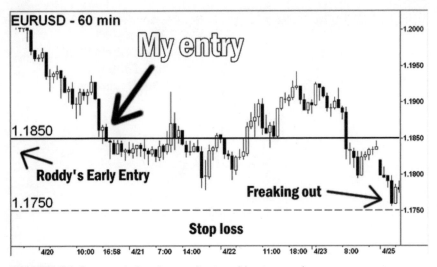

FIGURE 21.2   Harry's first live trade since blowing up the account.

way down below 1.1800 and was rapidly approaching our stop-loss (Figure 21.2).

But it never fell farther than 1.1757, and we narrowly escaped stopping out. This trade stayed open through one more scare, on May 13, and then it shot like a rocket to 1.2200 on May 27. We had held the trade for over a month, and gained 350 pips. We twice experienced drawdowns of 90+ pips, but we never stopped out. I had traded 1 mini lots, for $1 per pip. I had risked $100 of my account (100 pip stop loss times $1 per pip, or 2 percent of my account). I gained $350 on the trade.

That was a 7 percent gain in my account, for one trade. Could I repeat this again? Was it simply a fluke that I could produce a profit in my account? Could it last?

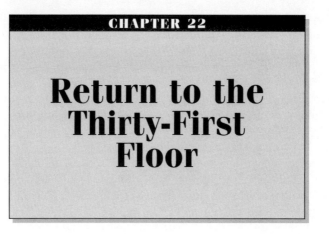

CHAPTER 22

Return to the Thirty-First Floor

I discovered the very next week why Anderson had been so kind to me. One evening not long after the EUR/USD trade was closed, he called up to the law firm and asked if I would pay him a visit downstairs. Downstairs on Floor 31, I found him working in one of the glass conference rooms off the trading floor. I knocked lightly on the glass and he waved me in. Once behind the soundproof glass, he welcomed me and asked how I was doing.

"I'm doing very well, Mr. Anderson. I want to say thank-you for providing some space for me to work. It has been a huge help. I don't know what to say, really."

He chuckled. "No, I suppose that I wouldn't know what to say in a spot like this, either. But you haven't only taken from us. You've planned some good trades, Harry. We made some good money from those trades, Harry. I'm sure we wouldn't have taken them without you. And they came at a time when the London office was having some problems, not to mention some of our own problems here, which you're already familiar with. Having you here took some focus off those challenges."

"I was happy to be a profitable distraction," I replied.

"Well, profitable is the operative word here," he added. "That's why I wanted to give you this," and he handed me an envelope.

"What's this?" I asked.

"It can't be a commission based on your trades, or a bonus, since you don't actually work for us. But we can consider you an outside consultant."

I desperately wanted to look inside the envelope right then. How rude of me. But who wouldn't want to know how much was in there?

"I appreciate this. I don't know how to every repay you. If I can ever help out, in any way, I don't even know how I would, but I'd be willing to do anything."

He replied so quickly that I imagined he might have been hoping that I would make that offer. He said: "If you don't mind, I would like to ask you a favor."

"Sure. Anything." Now I started to feel uneasy.

"There are some files upstairs that I'd like to take a look at."

Phew. That wasn't a big deal at all. Files, I could get those. We had stacks of Anderson/Ernest Wellington files upstairs. For all I cared, he could camp out in my cubicle and I'd bring him files and coffee until morning. "Which ones do you need? I can make copies and bring them down in the morning, or even tonight, if you need something right away."

"Tonight would be fine, Harry," he replied. "I need the some documents from a case entitled *Falkenburg v. American Banking Company*, and it's from at least a couple of years ago."

I remembered the file. It was a case nearly as large as the Anderson matter. But what would he want with that?

"I'm not sure I understand."

"Well, Harry, I'm technically not supposed to see those files, but I'd like to. There is some information from those proceedings that never made it into the court filings, some information about a few of our former traders that are now causing us some problems."

"I can talk to Mr. Johnson about it in the morning. I'm not sure what he's going to say about this."

"Harry, I'd prefer it if you didn't mention this to Herb. Or anyone else at the firm."

"What?"

"The *Falkenburg* case ended in a settlement right before the jury started deliberations. Part of the settlement agreement included the sealing of the files. Mr. Johnson has pretty much made it known to me that he can't help me out. That's where you come in."

Where I came in? I thought. This isn't where I came in! This is right where I would be stepping off. Anderson's kindness made so much more sense now that he was asking me to violate the trust I had with the law firm. Giving him access to those files wouldn't just cost my contract with the firm, but could land me in jail.

"I can't do that, Mr. Anderson." I looked him in the eye. "I just can't do that for you."

He looked down at the envelope in my hand. I looked down at it, too.

So he was offering money not for the trade ideas, but to buy some sealed case files! All along he'd wanted those files, and he thought he could get them through me. If I had been as dishonest as I'd been a few weeks ago, I would probably have taken the money and given him the files. But now I had a life ahead of me as a trader, and no reason to destroy the trust I'd regained with Mr. Johnson and the law firm.

I handed the envelope back to him. "I can't accept this from you. I have too much to lose."

He smiled warmly as if I'd just offered him a brand-new car or a back massage. He wasn't bothered at all, and I could see how he got his reputation for staying cool even when traders were blowing up, or the London office was losing money, or when he was being sued. "No hard feelings, Harry. I understand where you stand on this issue. That's all."

And then I left.

CHAPTER 23

Settling My Tab

Two more weeks passed. I hired a replacement at the law firm and planned to work alongside the newcomer for at least a month to make a smooth transition. I met in person with Roddy and Winnipeg George every evening in my cubicle at the law firm to plan longer term trades. We no longer met down on the trading floor, and I let them know that I no longer felt like I could take up space at Ernest Wellington without giving something back. They didn't care one way or the other—every day they still called me at least once every hour to give me a blow-by-blow account of how our trades were doing. In fact, they watched my retail trading accounts for me during the day so that I didn't have to take my focus off my work.

Roddy and Winnipeg George's secret was that they had raised nearly $25 million from their clients and they were setting out on their own. They had formed a hedge fund which they called, and I am not making this up, Paycheck Partners. By July, it would be up and running and they wanted me to join them as a trader. I wouldn't own any of the company (which I didn't care about), but at the end of the year, I would be paid 30 percent of all the profits from the trades that I made.

I talked to Harvey before I accepted the position, and he wondered why I was even asking his opinion. It was obvious to both of us that this was a chance of a lifetime.

Harvey and I had spoken in person every day since the day that he had shown up at Mass. Within a couple of weeks, he was repeating a lot of what he already had said, and although he always checked my notebooks to make sure that my wife had signed off on the trades that I took and the risk that I incurred, he kept telling me that he was no longer worried about what kind of trader I would become.

I could sense that he had less and less that he wanted to teach me, and more and more that he wanted me to teach him about what I was doing. He didn't need the information because he was going to trade like me; rather, he wanted me to teach him what I was doing so that I could prove that I was focused.

And I was definitely focused! I only traded support and resistance from the daily and four-hour charts. That doesn't include the retail carry trade, which I opened the very next week with $20,000, and which I talk more about in Appendix A.

A short time later, I reported to Harvey that I'd taken my 50th trade and that 35 of them had been profitable; 15 had been losers. My average winner was about 164 pips—less than I would have liked. I found that I had a hard time hanging on to the winners. The longer that I held a winning trade, the more worried I became that it might turn into a loss. But at least I was having winning trades in the first place.

The flip side of this was that the losers were really small. I averaged 67 pips per loss, much less than I had expected, and for the same reason. I just couldn't stand to watch myself lose money, and I was very likely to cut a losing trade fast and then get back in later, than I was to ride it out for a big drawdown.

I still traded for $1 per pip, and I'd made what to me seemed an astonishing number of pips: 4,774. I had nearly doubled my trading account. The next step would be to double the size of my trades from that point forward. Harvey took me to Little Italy to celebrate over a pound of olives, Italian sodas, and a mountain of pasta.

Harvey approved of my plans to double my trade size.

"You're going to find that you can make more money, more quickly from your trading at the firm," he said. "So you might want to pause in some of your own trading so that you can focus. Or you might find that you don't really want to work at the hedge fund—you just want to rent some space from them and trade there. Don't overcommit to any course of action right now. I have a feeling that you can do great things on your own."

"I don't know how I can repay you," I told him.

"Well, there is a little matter of payment that we need to settle," he replied.

"I'm happy to do anything that you want me to do. Pay you anything that you charge. I already get the feeling that you don't want my money."

"Right," he said. "I really just want your time."

"You have it. As much of it as you want. I don't know what I can really do to help you, but I am willing."

He smiled. "I want to bring a friend of mine to New York tomorrow, and I'd like for you to show him around the city and tell him about Paycheck Partners."

I wasn't sure about that. "The offices are in an old warehouse in Brooklyn. Are you sure you want me to take this person out there? He'll think I'm going to kill him and throw him into the East River."

"No, he won't think that. I want him to see how cheaply you can get by. I want him to see that a twenty-five-million dollar hedge fund just starting out has offices that are far worse than his own office. I'm trying to teach him the lesson on scaling down. Of becoming lean and hungry."

"Why not take him to Sisler's hedge fund?" I asked. "The amount of money they manage over there is far more impressive."

"Well, I could take him there. But this guy already knows about you. And he's driving me crazy. Sisler wouldn't be able to stand him for three seconds. Plus, you told me two months ago that you wanted to meet him. So, Harry Banes, you're going to meet Larry Ho tomorrow, and if you don't poke your eyeballs out by noon, I'll be surprised. See what you can teach him about not blowing up his account."

"I'll do my very best."

"I know you will, Harry."

And with that, Harvey stood up, finished off the last olive, and walked out of Di Palo Fine Foods.

Epilogue

When I tell aspiring traders that the most important laws of trading have nothing to do with entries and exits, they give me a strange look. Generally, they don't have much more to say to me, especially if they are looking for the next latest and greatest trading system. Harvey taught Harry in three weeks what Harry might never have learned otherwise: that the entries and exits were the easy part. It was the discipline and the attitude that came only after a lot of suffering and hard work.

There is a myth out there that a stay-at-home mom, or a union electrician, or a cardiologist can pick up the skill of currency trading with just a few hours a week or a few minutes per day, and soon they can be on the path to riches. The truth is that anyone peddling a trading system with that promise is a liar. They are appealing to our innate sense of greed. I was greedy when I first started trading. I wasn't any different from Harry Banes. I wanted something for nothing. And, like most new currency traders, I learned the hard way that although trading for a living could be the most profitable career in the world, it could also be the most expensive.

Another myth that still pervades the universe of new traders is that their initial losses can be considered "tuition" in the school of hard knocks. Well, that's crap. Imagine if your best friend knocks on your door one evening and announces:

YOUR BEST FRIEND: I crashed your car tonight. I totally wrecked it. But I want you to know, I learned a really good lesson.
YOU: What! What did you do? What lesson did you learn?

Your Former Best Friend: I learned that I should not smoke a pound of marijuana and drink a case of beer and then drive on the wrong side of the freeway. The good news is that I have learned this lesson now, and I am not going to do it again. Never again.

You: [speechless!]

Your Former Best Friend Whom You Are about to Kill: Oh, by the way, your iPod was in the car. I think you're going to have to get a new one.

Why do new traders talk the same way about losing their account? They say things like "Now I know that I should never risk half my account on a single trade," or "I've now learned my lesson to not just jump into a trade because I saw the market moving." I wonder: did they really need to experience the losses to know they were making a mistake? Some traders tell me that they needed to lose money before they could become really serious about trading.

I say that's hogwash. Maybe losing some money is a rite of passage for traders. Maybe most successful traders have experienced a damaging loss somewhere along the way. But they don't keep doing the same thing over and over. Right? If they did, they wouldn't be successful. And I see far too many new traders blowing up account after account after account, and making the same mistakes. That's why I say that the most important laws of currency trading have nothing to do with entries and exits. Here are the laws:

- Thou Shalt Never Lose More Than 25 Percent of Thine Account.
- Thou Shalt Test Before Trading.
- Thou Shalt Stand Accountable to Another Person for Thy Trades.

Harvey taught Harry those laws. I invented Harry and Harvey and Roddy and Winnipeg George, and all the others, in the hopes that you would gain something from reading about their experiences.

You've already noticed that Harvey didn't teach Harry how to draw support and resistance. He didn't even stick around to help Harry learn how to test! Harry had to do all of the hard work by himself. But the magic of it all lies in the fact that once Harry committed to obey these three laws, he never had to worry again. Even if his system of support and resistance trading broke down, he would be able to fall back on the three laws and create a brand new system.

It is possible to support yourself from trading. You can trade for a living. But you have to commit to obey the laws. If you were attracted to trading for a living because of the freedoms that it would offer, I applaud you. We all want financial freedom, and the opportunity to plan our own days and spend more time with the people we love. But to obtain that freedom, you have to be willing to sacrifice.

The sacrifice is worth it.

I know you can, too. I hope you stay in touch and let me know how you're doing.

P.S. In the Appendixes that follow, you'll find more examples of trades that Harry took in the two years after he joined Roddy and Winnipeg George's hedge fund. For even more examples, and information on the interest rates and carry trades, point your Web browser to http://www.HarryBanes.com.

The Retail Carry Trade

The retail carry trade is an adulteration of the same type of trade done by hedge funds all over the world.

To review: A hedge fund like Sisler & Company would borrow money at low interest rates in Japan, and then invest those loan proceeds in higher-interest bearing financial instruments. What makes the trade super-profitable is that they can actually invest two, three, five, or even ten plus times the loan amount because they are allowed to trade with leverage, just like a retail currency trader, or a stock trader who trades on margin.

In retail currency trading, every currency pair has a swap rate, or an overnight interest rate. If you are buying a high interest currency and selling a low interest currency—say, if you bought the GBP/JPY (GBP high interest, JPY low interest)—you would earn interest for every day that you held the trade. Actually, you only needed to buy it by about 4:45 P.M. eastern time and hold it past 5:00 P.M. eastern time the same day, and you would earn the interest. If you sold the same currency pair, you would be selling a high interest currency and buying a low interest currency. This meant that you would have to pay interest instead.

Each Wednesday was "triple interest day," or the day when instead of paying or charging one unit of interest, a currency dealer would pay or charge three times as much. Why? Because a currency transaction has a settlement date, and Wednesday's settlement date was Saturday. The currency market isn't technically open on Saturday or Sunday (until 5:00 P.M. or so), so a transaction opened on Wednesday can't fully settle until Monday. This means that any interest due or owed on the transaction would be triple. Remember, interest doesn't sleep: if you owe money on your credit card, you don't get to stop paying interest just because your credit card company isn't open on Saturday or Sunday.

When I discovered a few currency dealers who would allow me to open an account that did not earn nor would be charged interest, I discovered an astounding opportunity. This would allow me to open a sell position on the GBP/JPY and avoid paying any interest on the position.

I invited Harvey to the house one evening soon after I discovered the no-interest opportunity, and I presented the idea to him and Gini. It didn't take long for Harvey to realize that this no-interest game wasn't going to last forever. He encouraged me to take advantage of it as quickly as possible. This strategy did not require very much management and thus had a very low risk.

With Harvey's blessing (he was equally enthusiastic about seeing how well this strategy could work), the week after I found out about this trade, I deposited $10,000 with a No Interest Currency Dealer (which will remain nameless). At the same time, I opened a $10,000 account with Inter-Dealer Forex Trading, which paid slightly higher than average swap rates and which had excellent customer service.

In the No Interest Currency Dealer account, I sold 2 standard lots of GBP/JPY. At exactly the same time, in the Inter-Dealer account, I bought the same amount of the same pair. Then I held on. To say I was nervous about this is to grossly understate the feelings I had: I was terribly anxious about the outcome.

The greatest element and one calming feature of this trading strategy was that during the trade I was completely pip neutral: If the trade in one account was losing money, the trade in the other account was making money. And I had a 500 pip buffer—the trade could go against me 500 pips before the losing side would get a margin call. Roddy and Winnipeg George helped me to set up a model for determining when to withdraw funds from the winning account and wire them to the losing account, so that I could avoid the margin calls if possible.

From day one, I earned more interest than I thought possible. I was used to savings accounts at the local bank that would pay, back in 2004, about 1 percent per year. But by trading those two standard lots in each account, I was making over 1 percent interest on the total amount invested—the $20,000—every five days. Five days! I paid a spread to open the trades—but it only took a week to earn enough interest to pay back the spread that I'd paid to enter the trade in the first place.

In the first 12 months that this trade was open, I closed it six times on margin calls, and each time I closed it, I reinvested the gains that I'd made from the account earning interest. I made deposits as often as I could, to put more money into the trade. Within 12 months' time, I had over $60,000 invested in the trade; $25,000 of that money was interest profit. The other $35,000 came from my own deposits into the accounts. By July 2006, with no further deposits, the investment had nearly doubled to $116,000.

But that's just the small money.

In January 2005, after I had fully tested the strategy for balancing the accounts through real experience with the trade, and four months after I joined Paycheck Partners as a trader, I told Roddy and Winnipeg George that I wanted to take a million dollars of the fund's money and put it into a retail carry trade. I couldn't keep this savage profit taking to myself, especially considering that I felt I owed a great deal to my partners—the people who had made so much of this possible. They told me that under no circumstances would they give me a million dollars.

They gave me two million.

Yes, two million bucks. And the No Interest Currency Dealer took the trade. No questions asked. Remember: in the no-interest account, I was holding a sell trade on a currency pair that tended to go lower and lower all the time, which meant that they had the opportunity to make a lot of money from me because I was letting a losing trade stay open until a margin call in some cases. All they would need to do is to take the other side of my trade and not offset it by making a similar trade in the interbank market. By not offsetting the trade, all of my losses would be their gains.

This two million dollar retail carry trade is still perfectly lodged in my memory; I can still remember that on January 4, 2005, I put one million dollars on the sell side, opening the trade at 196.77. But I got a bad fill on the buy trade a few moments later, getting in at 196.90.

To make the margin calls less likely, I used a $500,000 slush fund account to wire money to each side of the trade that required an inflow of capital.

By February 4, 2005, the trade had gained $98,000 in profit.

In March and April, it gained another $220,000. Because I had so much more capital now, I then closed the trade and reopened it with the realized gains. I also got a call from the no-interest dealer—they were wondering if I wanted to do some more active trading in the no-interest account. I realized that they had probably not offset the sell trade, and they didn't like the exposure to the sell-side trade, and that some active trading would help. I decided to open a $250,000 account for the hedge fund, and from that point on, if I took a currency trade of any kind for the hedge fund in the regular accounts, I also mirrored the trade in the no-interest account. At least they were earning some spread on the trade and this kept the phone from ringing. At least for a while.

By December 2005, the carry accounts had a combined balance of about $3.5 million. That represented a better than 50 percent gain for the year on that original $2 million invested. Roddy was hysterical about it and wanted to put the entire hedge fund's capital into the carry trade. Of course he didn't mean that (I think), and in any case, all the other trading was going quite well so there was no need to do it anyway.

My take from those profits? It was 30 percent, just the same as for everything else I traded. Four hundred, forty-nine thousand, five hundred, forty-three dollars. And sixty-two cents.

If you're thinking that the retail carry trade sounds too good to be true, well, you're right. At least for the time being, it's no longer possible. In July 2006, I had the no-interest side of the trade going in four different accounts with four different currency dealers. The trade had produced a 43 percent gain for the year up to that point, but then suddenly all of our dealers turned us off. One by one, in a matter of two weeks, each dealer called me and said that no matter how much regular trading I was willing to do in those accounts, they could no longer offer me a no-interest account.

We had gamed the system for as long as we could. In total, we had earned over three million dollars in interest profits, using nine different trading accounts.

How I Got Six Hundred Pips

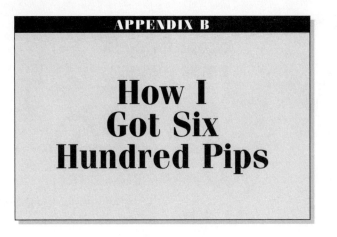

This was a trade from late 2005. For some time I'd been adding the stochastic oscillator to the horizontal line trades, and it had tested very well. This was one of the first examples when I used the stochastic to filter the trade.

I looked for times when a currency pair would pause at a level on the way up, and then on the way down. It was okay with me if the pair broke the level in between, as long as it did indeed pause at support and resistance separately.

In August 2005, I noticed that the GBP/USD had paused at about 1.7800 on the way up (a month earlier, in July). Then in late August, it had tried to fall lower and stopped near the same number—at 1.7820. In fact, the support had been so strong this time that the pair jumped upward 600 pips in just a few days. This was a good candidate, so I made sure to watch this pair every afternoon to see when it got close to the 1.7820 number again (see Figure B.1).

On September 23, the currency pair dropped all the way to 1.7820. I had found that if I checked the stochastic oscillator first, I could better time the buy trades. As long as the oscillator showed that the pair was oversold, I had two pieces of information in my favor: It was hitting a line that was likely to demand respect, and it was oversold.

The stochastic showed the pair at oversold levels, so I bought a starter position at 1.7810 (it had fallen a bit before I could get in). I determined that if the 1.7820 area proved strong enough to reject the currency pair, I would add another position. I placed a stop loss 100 pips away, added a profit target at the recent peak that it reached at 1.8500, and left it alone.

FIGURE B.1 Monitoring the GBP/USD.

Five days later, the trade stopped out at a 100 pip loss (see Figure B.2).

But this wasn't the end of the position. Now that the level was broken, I was willing to buy the pair if two conditions could be met: first, that it fell at least 100 pips lower and then rose back upward; second, that when the pair hit the level, the stochastic was above 80, showing an overbought

FIGURE B.2 The trade stops out at a 100 pip loss.

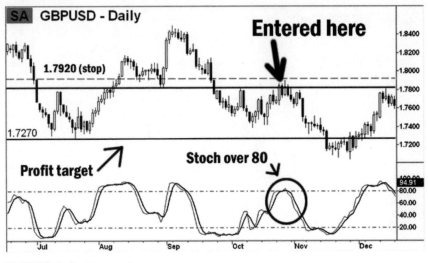

FIGURE B.3 Time to buy.

situation. On October 6, the pair rose up as high as 1.7812, but the stochastic was stuck near the lower range, not even close to 80.

But October 26, the pair not only rose up to hit the 1.7820 level, but it also found itself in an overbought area. That meant it was time to buy. I sold a starter position exactly at 1.7820, set an order to buy back the position at a loss if it went 100 pips against me, and set a profit target at 1.7220, six hundred pips lower and an area that marked a recent low (see Figure B.3).

This trade was open for about 20 days, and it netted the full six hundred pips. Along the way down, I had added several positions onto my winning trade so that the total gain from this trade was $240,000.

Index